Chords

and

Stories

Chords and Stories
Ron's Song

RON SWINDALL

iUniverse®

CHORDS AND STORIES
RON'S SONG

iUniverse books may be ordered through booksellers or by contacting:

iUniverse
1663 Liberty Drive
Bloomington, IN 47403
www.iuniverse.com
1-800-Authors (1-800-288-4677)

Because of the dynamic nature of the Internet, any web addresses or links contained in this book may have changed since publication and may no longer be valid. The views expressed in this work are solely those of the author and do not necessarily reflect the views of the publisher, and the publisher hereby disclaims any responsibility for them.

Any people depicted in stock imagery provided by Thinkstock are models, and such images are being used for illustrative purposes only. Certain stock imagery © Thinkstock.

ISBN: 978-1-5320-2393-4 (sc)
ISBN: 978-1-5320-2392-7 (e)

Library of Congress Control Number: 2017909706

Print information available on the last page.

iUniverse rev. date: 07/24/2017

Dedication

It has been a few years now since my good friend Brenda Dotson Salyers mentioned that it was probably time for me to start writing my memoirs. Very special thanks to her for having confidence in me. If not for her, I might not have started this project. Somehow, she has made me feel that I can actually write, so it is appropriate that I dedicate the book to her.

I also dedicate this work to my wife, Vickie Lynn Sturgill Swindall. Her love, encouragement, and inspiration have been at the base of most of my successes in education, music, business, entertainment, and life in general.

Contents

Acknowledgements

I had some wonderful teachers that were instrumental in teaching the skills necessary for communicating by pen. The foremost of these was the late Grace Beverly Edwards, my English teacher during my junior year in high school. Thus, she is, in large part, responsible for this creation.

Much of the ancestral information used in the first part of the book could not have been shared without the research about the Swindalls and Austins by my late cousin, Hetty Swindall Sutherland and her husband, Elihu.

I gleaned more interesting facts from my cousin Robert Mullins and his work on the Osborne and Mullins family history.

The book compiled about the Gilliam family by Kenneth Brummett was also very useful.

Additional interesting stories and facts were provided by my Aunt Lena Swindall Roberson and my late cousin, Ruby Vanover Beverly.

Special thanks go to Ron Flanary and Sharon Hatfield for their contributions in the life stories of Joe Flanary and Glenn Smith.

A writer can read over the material many times and still miss grammatical errors, misspellings, and incorrect information. I appreciate the editing help of my daughter, Michelle Swindall Sisson and my wife, Vickie Sturgill Swindall in helping me to locate some of these problems.

I would certainly be remiss if I did not mention my appreciation for the many photos used in the book. Photos were taken by The U.S. Army, Dolly Countiss, Sharon Hatfield, Tim Cox, Paul Hughes, Uncle Homer Swindall, Uncle Curtis F. Mullins, Morris Burchette, Helen Dotson, Ronnie Clark, Brenda Dotson, Don King, Terry Gibson, Sterling Gilliam, Grace Helen Edwards Stinson, Shannon

Scott, Danny Stanley, Jay Corder, and Vickie Swindall. I took a few of them myself.

Also, a special thank you is in order to all of those folks that gave me permission to use one or more images of them in my book.

Introduction

I'm just an ordinary guy that is proud to be from Indian Creek, near the little town of Pound, Virginia. In my opinion, there's no better place on earth to call home. My life has been full. There were wonderful, nurturing, caring parents. I had a very normal childhood, yet it was extraordinary in some ways. There were enjoyable and interesting years as a young man, and I was fortunate enough to go to college and earn an advanced degree in biology. I've been around a little, but not much. As a performer, I've played and enjoyed a lot of music, but I don't have delusions of grandeur. Many folks say that I had success as an educator. My wife and I have been happy and successful in marriage, and we have a great family with a girl and two boys. We all fished a lot, and spent many days camping and enjoying the outdoors. I don't regret a single day. I've worked and survived for several decades, and I've enjoyed life. I've been able to travel some. I'm somewhere near the end of this life's journey, but I still have hopes, desires, and aspirations. I've been lucky in many ways to have realized some of my dreams. Death has already been met face-to-face a few times, and it's never become any easier. Life is precious and delicate. I have faith in a living God, and how could we not all have this hope? Like most folks, I have made a lot of hasty and foolish decisions and a few were regretful. I have experienced some things that have given me a bit of wisdom, but not enough to impress nor overwhelm anyone. I have seen both equality and inequality in human beings, and I prefer the former. I'm thankful for my daily bread, my wonderful wife, and my children, in addition to a multitude of extended family and great friends. I am thankful for my life.

I am lucky to be capable of remembering so many details about my life, plus the names of many people whom I have encountered.

But at the same time, it has placed me into a quandary. Which details are really interesting to others, and which names should or should not be included? If I had chosen to include all names and details, the sheer length of such a discussion would be overwhelming, and it would be more likely to elicit boredom. Even though the dilemma has not been fully resolved, decisions have been made which will hopefully improve the reader's opinion of the subject matter.

I suppose you could label these pages as memoirs, but be assured that the writing is not only about me. I have been touched, inspired, loved, resented, taught, helped, hindered, ignored, encouraged, coached, mentored, mistreated, and befriended by countless other human beings, and the most important ones are found in this writing. I have included the most information and have written more detailed sketches about my closest and most faithful friends and family, including those that have passed on. I have felt a comforting type of satisfaction in recalling stories about them. I have brought them to life again in my own mind. I would hope that these bonding feelings might also be contagious for others who knew them, and perhaps this might even offer an encouragement to read more of my renderings.

I have started my memoirs with quite a large section about the ancestry on both sides of my family. You may or may not find this interesting. I believe that most of my immediate family will elect to read the entire treatise. Many of the extended family will pick and choose, and friends will skim over the work, looking for certain words and phrases even more. Because of this, I have chosen to write most of the book as a newsy description of my experiences with some of the people and ideas that have affected me and local history during the past 70+ years. I have included several curious true stories and other thoughts.

I probably haven't changed as much through the years as many people in my age group. I still love sports, theatre, music and the outdoors. I love the beauty of our mountains, the protection from the elements that they offer, and the wonderful recreation. The fact that many folks here are backward and resistant to change is sometimes upsetting, but these same qualities also create some strengths which I admire. My philosophy of life has bounced around a slight bit during my days on earth, but the basic content has remained the same for most of my years. Like all people, I have likes and dislikes, beliefs, passions, talents, skills, and knowledge, or otherwise complete lack of knowledge about many things.

I am, or have been, a career educator, collegiate professional, retired teacher, professional musician and retired businessman. I've dabbled in other things as well, many of which I still know very little about. I am a husband, a father, and a grandfather ("Poppy" to my grandbabies). I am an amateur writer. However, if anyone finds at least some of my effort to be interesting and sometimes well expressed, I give almost sole credit to my high school English teacher, Grace Edwards. She inspired me, taught me the basics, then encouraged me to write. Even though she would have known little about the contents of my master's degree thesis, she is, in many ways, also responsible for its success.

The teaching profession has been my life's work. I have enjoyed my career, and continue to have a desire to share some of the knowledge that I have amassed. I have always been highly in favor of new ideas and freshness in education. I believe very strongly that public education is one of our hopes for a bright future that must be maintained and supported by everyone. I know that home schooling and private schools must exist for various reasons, but neither should ever become a replacement for the one thing that can insure a strong future for our nation.

Before, during and after my teaching career, I have "moonlighted" as a backup stage musician. My role in music through time has mostly been as a lead guitarist in a band. More recent efforts have been focused toward vocals. My guitar has always been a good and consistent companion. It has helped me to entertain myself, bring fun and joy to others, and buy food. Music has been a wonderful and fruitful pastime.

I feel justified in documenting these thoughts, because I feel that my life has been full, varied, worthwhile, and sometimes interesting. I still have something informative and useful to offer. I would want most of the events in my life to remain unchanged even if I could travel back in time.

I want to disclose to the reader to be aware that all of my ancestral information is gleaned from written records in deeds, Bibles, marriage certificates, birth certificates, some documented written history, and a lot of oral history. Some of the particulars from centuries ago may need to be taken with a "slight grain of salt," but I hope that they are close to factual. You certainly may not agree with some of my facts, assumptions, philosophies, or other statements. That is to be expected.

My Father's Family

THE SWINDALLS

The Swindall people that moved into Southwest Virginia were mostly from the Counties of Ashe or Allegheny in North Carolina. Both of these regions are just across the state line from Grayson County, Virginia where many of the Swindalls originally settled after leaving far eastern Virginia. The family within my own lineage has been traced all the way back to a Thomas Swindle in Lancashire, England. After Thomas, the family has been roughly followed down through several generations as follows: Timothy Swindle, father of John Swindle, who was the father of John Swindle, Jr, the father of Elizabeth (Betsy) Swindle, mother (unmarried) of John Wesley Swindall, who was the father of James Swindall, the father of Morgan Tennie Swindall, who was the father of my dad, William Edward Swindall, father of Ronnie Edward Swindall (me), father of my own children Michelle, Nathaniel, and Reuben. This is a total of eleven generations.

It should be noted that both John Wesley and his brother Eli spelled their last names as "Swindall," and this was followed in suit by their descendants. Maybe the spelling was changed by their mother, or perhaps they themselves made that decision. Another possibility is that someone taking census at some time during the mid-1800s may have spelled the name incorrectly and it just stuck. In either case, the spelling has remained the same for several more generations.

Many of us have really strong ties to our own hometown. I have those ties and tales about "the Pound," Virginia and surrounding area, where I grew up. Many families have great stories about their heritage and ancestors. I have a few, handed down by older relatives like Hetty Swindall Sutherland (1901-2004). She and her husband, Elihu, worked tirelessly for years tracing the roots of our Swindall and Austin families. They collected related information and stories that could be assembled into book form. It's wonderful that we have their work, and that of others like Jack Brummett who assembled information about the Gilliams.

The first Swindalls came to the headwaters of the Pound River region in what is now Wise County in the middle 1800s. John Wesley Swindall (1826-1900) and his wife Mary "Polly" Phipps Swindall (1834-1907) left Ashe County, North Carolina in about 1855. Traveling with them to the area were their sons, James, who was my great-grandfather, and his brother, John Calvin. They first settled on Camp Creek beside Pound River near Norland in Russell County. The actual location may be referenced by considering a route from highway #83 between Pound and Clintwood. When traveling to Clintwood on this road, a left turn on Camp Creek Road leads over a steep hill and eventually down to Pound River. The Wes Swindall family first settled on land in the community just before crossing the river. The homestead was located in a hollow on the right side of the road. This part of Russell County became Wise County in 1856, then Dickenson County in 1880. My Melvin Tennie Swindall grandparents lived in this same community later for a period, and my father was born here.

There are many rich stories about John Wesley Swindall, who became one of the first Justices of the Peace in Wise County later in 1860. Wes chose to leave the South of the Mountain and move his family into Kentucky as the Civil War started. This was because he had no interest toward either side. Later, however, he became the only resident of the area to fight for the Union because of the way he was mistreated by rebel soldiers. When he brought his family back to Virginia after the war, he purchased land in the Osborne's Gap area, where he was a postmaster after Dickenson County was formed and encompassed his community. This community can be located by traveling on further down the river on the Camp Creek Road, then turning left on the Osborne's Gap Road. A few miles up a steep hill along this road leads to the last M.T. Swindall property just beside the road on the left. Up the hill a few more feet is the little Osborne's Gap church/school which sits on a ridge in front of the M.T. Swindall cemetery. About a quarter mile further on, the Wes Swindall family cemetery can be seen on the left side at the top of the hill. The "Flats" where Wes and Polly Swindall raised their children can be seen within a few hundred more yards. One of their children, Mahlon, built a home and stayed in this same community.

It is interesting to develop a perception of the value of certain items of property in the middle 1800s. Polly's father, Joseph Phipps, passed away in about 1851, probably near the time of her marriage to Wes. This was before their move to Virginia. Wes and Polly inherited some of her father's real estate and other possessions. It has been noted in the Ashe County, North Carolina records that Wes was indebted to a man named J.S. Parks by note in the amount of two-hundred fifteen dollars and sixteen cents. To satisfy this debt, the records indicate that, "Wesley Swindle doth hereby give all his undivided interest in the personal estate of Joseph Phipps deceased; also one four horse 'waggan' and one two horse waggan, two woodworks of waggans and mare, twenty-one head hogs, and the present standing crop." Even for a person who cannot identify some of these possessions, it should seem to be excessive for payment of the debt in question.

It is not a proud discussion that any of our ancestors ever owned slaves. This is certainly true for the Swindall family. How on earth can one man own another? However, the record in North Carolina shows by bill of sale and a recorded deed that Wes Swindall and wife Polly of Ashe County, North Carolina sold to Preston Phipps, her brother of Russell County, their full distribution share of four certain negroes. These poor people that were unfortunately bartered like cattle were as follows: one woman named Vitale, one girl named Ceil, one boy named Sam and another boy named George. There is hope that the sale came about as a result of a change in conscience.

The more likely reason, however, is that Wes and Polly were trying to recover part of a previous investment when they feared that abolition would become more than just talk.

In reality of course, emancipation did occur later. It was passed by Congress on January 31, 1865, and ratified on December 6, 1865. This 13th amendment abolished slavery in the United States. It provided that "Neither slavery nor involuntary servitude, except as a punishment for crime whereof the party shall have been duly convicted, shall exist within the United States, or any place subject to their jurisdiction." What a wonderful testament to compassion and common sense was exhibited by the drafters of this law, which was favored by Abraham Lincoln and his supporters, then passed by the legislature at that time.

The American Civil War started in April, 1861. Wes Swindall took his family and moved to Kentucky after the war started. According to one of Wes's sons, John Calvin Swindall, rebel soldiers whipped his father in an incident that occurred not long after their first move to Piketon, KY. Rebels came to his home and tried to force Wes to join their ranks. When he refused, they beat him up. After this, the family raised some corn on Coon Creek, and more rebels came and took everything they had. This included a quilt that Polly had tried to save by hiding it in the creek.

Soon after these incidents, the family moved to Tom's Creek near Paintsville, KY. Wes joined the Union army in 1862 as a private. After this, they moved to Louisa, Kentucky and he became a Sergeant. His infantry group was involved in small battles and skirmishes in KY and WVa. They stayed in Louisa until the war was over and moved back to Osborne's Gap.

Because Wes had fought for the Union in the Civil War, he became a Republican. Part of his army pension application filed in

November, 1886 is seen above. He did receive a pension from the U.S government for his service during the civil war.

Wes' brother Eli (b.1837) and his mother Elizabeth (1801-1874) also came together to the South of the Mountain at about the same time as the Wes Swindall family. Eli married Elizabeth Anderson. Wes and Eli's mother, Elizabeth ("Betsy") lived with Eli and his wife, and they purchased and settled on what is now the Camp Jacob property. This was a few miles from Wesley and Polly on another road leading back toward Pound.

Eli had several children and thus gave rise to another "set" of Swindalls. Eli and his wife are both buried in the old Pound, Virginia graveyard. When my great-great-great-Grandmother Elizabeth passed away, she was buried in an unmarked grave across from Eli's home place. This unmarked grave is somewhere near the western corner of the Camp Jacob property, about 150-200 yards up the hill.

Near the end of her life, Polly lived with my grandfather M.T. until she died in 1907. He was more like a son to her instead of a grandson. M.T's mother, Ruth, had passed away when he was just an infant, and she and Wes had taken him into their home and raised him. Polly and Wes are both interred in the J.W. Swindall cemetery, located at the top of the hill in Osborne's Gap. It is notable that my great-grandfather James and my great-great-grandfather Wes both died within only a few days of each other in the year 1900. They both had contracted typhoid fever. They had been exposed to the disease while carrying out the dead from the homes of those that had been stricken. Several of Wes's offspring and other Swindall descendants are also buried in this cemetery, including my great-grandfather James.

My great-grandfather James Swindall (1852-1900) was a farmer much of his life, but he also became the high sheriff of Dickenson county in the 1890s. James first married Ruth Vanover. They had four children. One of the members of James and Ruth's family was my grandfather, Morgan Tennie Swindall, whose children and grandchildren called him "Poppy."

James was married two more times and had two more children.

5

His second marriage was to Amanda Stanley, and this marriage resulted in one of Poppy's siblings that I met and knew for a short time. She was thus Poppy's half-sister, and her name was Emma. My Dad called her Aunt Em. When I was a small child and we went to visit her, she was nearly 90 years old. She loved to see my father come to visit and was always very emotional, crying whenever we went to her little cabin beside the Pound River near Camp Creek. She had been married to Shade Holifield and they had five children. I remember two of them, Edna and Egbert or "Ag," which were my father's "half" first cousins. One of Em's daughters by another marriage, Hettie, married Logan Childress. One of their sons was Kenneth Childress, my third cousin. I have a music connection with him. Kenneth was a fine musician. He played guitar and sang in some of the early bands around Clintwood, and he was especially known as a great vocalist. Even though we never worked together professionally, we followed each other's music through the years and we had a lot of interest and respect for each other's music.

James' third marriage was to Nancy Hibbitts. This marriage produced only one living child, Nancy Eunice, who was at one time married to Charlie Ison. Another child died in infancy.

The South of the Mountain region was inundated in the late 1800s and early 1900s by Austins and Swindalls. The Swindalls owned much of the land in the Osborne's Gap area, and all the way down to the Pound River on Camp Creek. Many of the Austin families had also settled in the South of the Mountain closer to Pound, in the Almira section. When I visited my Aunt Nora in the 1950s, she lived on the side of the hill overlooking the "Flats" where the old original Wes and Polly Swindall home place was located. While there, I first learned about the existence of some relatives which were Swindall "offshoots." The flat bottom and some of the surrounding area was where Mahlon Swindall had lived, near the final Wes Swindall home. Mahlon was the brother of my great-grandfather James. Mahlon and his wife raised several children in this community. A few of them were Jim, Pauline, Draxie, and Russell. Pauline (Keen) lived a "stone's throw" from my Aunt Nora, on some of the original Swindall property. My first cousin Janice and I played with Pauline's children. I fondly remember one of them that we called "Mosie." His actual name was Russell Moses Keen, named for his uncle Russell. Recently, I have met another Ron Swindall (Ronnie Carl Swindall) that lives in Montana and is the son of Russell. I have learned that Jim's son, (also named Jim) lives there in the flats on the right and that his brother Charlie lives near him. Bill France and Draxie, Mahlon's daughter, lived just around the hill on the other side of the flats.

Another musical relative whose family originated in the Camp Creek area was Ron Shortt. He is known widely for his storytelling and his mountain music. He is the great-grandson of J.C. Swindall. His grandmother was Carrie Swindall, and his father was Thadys Shortt.

MORGAN TENNIE SWINDALL

My paternal grandfather was M.T. Swindall. He was widely known as a fine person. He left a legacy of being charitable, considerate and honest. One of the notable stories about him was his interest in the education of his own children and other young people in the South of the Mountain. My grandfather M.T. and Rufus Swindall provided the land for the county to build the Osborne's Gap school in 1906. The building was built by Roland Wheatley and one other helper. The officials agreed and signed a covenant stating that the property would be deeded back to the original owners should they ever stop having school on the property. School started there through the 7th grade in 1907 with about 30 students.

All of Poppy's children went to school at the Osborne's Gap School. My father completed fifth grade in the school. Lena, the youngest of my dad's siblings, finished 7th grade in 1942 and went on to graduate in 1946 from Dickenson Memorial and Technical School in Clintwood. The county stopped having school at the original Osborne's Gap School sometime in the late 40s and the property was, as promised, deeded back to Poppy and Rufus. My Uncle Joe Carson and others started having church worship services there. Soon afterwards, my grandfather secured complete interest in the land from Rufus. At that time the county started having school about 100 yards past Bill France and cousin Draxie France's home. The building was on what is thought to be original Swindall property owned by Wes Swindall. Leonard Sowards taught there. I even attended school there as a visitor with my cousin Janice while staying a few days with my Aunt Nora when I was on vacation from my school.

My Aunt Lena told me a story about a fellow named Doc Boston that came to the Osborne's Gap school and performed dentistry for the children. He was paid with money raised through pie suppers and cakewalks held at the school. The doc also made impressions for the neighborhood adults that needed teeth. He was arrested once while there, probably for public drunkenness. Poppy bailed him out of jail but he accused the doc of drinking a barrel of cider that he had made.

None of the Swindall boys were called to fight in the first world war, which started in 1914. My dad was only 6 years old. This family, however, did not escape the Great Depression, but as poor as the family was, they didn't pay much attention to it. Even though Poppy and his boys made moonshine whiskey in the 1920s, they managed to stay out of trouble with the law. Other than this, he stood on good country morals. He taught his children to be honest and loyal. They were taught never to steal or lie.

Southern mountain hospitality was shown toward people that walked for miles on the country road. The old road passed right by my grandparents' house. Poppy always asked the travelers to stop and rest awhile and have a bite to eat.

Out of necessity, farm people that lived out in the country had to be self-sufficient. During a recent visit with my Aunt Lena, she related to me some stories about her growing up years. She told me that she and my cousin, Ruby Vanover, rode Poppy's old mule to the mill. They carried corn on the mule to get it ground at the mill. The meal was used to make cornbread.

Cousin Ruby also left some stories about growing up in the mountains. For a large part of her life, she lived near Poppy.

Ruby told us, "Poppy made molasses. The juice from the sugar cane was used to boil molasses. Horses were used to help with the crushing of the sugar cane. The juice was boiled in a large flat container until it was thick enough to put in glass jars. While it was boiling, everyone around could taste the hot, delicious syrup."

My grandfather M.T. passed away in April, 1949 from pneumonia. I remember the night well because it was so cold. The family had been called in because of the seriousness of his condition, and most of them were in Clintwood at the little makeshift hospital there. I was left at the home place with my Uncle Carson. When it was time for bed, we slept together in a feather bed in the side room. I thought I might just freeze to death, there was so very little heat. I was only six years old. The funeral was very sad. Poppy had passed at the relatively early age of 61. He was interred behind the old school/church on the hill and was the first of several to be buried in what has now become the M.T. Swindall cemetery. It is interesting to note at this point that the Swindall men were mostly only living into their 60s, my father included. My Uncle Glen was an exception, living well into his 90s.

THE GILLIAMS

Jack Brummett describes John Gilliam as a pioneer, a patriot, a soldier, and a leading citizen of Wise County, Virginia. He is important in my lineage and in the history of our nation.

John Gilliam was selected by future president Garfield in the 1860s to lead his Union Army forces against the Rebels during the bloody battle at Pound Gap during the Civil War. He is my great-great-great-grandfather. His son was Martin L. Gilliam, my great-great-grandfather. Martin was born in 1835 at Cooper Creek, Scott County, Virginia. He was a farmer. He married Sarah Jane Skeen in

1855 in Whitesburg, Kentucky. Sarah was born September 19, 1839 in Russell County Virginia, the daughter of Stephen S. Skeen and Susanna Kiser. They had a daughter named Martha Jane Gilliam. This was my grandmother Hettie's mother. Martha Jane's father, Martin died of pneumonia September 7, 1862 in Louisa, Kentucky two months before my great-grandmother Martha was born.

Due to very poor economic conditions in Wise County caused by the war, Martin's wife, Sarah left Virginia and went to North Carolina with a logging company. She worked as a cook for the company after Martin's death. She had to leave her five children in the care of their grandfather John Gilliam. Sarah Jane later had two other children with Stephen Ward. They were never married. She died July 1917 in Wise, Wise County, Virginia. She was buried in the Gilliam Cemetery on Turkey branch in Wise County.

THE AUSTINS

My father's mother descended directly from the Austin and Gilliam families. Many of the Austins originated like so many others, from Northern Virginia. They made their way into Southwest Virginia, settling first in Smyth and Grayson Counties. It's interesting to note that one of the Austins, Stephen Fuller Austin, was born in Smyth County near Wytheville in 1761. His family moved to Texas where he became a notable public servant. He is many times referred to as the "Father of Texas." The city of Austin is named for him. It appears that he is a distant relative.

The known Austin lineage extends back to 1680 with my five times-great-grandfather John Austin and his wife, Hannah. They were possibly from Halifax or Pittsylvania County, Virginia. Their son, John Austin, Jr. and his wife Mary Maybee had a son, Bartholomew ("Bat"). Bat married Anne Reeves from New River Plantation in Grayson County, Virginia. She was the daughter of George and Jane Reeves. Bat and Anne lived on Rock Creek in

Allegheny County, North Carolina. They sold the farm there and moved near Cumberland Gap in 1830.

Bat died before the Civil War. Anne came with her son Jessee to Wise County, Virginia. She was born in 1773. She died in 1870 at the age of 96. Before she died, she selected the site for her burial and was the first to be interred in the Austin Cemetery. Her headstone was carved by Doctor Lawrence Haddon, a neighbor that lived nearby on the South of the Mountain Road.

Bat's son Jessee and his wife Margaret Douglas Austin were later buried here also. Each year, usually in September, the descendants of the Austin families schedule a family reunion and memorial service under the shed at this cemetery. The cemetery is located in the Almira section of Pound. It can be found by traveling from Pound toward Jenkins KY on U.S. Route 23, then at the foot of the mountain, turning right onto South Mountain Road, route 630. It is located on the right side of the road within just a few miles. It is interesting to note that the original Austin property is located near here, and that the road leads back to the Pound River. Another branch of this road goes to Osborne's Gap where the Swindalls lived.

My great-great-grandfather, Jessee Austin was married to Margaret Cox Douglas at Old Town, Grayson County, Virginia in 1855. They moved around quite a lot (a farm on Toe River, Ashe County, North Carolina in 1855, on to Russell County, Virginia in 1857, then to Elkhorn Creek in Kentucky, which is now named Jenkins, in Letcher County). They finally came back across the Cumberland Mountain to a tract of land beside the Pound River at Bear Pen and White Oak Creeks containing 2,422 acres. They and some of their children spent the rest of their lives here. This tract of land was about five miles northwest of the town of Pound. Some of it spanned all the way from the Kentucky line to the Pound River. Jessee was a farmer and a Baptist preacher.

Among their children was my great-grandfather, William Douglas Austin, a traveling merchant and farmer. He made frequent trips into Gladeville, now Wise. He was born in Grayson County. He courted and married a girl he met in Wise named Martha Jane Gilliam, and they had several children. They had a farm near the Pound River across the low water bridge from the Chant Kelly farm. One of their children was my grandmother, Hettie Jane Austin. She later married my grandfather, Morgan Tennie Swindall, and they were the parents of my father, William Edward Swindall.

HETTIE JANE AUSTIN SWINDALL

My paternal grandmother, Hettie A. Swindall was another of those women that knew what life was all about. She lived hard, worked hard, loved hard and had a passion for her Lord. She knew how to take care of her family, and she took pride in keeping them all happy and well-fed. My wife and I still take pride in knowing that some of the recipes that we use were handed down from her, and probably even from her own mother and grandmother. Hettie made barrels of pickled corn and beans. We just recently made a pickled mixture this fall called "chow-chow" that my Aunt Lena handed down to us from these archives.

Grandma Hettie loved me and whenever I would visit she always seemed to dote over me. She would always ask, "Now, are you hungry, honey? Let Mamaw fix you something to eat. What would you like?"

It didn't take long to fire up the old wood stove and have a tasty meal. She kept a drawer full of cornbread and biscuits. When any other children and I came in hungry, we snacked on bread, fresh churned butter, fried apples and cold sweet milk. During the summer months she placed her sweet milk and butter in a water bucket and lowered it into a well near the house to keep it cool. My dad had dug the well when he was a young man. I was lowered into it once to clean it out. Grandmother also made gingerbread for the children. She made gingerbread men, and put raisins for their eyes. She put a nose and mouth on the little man and each child could have one for their very own.

The hereditary origins of the musical abilities in our Swindall family are obvious. Grandma Hettie had a beautiful voice. She sang many of the old mountain songs for her family. A few of those songs (some of which I have also learned) were: "Barbara Allen," "Pretty Fair Miss," "If I Ever Prove False to You," "Ten Thousand Miles," "My Old True Love," "Going Up Cripple Creek," and "The Blind Child's Dream." Many years later, my dad still played these songs and others on the banjo.

As cousin Ruby said, "There were times when Grandma sang a little jig, and a twinkle would come into her eyes. Then she might say, 'I shouldn't have done that' after also dancing off a few steps."

In 1937, a man came through with a recorder that cut a record on the outside of the cylinder. He was collecting and preserving some of the mountain songs of that time period. He made recordings of my grandmother as she sang some of the old songs. These were filed and stored in the Library of Congress, and they can still be found there.

There was no electricity in those days. At night, all reading was obviously done by lamplight. A stove iron that was heated on the cook stove surface was used for any ironing that was needed.

Hettie made lye soap. It was very strong, but it removed the dirt from the clothes. She drew water from the well and put it in a huge kettle over a fire. Then she put the heated water in a tub and washed her clothes on a wash-board.

WILLIAM EDWARD SWINDALL

My father, William Edward Swindall, was born in a little cabin in Norland, Virginia on Camp Creek near the Pound River on February 10, 1908. The cabin was where his great-uncle Joe had lived. Tennie and Hettie later purchased about 55 acres of property in Osborne's Gap from his Aunt Elvira Swindall Hopkins and her husband Solomon Hopkins. They lived in this home place most of their lives except for about a year (1913-1914) when they resided in Jenkins, Kentucky.

My mother and father were married on August 11, 1942. They had met at a boarding house in Jenkins, Kentucky where my mother worked. At that time my father held a job as a miner with Consolidation Coal Company in Jenkins, Kentucky. My dad's friends and family affectionately shortened his rather sophisticated name to "Bill Ed." My great-grandfather's name, William, was passed on down to my dad. My father's middle name, Edward, was given to me, and I have in turn passed it on down to one of my sons, Nathaniel Edward Swindall. As of this date, I hope it might be passed on down again to a future grandson.

Bill Ed eventually had 9 siblings. There were two sisters and seven brothers: James Carson (Joe), Nora, Alphus, Clayton, Glen, Arthur, Homer, Thelmer and Lena. The family would have been a total of ten had it not been for the death of an infant, Leonard Cecil. Bill Ed grew up in Osborne's Gap, located in the South of the Cumberland Mountain, about seven miles from Clintwood, Virginia.

Dad spent his early adulthood, as many young men do, busy with a variety of interests. He was always interested in working and trying to make money to buy his own clothes and other things he wanted. He worked hard at a variety of jobs over the years and even made some moonshine whiskey. A good profit was made on the moonshine that my dad made because he never really drank any of it himself. There was always a 32 special Smith and Wesson pistol in his pocket for protection. When he was in his thirties, he left home and went to Toledo, Ohio to work in a factory. He returned later and settled for a period of time in Kentucky where he worked in the coal mines in Wheelright and Rockhouse. He was involved there in helping to form the U.M.W.A. Nearing 1940, he settled into a very stable job with Consolidation Coal Co. Bill Ed loved music. He played claw-hammer style banjo and strummed the guitar for his own enjoyment, and when he was younger he often played for others along with his brother Arthur and some of his Austin uncles.

My father was inducted into the army on May 27, 1943. He was sent first to Fort McClellan in Alabama on June 10, 1943 for his first round of basic training. He was in the infantry. He went on to Fort Custer in Michigan on December 1. I was only 7 months old. My mother and I followed my father to Fort Custer near Battle Creek, Michigan by bus and took a taxi toward the army base. While on the way, my mother met and discussed her dilemma with a lady that offered to take us into her home. We stayed with her and her husband for a few days. Her husband even volunteered to drive us all the way back to Kentucky later.

In a short time, my father shipped out to Texas, and we once again left for Jenkins, Kentucky where my maternal grandparents lived. His training continued at Camp Fannin in Tyler, Texas. My mother and I rode a train to Tyler and stayed there until he shipped out again, this time to Camp Barkley near Abilene. All of this activity was occurring before I had even developed a memory of my father. On April 30, 1944, my father received another stripe and became a *PFC*. Dad never cared for the army life in any way, and thus he had little incentive to try to make a higher grade after that. He just wanted to finish his hitch and get home. This he did, but it was over a year later.

Mom and I traveled back home again and spent a short time with my grandparents. Dad trained in Texas as a guard for German war prisoners, which would be one of his duties while stationed in France. He moved around quite a lot during the next few weeks, and contracted a lung ailment that landed him in the hospital for several days. From there he went to Fort Ord in California in May.

After a short stay at Camp Myles Standish in September, 1944, he shipped out from Boston Harbor aboard the *USS West Point*. This was a former cruise ship acquired by the U.S. Navy for troop transport. He arrived first in Liverpool, England on October 12, then to Hampton and Cheshire, England on October 13, and from there he was transported to Lazonne, France. After a few months in Lazonne, he travelled to Mourmellon, France on March 3, 1945.

For the next few months in France, my dad's job was guarding German prisoners of war and standing guard in a guard tower on the base.

A few of my friends' fathers never came home from the war. I have always felt lucky that my father was not in the thick of the battle. He did not enjoy his time away from home during the war, but he was able to travel a lot and see a lot of sites that he would not have otherwise seen.

William Edward Swindall left France from Le Havre, France on October 26, 1945. He came across the Atlantic Ocean on the good ship *General Breckinridge,* and he arrived with a lot of other happy soldiers in Boston Harbor on November 4, 1945. He was mustered out of the army with an honorable discharge on November 4, 1945 at Fort George Meade, Maryland. He was sent on his way with a final payment of $329.04, which included travel pay back to his home in Virginia. After a train and bus ride, he arrived home to his wife and son (me) during the first week of November.

MY BROTHER

Dad was rooming in Wheelwright, Kentucky with my Aunt Nora's family when he worked in the mines there in the 30s. He had been dating a girl named Goldie George from Melvin, KY. After a while their intimacy eventually turned sour and they broke up. She later left word that she wanted to see my father but he was not interested. It turned out that she was pregnant. My dad told others that he thought he was probably the father, and he showered the child with toys and bought him clothes, but he refused to marry Goldie. In the late 1930s, my father was still not interested in settling down. Of course, this all happened long before my dad and mom hooked up. One day, a couple of years later and at a time when my father was not present, Goldie dropped the child off in Osborne's Gap with my grandparents. Goldie told them that Billy was their grandson, and that he was being physically abused by her brothers and she was unable to both protect him and work. She had named him William Edward Swindall, Jr. When my mom and dad were married in 1942, Billy was almost 5 years old. While my father was in the army he occasionally sent money to my grandmother to help purchase clothes, etc. for Billy

Most family members accepted Billy as a member of the family. My mother never did. Billy probably resented me and wondered why I was so lucky to have been accepted and he was not. My dad's youngest sister, Aunt Lena S. Roberson, told me that Billy always wanted to be accepted and to be a part of the family.

Through the years until Billy finally left in 1953 I always saw him around when we would visit my grandparents, all seen here in this photo. I never understood that he was my brother! My mother (and father, and the rest of the family) always kept it from me. In these later years since I finally have realized the truth, I consider the story to be one of the greatest tragedies of my life. I always dreamed of having a big brother. I had one but didn't know it! I saw him with cousin Charles occasionally and I noticed that they were close buddies. Charles told me that Billy was like a brother to him as they were growing up.

My grandparents reared Billy until the summer he turned 16. I was 10 years old at that time. Goldie had been spending her summer vacations with him at Grandma and Grandpa's but told them that she wanted him to spend the summer with her in Baltimore this time. Grandma pleaded with him to not go. She said "I know if you go I'll never see you again."

Goldie assured her that she would bring him back before school started. That did not happen. Goldie may have kept him with her because he was now an asset to her, since he was able to get a work permit at age 16. He wrote a few letters to Charles during the next couple of years and corresponded with my grandmother until the early sixties. It was learned that he had moved with Goldie from Baltimore to Tonawanda, NY. Goldie had married a man whose last name was Wright and he had a daughter who was 2 or 3 years younger than Billy. Our family that lived in the Fairfax area said the Wright fellow abused Goldie and that he had brought Billy to my dad's brother Arthur's home one time. He told him he couldn't get along with Billy and asked Arthur to keep him. Arthur turned him down.

We never saw him again after this. Many years later when the family began to search for evidence on the computer again, Cousin

Charles learned that Billy had a Social Security card issued to him in Baltimore that very summer. It was likely that Billy had no desire to come back to the mountains after leaving that summer. He had nothing waiting on him back at Osborne's Gap but hard labor as an unpaid servant on a dirt farm. He promised others that it wouldn't always be that way. He was determined to leave, get a job and one day come driving back to show off a fancy car. He never returned. Now we know that Billy died October, 1971 somewhere in the Caribbean. We do not know why he was there. According to the records, someone did receive the $350 that Social Security pays as a death benefit.

The photo below was probably taken by my uncle Homer Swindall, and it likely is the only one in existence that I was in with my brother. I am standing inside Billy's wagon (purchased by my Dad). Billy is on the right side. Our first cousins are my Aunt Nora Vanover's children, L to R: Janice and Charles, and Clarence sitting in the wagon.

From internet research in the Social Security Administration records, we have confirmed that he was born June 28, 1937 and died October 16, 1971 at the age of just 34. My cousin Noel found some information on an internet site called Find A Grave. If it is all correct, Billy was laid to rest in the Glen Haven Memorial Park, plot A in Glen Burnie, Maryland. His wife was Janet C. Swindall (1936-1986). They had a son, Wayne Edward Swindall, Sr. We know very little about Edward's life at this point. My cousin, Charles Vanover, made contact with his grandson, Wayne. He has given us some more information about Edward.

I miss my brother, even though I never really knew him very well. As of this writing, I am continuing to pursue the possibility of learning still more, and especially now, because we want to know more about Billy's son, Edward, and other descendants.

William Edward Swindall, Jr.

From the picture of the grave marker that we have now, and from Wayne's information, we have learned that the grave of Wayne Edward Swindall, Sr. is located at the foot of Billy's grave. He was Billy's son, and he was born July 17, 1956 when Billy was only 19 years old. Wayne passed away on August 27, 1998. Based on an etching on the marker, Wayne Edward may have also been a musician.

My Mother's Family

Well, the kerosene that I drank didn't kill me. The story: My mother Louella and I had arrived for a visit at my maternal grandparents' home in Rocky "Holler" over in East Jenkins, Kentucky that warm fall day in 1945. (Don't ask me why it's called East Jenkins when it is actually west of the town of Jenkins). Kerosene was a common material used for starting a fire in the cook stove or fireplace in those days. Small containers of it were usually kept handy for that purpose. My grandmother happened to have a drinking glass filled with the clear liquid sitting on the porch. I had been playing in the yard and had gotten thirsty, so you can already guess what was going to transpire. Yep. I picked the glass up and took a large swallow before I realized that it didn't taste quite right. The next few minutes are a little foggy in my memory. The way I understand it, my grandmother (Mamaw, as I called her) gave me something to help me to regurgitate. Of course, she probably saved my life in the process, or at least prevented some degree of real sickness or brain damage (maybe). Who knows what great accomplishments and goals I might have eventually achieved if only I hadn't gotten thirsty that day? Ha.

THE MULLINS

I would like to credit Robert Mullins, my first cousin and the son of my Uncle Roy Mullins, for offering the results of his research about both the Mullins and Osborne families.

Mullins is the anglicized version of the French Huguenot name *Desmoulins* (millers). The Huguenots were a much-persecuted religious people (Protestants) of Normandy in northern France. Because of persecution by Catholics, many French Huguenots left France and went to England. Several thousand came to America, either directly from Normandy or through England. They settled mostly in New York, Virginia, and South Carolina. The Mullins of Beefhide in Kentucky could have been descendants of the French Huguenots that settled in Virginia, since many of the settlers of eastern Kentucky were from Virginia.

Many of our family members have assumed, because of the small stature and the demeanor of the Mullins families that are directly related to us, that we are Irish descendants. This surely is a possibility. Consider the ancestral backgrounds of the many women down through time and how this has influenced the DNA of their descendants. I am not schooled as to the nature and intricacies of these many bloodlines.

JAMES ROY AND LAVONA O. MULLINS

My maternal grandparents, James Roy Mullins and Lavona Osborne Mullins were married in April, 1923. Lavona was sixteen years old. The picture here was taken near the time of their 50th wedding anniversary. My mother Louella was born August 11, 1924, the eldest of eleven children in the Mullins family, all born by 1944. Louella was born in Myra, Kentucky, a tiny community between Jenkins and Pikeville in extreme eastern Kentucky. She came into the world just five years before the Great Depression (1929-1939), the deepest, longest-lasting economic downturn in the history of the Western industrialized world.

As my mamaw Mullins described my mother's birth to me, she said, "Your mother was born one evening during a hailstorm, and that's the reason for her disposition."

Mom was known to be headstrong and somewhat stubborn, like many of the J.R. Mullins family. She was a diligent, dedicated hard worker most of her life until she became ill with Alzheimer's disease in 2007. Her 10 brothers and sisters in order of age from oldest to youngest were Ruth, Roy Jr, Thelma, Ada, Curtis, Virginia, Eugene, Elaine, Rebecca, and Carol. During the early years of most of the Mullins children, their subsistence was mainly from farming. They existed by keeping a cow, raising pigs and chickens, and growing their own vegetables. The family was poor and there was very little money for any "foolishness" like candy or fancy clothing. Louella was, however, able to complete school through the eighth grade by 1938. Curtis was the first in the family to finish high school in Jenkins, Kentucky.

The J.R. Mullins family moved to Burke's Branch between Virgie and Pikeville, Kentucky and eventually into another home where they ran a boarding house mostly for the local coal miners. My grandmother and grandfather were always looking for ways to make some extra money. At one point in time, they even tried to make some moonshine on the stove to sell, until my grandfather ("Papaw") was caught and carted off to jail, but just overnight.

It appears that a lot of families did this at that time, but they were cautioned not to sell it, or at least, "don't get caught!"

Papaw also worked for a period in the coal mines and he worked as a laborer in a sawmill for the vast Ritter Lumber Company, incorporated in 1901 by William M. Ritter. The company quickly became one of the largest lumber and sawmill companies in West Virginia, Kentucky and Virginia. Through the years my grandparents tried selling commodities and Electrolux vacuum cleaners. Papaw eventually got a job as the school custodian in the Burdine, Kentucky elementary school, and he later became a custodian in a hospital in Farmington, Michigan. This allowed him to further build his retirement income. When he retired, he and my grandmother moved from Michigan and settled in Pound, Virginia in the early 70s in a house and property that they purchased from me. They lived there comfortably during their final days on earth.

James Roy Mullins was born on Beefhide Creek near a community now called Dorton, Kentucky on September 6, 1902, one of fourteen children of Joseph Mullins (1865-1934) and Delena Reese Mullins (1873-1970). Papaw's parents were married in 1889. The Joseph Mullins family lived on Beefhide Creek in Pike County, Kentucky. The family was relatively poor. They farmed and raised a few livestock.

Great-grandmother Delena lived until age 97. One of the features that I and many other people that knew her remember about Delena was her constant winning smile. My family and I visited her many times as I was growing up. One of the last times that I saw her, a photo was made shortly after my daughter Michelle was born. The photo was unique because it displayed five total generations of Delena's family, including Michelle, me, my mother, Papaw and Delena.

Great-grandfather Joseph Mullins, who died at age 69, was also an elementary school teacher for a while. He got his education at Gladeville "College" which later became Wise High School. It was located in Gladeville, Virginia, which later became the town of Wise, named after the Governor of Virginia at the time. Joe was rumored to be "ill-tempered," and according to my papaw, some of his children suffered physical abuse from him. He was the son of Smith Mullins (1831-1898) and Sarah Craft (1837-1898). Smith's father was Booker Mullins, born sometime around 1800, and Polly Newsome was his mother.

In his lifetime, my great-great-great-grandfather Booker Mullins had accumulated 3000 acres of land in the head of Beefhide Creek which stretched across the divide into Letcher County. Booker and Polly only had two children, Smith and William. William inherited the Letcher County land, and Smith inherited the property on Beefhide which many of his children and their children in turn inherited. They all lived there for many years thereafter. This large tract of land has greatly diminished into a few small scattered plots of land today.

THE OSBORNES

My grandmother, Lavona Osborne Mullins was born November 1, 1907 in Pike County Kentucky, one of 16 children. She was the daughter of Grover Cleveland ("Cleve") Osborne and Rebecca Tackett Osborne. My parents and I visited these great-grandparents a few times in the late 50s when they lived on Pond Creek just outside of Portsmouth, Ohio. Cleve always seemed to like me, and I remember playing an old upright piano that he had sitting out on his porch. He always smiled, and he seemed to enjoy hearing me play a song on it. I remember playing songs like "Sentimental Journey" and

"Red Sails in the Sunset" for him. He would sit and listen carefully, then he'd say, "Ah, that's really pretty. Play it again."

When Grandpa Cleveland was in his eighties and we were visiting one time during the summer in 1959, he sat and listened to me play a little. Then he said, "You play so well. I will give you the piano if you can find a way to come and get it."

I schemed a while about a way to move the piano back to our home in Virginia, but unfortunately that never happened.

Great-grandfather Cleveland Osborne was born September 22, 1884 on Indian Creek in Pike County, Kentucky. The lineage of the Osbornes has been traced exceptionally well through the years. Cleve's parents were Stephen Alex Richer Osborne (b.1865) and Montana Coleman. Stephen's parents were Jessee Bowling Osborne (b. 1830) and Sarah Greenfield Johnson. The parents of Jessee were Hiram Osborne (b. 1798) and Nancy Mullins. I have wondered about the chronological events in the lives of all of the ancestors on both sides of my family and where they settled at certain times. I have speculated about the possibility that some of them might have even known each other, especially since the entire eastern Kentucky and southwest Virginia region was so thinly populated in the 1800s. It seems likely that some of the Austins, Osbornes, Mullins, and Swindalls might have crossed paths and could have known each other.

Hiram's father was Solomon Osborne (b. 1765) and his mother was Hannah Bowling. Thus, Jessee's middle name Bowling was derived from his grandmother, Hannah Bowling. Names were often handed down like this. My mamaw had a brother named Jessee, and he named one of his sons Jessee. Also, Solomon, for example, was the namesake of his uncle Solomon that was killed by Indians in 1766 in Watauga County, North Carolina.

In 1805 Solomon Osborne and his family moved from Scott County Virginia to Pike County Kentucky and first settled at Elswick Branch. After two years, they moved to Indian Creek in Pike County, which was still almost uninhabited and mostly wilderness at that time. This is where Hiram was born and raised. Solomon lived here until he died in 1851. Solomon's father was Enoch Osborne (b. 1745) and his mother was Jane Hash.

Enoch's parents were Ephriam Osborne (b. 1723) and Elizabeth (Betty) Hardin. Ephriam was a fur collector and at one point in his life he was a serviceman in the employ of Christopher Gist on the Yadkin River in North Carolina. Gist was a surveyor that worked with George Washington to survey much of the land in Virginia. Especially notable was his work in the area of Pound Gap on Jenkins mountain. (The first high school in Pound, Virginia, Christopher Gist High School, was named for him many years later). Ephriam Osborne's wife Betty was related to Ms. Gist. To help place this in perspective, Ephriam and his wife settled ten miles north of the Gists on the Yadkin River at about the same time that Gist brought the Boones to their first North Carolina home. Daniel Boone was about thirteen years of age at the time. The record indicates that Ephriam and his family moved from Rowan County in North Carolina to Grayson County in Virginia about 1757, and that he lived there until his death in 1795. Ephriam and his son Jonathan were in the battle of Point Pleasant in Bland County, Virginia. The Battle of Point Pleasant is known as the Battle of Kanawha in some older accounts. This was the only major action of **Dunmore's War**. It was fought on October 10, 1774, primarily between Virginia militia and Indians from the Shawnee and Mingo tribes.

It is interesting to note that Ephriam's father Jonathan Osborne (b. 1697), was born in Warwick, England and landed at the James River Settlement, King and Queen County, Virginia in October, 1720. Ephriam's mother was Gretta Holman. Jonathan was a member of the Colonial Assembly of Virginia in 1741. Colonial Assemblies were the first official forms of popular representation founded in the American colonies prior to the Revolutionary War. According to research done by Northern State University in South Dakota, they provided the initial taste of self-government for the colonies and served as the forerunners for future representational bodies that emerged during and after the Revolution. In 1744 Jonathan joined the King's Royal Guards, and in 1745 - 1746 he was at Port

Royal in Virginia, one of the first important ports located on the Rappahannock River.

Jonathan's parents were James Osborne (b. 1674) and Ann Carter. Both were born in England, one at Warwick and the other at Stratford. They would be my nine-times-great-grandparents, and I would be a member of his 12th generation of descendants. My children would be the 13th generation of descendants from James Osborne.

Early Childhood

BIRTH AND FIRST MEMORIES

I was born in the wee hours of the morning at the old Catholic hospital on lake side in Jenkins, KY on May 11, 1943.

I weighed in at eight and one-half pounds, and my mother immediately had her hands full. My dad's sister Nora Swindall Vanover suggested the name 'Ronnie' for me and I was dubbed Ronnie Edward Swindall. I was not a "baby boomer," born after World War II. I was a full-fledged war baby, born right "smack dab" in the middle of the biggest war in history. My mom was a young girl of eighteen, whose husband of 9 months was inducted into the U.S. Army only 16 days later on May 27.

My Aunt Lena and cousins, Ruby and Arbutus sometimes took turns spending the night with my mom and I while dad was in the army. He had sold the car before he left because mom had not yet learned to drive. The girls even helped carry me all the way over Camp Creek Hill to visit with my grandparents.

My first memory of my father when he returned from the army was not pleasant. I did not know him, and I cried when he first tried to hug me. I vaguely remember that he had gotten some strawberry ice cream to try and win me over. It did not work. He seemed frustrated by this. I slowly got used to him being around, and our relationship improved as he spent  more time with us. He had gone back to work in the coal mine in Kentucky. He bought a little Chevrolet coupe to drive to work. There were no seats in the back, so I stood behind the seats.

Before he had left for the army, my father had purchased a small plot of land beside the road on Georges Fork. It was on highway route 83 near the Camp Creek Road intersection between Pound and Clintwood, Virginia. He bought it from his cousin Theodore (Ted) Swindall, and he built a two-story frame house on the lot.

My mother and I lived in this house while my dad was finishing his service obligation, and my mom tried to run a grocery store on the top floor. It was unsuccessful because groceries and other goods were extremely hard to come by during the war. We had little to sell and nobody had much money to spend anyway. Before my Dad returned, my Mom and I subsisted on the monthly check that was sent for support by the U.S. army.

Dad, Mom, and I settled into a happier existence in those days after the war. He worked, made money, bought a new car, and we all made neighborhood friends. Since he had been drafted while employed by *Consolidated Coal Company* in 1943, he was offered his job back when he returned home from overseas. He accepted it and began to settle down into the more pleasant routine of home and family. My mom joined the home decorating club and enjoyed some of the arts and crafts offered through the county extension service. But we were soon making plans to leave Georges Fork, buy a piece of property, and build a new home in Pound.

My dad's illness during his second year in the army may have been a Godsend in a way. It prevented him from shipping out to take part in the landing at Normandy Beach in France on D-Day, June 6, 1944. He was able to draw a service related disability check from the veteran's administration. He had a lung problem during the rest of his life. As a result of this he died from lung and heart failure at an earlier age than usual on August 22, 1974. He was only 66. My mother continued to receive this VA benefit after he passed away.

GEORGES FORK

In the next house down from ours and also on the right was a family of four. I cannot remember their last names, but the children were David and Delilah. They had briefly been my first neighborhood playmates. They soon moved away.

The next family to move into that house were the Kennedys. "Brother Boy" (Arnold) Kennedy was another one of my early childhood playmates on Georges Fork before we moved to Pound. I remember him well as being very mild mannered and pleasant. He had an older sister, Rosetta, that I didn't know very well.

The next house down the road past the Kennedy house on the same side belonged to Corbett and Mary Mullins, very close friends of my mom and dad for many years. The two couples loved playing cards together and spent many hours enjoying "setback."

These houses were all across the main road from the Camp Creek Road intersection. At about that same time, the Jarvis Vanderpool family lived on the other side, on the hill to the left and above the intersection. Janice V. and I were also early childhood playmates. Earl and Jerri Owens lived in the big block building on the left of the turnoff. They had one very young child and I did not learn his name. On down the road on the right, there was the little grocery/general store that was owned by Lacie Davis and Burl Shortt, the uncle of cousin Ron Shortt.

Next, on the hill, was the home of Hillman and Georgia Cassidy. Mrs. Cassidy was a dear friend of my mother. We visited her often through those early years. I found out later that Mrs. Cassidy's maiden name was Beverly. She was Walton Beverly's sister and they were relatives to Papaw Mullins' side of the family. She had an almost total hearing loss which she suffered during a fall. They didn't have children. The Cassidys had a huge bulldog that I always feared when we visited. Mr. Cassidy was a miner like my dad. He had a huge low booming voice.

There was a large house on the hill across the main road from the Cassidys and I can't remember who lived there. My mother was friends with the lady of the house because her husband was also away at war. They had a little girl named Rosella. We used to sit on the couch and hold hands and she became the first person of the opposite sex that I really noticed. She was, of course, my sweetheart for a short time. I was 3-4 years old. Cousin Ted Swindall and Eura moved down the road later to near the spot where Ted's son Tommy and wife Jewel would live.

Up the road about a mile from our home on Georges Fork in a community called Baden was the community post office where my mom and I would go to collect our mail. The only thing I remember about the place was the long sidewalk going up to the house where the P.O. was located, and the fact that a dog once bit me on the ankle as we were leaving. There was no damage except to my feelings. On this road was the school where I started my education and near where my friend Billy lived. The old school building is long gone, but the house that my father first built, which was our home when I was a small child, is still there.

Two other very important early childhood playmates were my aunts, Rebecca Ann and Carol Sue, seen here with me in this photo from the 40s. It was taken in front of our home on Georges Fork. They were my mother's sisters, but they were about the same age as me. I saw them and enjoyed their company when they came to visit, or when we went to Jenkins, where my grandparents lived.

Another relative to whom I always felt very close was my Uncle Gene. I looked up to him, and I always looked forward to visiting at my grandparent's home in KY, hoping to find him there so we could spend time together. This was always such precious time. He was a few years older, and we loved to play Tarzan. I was Boy, and he carried me around on his back, running, climbing trees, etc. We were also on the constant lookout for the ever-elusive Jane.

Elementary School

FIRST GRADE

It is my opinion that my classmates and friends in my age group have lived through the greatest era of time that America has ever known, or probably ever will. The latter part of the twentieth century may well go down in history as being the most creative period for arts and music, the years of many technological advancements, and one of the most prosperous times in history. We are certainly lucky.

I was a growing, learning, curious youngster when my dad changed jobs and started working at Meade Creek, near Pound, VA. In a couple more years I was six years old. The Virginia school rule at the time was that a child must be at least six and one-half years old in order to enter the first grade. In August of 1949, I was only six years and three months old. My mom had always read to me, and had actually even taught me to start reading. The teacher was impressed by this and made an  exception for me. I started school in a one-room school at Georges Fork, within walking distance of our home. My teacher was Ms. Bertie Phipps.

It was a difficult period of time for Ms. Phipps, with about 20-30 kids in grades 1-5.

Much of my free time from school was spent outdoors, either playing with other kids, or in our backyard, or even in the little creek that flowed behind our house. I loved to watch the little minnows swimming around in the water and to study their movements. I have been an outdoors person all of my life.

One of the first friends I made in school was Billy Moore, the son of Willard Moore. We spent recesses playing together and I was even allowed to visit Billy at his home which was just a short distance above our home on Georges Fork. In later years, Billy moved to Pound. He became a classmate and a teammate on our football team. Mr. Moore had some ponies, and I was impressed by the fact that Billy had a pony of his own. A selling price was made to my dad for one of the ponies. I remember getting very excited, because dad had actually considered buying it, but he soon realized that it wasn't practical for us at the time.

My dad stopped working for Consol on September 9, 1947. He took another coal mining job as a shot fireman for Clinchfield Coal Company in a mine located across the mountain at Meade Creek, close to Pound, VA. We were still living on Georges Fork at the time.

By the time I had finished first grade, my parents had definitely decided that we should move to Pound. They thought I might be in a better school situation, and that my dad would at least be a little closer to work and not need to drive across a mountain every day.

MOVING TO POUND

The Korean War started in 1950. I was 7 years old, and a second grader. My dad was not drafted into the army at this time. He had reached age 42, and they were calling younger men. There were 36,584 American soldiers killed in this horrible conflict and about three times that many were wounded. North Korea was a communist country, under the influence of the Soviet Union. Our interests stemmed around the fact that South Korea should be protected from the spread of communism. My uncle, Roy Mullins Jr. was in the army during the war but he was lucky to have been stationed in Germany and was not sent to Korea.

When we moved to Pound, we moved first into a little rental house owned by Leonard Barnette. It was located on the left side of the main highway just above the turnoff to Killen Hollow. The closest school was a little one-room school on the old road, called Hillman school. My mother did not like the idea of me attending another one-room school. She decided to pay tuition and send me down to the town of Pound to attend school at the little elementary school on the hill near the Methodist church. I started second grade there in the fall of 1950. My teacher was Mrs. Almon. Other than learning new math skills, I remember that she was a stickler for teaching vowels and word sounds to her students. That became an asset for us all as we learned to pronounce and spell. The school system in Wise County was struggling with funding. It was necessary to have two sessions of second grade, one in the morning and one in the afternoon. I rode the bus to and from school and attended the morning session. There was no school cafeteria at the time, so I carried my lunch in the same Lone Ranger lunchbox with the thermos of milk that my parents had purchased for me to use in first grade.

The kids in the morning class were allowed to have lunch before getting on the bus to go home. I remember a few of my classmates, like Herman Meade, Lynne Fleming, Betty Hodges, Gloria Hopkins, Sue Hensley, Newton McCoy, Rose Ann Swindall, and a big kid named Dan. He was strong and a little too playful at times. One of his joys was to chase a little guy down during recess and just hold him. He meant no harm, and this activity gave him purpose. He probably felt he was gaining affection by doing so.

The kids ran around screaming and avoiding Dan's attentions, yelling, "Look out! There's Dan."

I was caught a few times and it both annoyed and scared me. One day I turned and plowed my little fist into his stomach as hard as I could. Of course, he immediately turned me loose and he started to cry. I was elated at first, but later felt bad about it. He didn't tell the teacher and nobody else tattled on me. He always avoided me after that.

I remember a couple of incidents that happened while I was in second grade. When Rose Ann and I met for the first time she was extremely excited to know that she had a bona fide cousin in her class. She began showering me with gifts that she had purchased downtown, and of course, I accepted the candy and coloring books and other items with grace. This continued until my mother began wondering where these items had come from since she didn't buy them for me. She asked me to return them, and of course I did. Rose Ann's mother Grace Edwards had also gotten wind of these exchanges by that time. Then it was not a fun experience.

Another thing occurred when it was Lynn Fleming's birthday. There was to be a party and I had been invited, but I had forgotten. On the day of the birthday she asked me at school if I was coming to her party. I admitted that I had forgotten, but after school I ran downtown to the Federated store and bought several items that I thought she might like. I charged them, telling the clerk that it was ok with my parents that had already established an account at the store. When I arrived at home with the gifts, it was again not a pleasant scene. I had overstepped my bounds and my mother was angry. She did, however, take me back down to the party that evening.

My good friend, Brenda Salyers sat behind me in school. One thing that she told me later was memorable and funny. She said that she always marveled at how clean my neck and ears were and how my clothes always looked so clean. It exemplifies why I was luckier in some ways than a lot of kids in my age group. Most families had at least three or more kids to feed and maintain, so the work of keeping them clean and in line was much bigger than the one that my mom had, since I was an only child. There were both advantages and disadvantages in growing up as an only child.

Home for me during this time was not a very interesting and

exciting place. The rental house was perched on the side of a hill. The yard was dirt and weeds. We were always straining out the wiggle worms (mosquito larvae) before using our water from a spring on the hill above the house. There was an outdoor toilet but it was not often used in the dead of winter, except to empty the "chamber pot." I will not describe the "potty" alternative at this point because it was not pleasant, but we were accustomed to it. Our family had always had this situation, and most households in the middle of the twentieth century had little or no indoor plumbing, and experienced the same conditions. We really didn't know the difference, but this would soon change for us.

The entire one-bedroom house was small, but my bedroom was the epitome of smallness. I think the room had been designed as a pantry or a large closet. In any case, my half bed fit into the room with no space on either side and I had to crawl into it from the foot of the bed. The only positive side of living here was the fact that our friends, the Bills, lived next door. They didn't have any children at the time so the small size of their house was less of a problem for them. Regina and Sterling Bills became extremely good friends of our family. This friendship continued for many years even after they had moved away, and we lived in our new house up the road.

Sterling Bills was a young guy, and fun to be around. We picnicked, and we made day trips together to High Knob and to the Breaks of the Mountain Interstate Park. He and his wife loved to go swimming on the South Fork of Pound River. They had located a wide and fairly deep bend in the river about three miles up the South Fork road. We went there often during hot weather in the summer. Sterling got a job in Louisville, KY in 1951 and they moved away. We visited them there a couple of times.

My dad had previously purchased an eight-acre tract of land, along with a house that had to be torn down. My dad hired some help and made short work of the structures. Afterwards, he and my mom looked at house plans and selected one.

While we continued to cope with the living conditions in the rental house and property, he cleared the land further and contracted a bulldozer to level the earth. The contractor began landscaping a future yard. Dad decided to use glazed tile for the walls. He made a deal with his cousin W.F. ("Bud") Austin to help purchase and haul the tile from Ohio. This was a similar tile to that which Bud had used to build his Austin Motel in Pound many years prior. Dad contracted more labor and skilled help and began pouring the footer for the new building. Twelve years later when U.S. 23 became a four-lane highway, the house was moved by Leonard Barnette. The moving contractors struggled for days to cut through the footer. It was over a foot wide and over a foot deep, and it was laced with steel rods.

Ked Hibbitts from Clintwood laid up the tile for the outer walls. My parents and I made trips into Scott Roberson Hollow at the foot of Indian Creek Mountain to secure the services of a skilled carpenter named Willard Addington. He was an artist and a very meticulous worker, and he loved to work with oak. My father actually did a considerable amount of the construction himself and it seemed to me that the house was built quickly. My dad had purchased a little 1950 model Chevrolet pickup at the time and he used it to haul building materials. He purchased floor joists, studding, rafters, white oak flooring, moldings and other building supplies from Short Lumber Company on Indian Creek. This was a business that was formerly located in the deep curve between the former Buck's Drive-in and Nifty's Signs. One of the amazing considerations within all of these changes was the way my father and mother managed to buy property and build a nice new home. They accomplished this with funds from their sale of the old property on Georges Fork plus a bit of savings, his wages from the mines and a lot of penny-pinching. There was no mortgage nor debt. We moved in during 1951, and for the first time, we had indoor plumbing!

All of a sudden I had a bedroom of my own, and since we also had a planned guest room, I wasn't even required to give it up for company! A sidewalk led to the front entrance of the house. The front porch door entered into a fairly large living room with a picture window in the front, and a fireplace between two higher small windows in the outside end. Willard had fashioned an arched double doorway with oak framing leading into the kitchen/dining area. Four windows in the back wall of the kitchen allowed my mother to be able to look into the back yard and the garden while cooking or washing dishes. The kitchen opened to a covered breezeway which housed the ductwork running from the furnace room, which was on the right side as one looked from the front of the house. The furnace room was the location of the heating system, consisting of a large coal fired Sunbeam furnace and the coal bin. There was room for can house shelves, a small cook stove, and even a bed.

Back in the house, the other end of the living room opened into a small quadrangle hallway leading to the three bedrooms and the bathroom, which was on the end next to the outside wall. My bedroom was in the back corner of the house with mom and dad's bedroom being located in the front corner. The third bedroom, located in the middle back, was removed by a later owner when the wall was torn down between the bedroom and kitchen to make room for a formal dining room.

My father made improvements and convenient additions to the property as time and money would allow. We had a large garden laid off behind the house and dad built a smokehouse to accommodate salted pork from yearly butchering, plus tools and storage as well. He worked on the yard and landscaping, and built a rock ditch to re-route and take care of the heavy runoff from the hollow behind the house.

I rode the school bus to school every day. During all of my school years, the lower Indian Creek bus which covered the area from Killen Hollow up to the New Camp was number 27. It was driven by Mr. Earl Bolling, a math teacher at the high school. He was my algebra I and algebra II teacher a few years later. I caught the bus each day just below our house in front of Barnette's store where all of the neighborhood kids waited. There were days when I was late getting there and I missed the bus, sometimes while I was running down to catch it.

Through the ten years that we lived there, which were most of my impressionable growing-up years, we did well as I struggled with puberty, peer pressures, school, and various other adjustments.

Money was still relatively tight and I didn't receive everything that I wanted by any means, but I was still probably luckier than many of the kids in my age group simply because I was an only child. One of the gifts that I received as an eight-year-old was a rod and reel. I had been using a cane pole to catch the bluegills, suckers and horny heads from Indian Creek, which ran down toward "the Pound." I would bring a couple of the larger ones home from time to time and ask my dad to "fix" them for me. He seemed to not mind doing it because I think he wanted to encourage me to enjoy fishing. I was occasionally known to try and dam up the water in the ditch that ran beside our house to try to keep the fish alive that I had caught. My dad and I made a few trips to South Holston Lake, but we were never very successful. I have, however, always been fascinated by water and what lurks underneath the surface, so I was "hooked." I loved to fish anywhere I had a chance, and the sport has become a lifelong hobby for me and my family.

In third grade I was deeply in love with Betty Hodges, a curly headed little classmate. We exchanged notes, passed on of course by another of our friends, and we developed a mutual attraction. I was overwhelmed by her note that said she "liked" me. I was quick to respond and we became sweethearts. Our dads worked together, and the next time I saw my Aunt Nora she quickly told me that the Hodges family were really good people because they went to church with her. Whenever there was any kind of assembly, we sat together and held hands. I thought it was great. For example, the high school seniors at Christopher Gist gave their senior play performance on the stage of Pound theatre, for the final time that year, and I sat mesmerized with Betty. The next year the new Pound High School building opened and they finally had their own stage there. We were then bussed over to the new high school to see the plays. Our great romance did not end until fifth grade.

Our third-grade teacher was Ms. Cornett. She really liked me. During our yearly health screening and testing of eyes, she discovered that I was quite nearsighted. She informed my mother that it was probably affecting my ability to see the board and other objects in the room and could cause learning difficulties. Naturally, my mother became quite concerned about this and made an appointment with Dr. Henderson, an eye, nose and throat specialist in Norton. After testing me, he prescribed and sold us a pair of glasses. I received the new spectacles by mail a few days later and I was shocked at the clarity I gained while wearing them. I had just entered an all new era.

So, I was now a bespectacled third grader. To my dismay, some of the less caring kids immediately started making fun of me, calling me "four eyes." This really hurt my feelings, but I knew that I was going to need to cope with it. Unfortunately, I don't remember any other kids with poor eyesight that were friends to which I could relate, except a couple of girls, and of course nobody called them names.

One of the problems which was ongoing for quite a while was the fact that the glasses were real glass and they had plastic frames, both easily breakable. Well, sure enough, while playing football in the yard, it happened. When I went inside to tell my mother, it was as if I had just killed our pet or something even worse. We had to go back to the doctor and order another pair. There was no other alternative if I wanted to see. This happened a few more times down through the years, always with severe chastisement.

The next year after third grade I went to school down at the old Christopher Gist High School building which was now an elementary school. Fourth grade was a bomb! I ended up in Ms. Hughes' class. Because of our lack of rapport, I feel like I failed to progress very much that year. I suppose I was lucky to pass on to the fifth grade. I don't remember a lot about the year other than it seemed as if there were two or three kids on the playground that always wanted to fight, and I had no desire to do so. I wasn't afraid of the kids, but I was wary of getting in trouble or perhaps hurting someone. It just made no sense at the time. The playground was a little better than what we had at the little school on the hill, but it was always either muddy or dusty. I knew that my parents probably had it worse when they attended school.

One of the activities that I enjoyed was marbles. I was always amazed at the skill and accuracy of some of my playmates as they cleared the ring. I always lost. Another game during recess was basketball, but it wasn't as much fun without a net.

We also played quick games of softball and dodge ball during recess.

Another one of the activities that I will never forget had no particular name. When we had winter snow, we always looked forward to the times when the sidewalks were covered. We started working the sidewalk runways as soon as we arrived at school on those mornings. By morning recess, a good length of our sidewalks were perfect slides. The idea was to get in line with the rest of the boys (girls did not participate), and run toward the packed ice/snow. When we hit the beginning of the slide, we locked our legs and slid as far as we could go. As time went on, the slide became longer and slicker. If one was lucky and careful, several great thrilling runs could be made without wiping out. I loved it!

From one of Brenda Dotson Salyers' memories: "In fifth grade I turned a cartwheel on the playground, landed in a mud hole and splashed Ron. Next day he told me that his mom said for me to never do that again. I didn't, but Ron, in my memory, is the guy who sat me down in the dirt in front of the third-grade rooms and drew in the dirt to explain multiplication to me."

The elementary school did not have a cafeteria, so we had two lunch choices. We could either bring our own or walk over into town during the noon hour and eat at one of the restaurants. I mixed it up. I brought my lunch most of the time, but I walked over to Wright's Restaurant a few times for a hot plate, or to the Pound Cafe for a hot dog. One time my mother made arrangements with the Pound Cafe owner to pre-pay for my lunch for a few days. The "exorbitant" price for a hot dog and sixteen ounce Pepsi was twenty-five cents! Also for a quarter, I would occasionally just walk out to Lloyd Mullins' store, which was located only a few steps down from the school on the same side of the road and get a sandwich and a drink. At lunchtime, his wife Florence would be making bologna sandwiches with tomato and mayonnaise for several kids lined up in front of the counter. The little candy shops in the basement of the Federated store and the United Discount store seemed to flourish during this time, when the school children had a little change in their pockets and more time to spend it. This was soon to be a thing of the past as new schools with in-house cafeterias were built.

Fifth grade was even worse than fourth grade for me. It is absolutely my worst memory of school. Betty Hodges and I broke up, which was bad for me. For some reason, Ms. Jewel didn't like me. Was it the way I looked or did she resent me for some reason? She was never nice to me. She seemed to have it in for me from the start. I made low grades in the subjects in her class, no matter how hard I worked. I also seemed to get bad conduct grades, but I never really knew why. I was lucky to get through that year. Anyway, I really believe that music saved me from making a wrong turn in the road at that time.

SCHOOL, MUSIC, AND OTHER DIVERSIONS

As bad as school was for me in fifth grade, two wonderful things happened at home and at school during my 1953-54 school year. My dad presented me with my first guitar, and William Duckworth moved to Pound to teach music and start a band. My whole world was changing for the better. Mr. Duckworth recruited band members based on instrumentation needed for the band. I'm sure that he tried to cater to the desires of some of the upper classmen, but in my case, he quickly decided that I should play snare drum. He said that I probably could not play my dream instrument, the trumpet, because my embouchure was not made right. I joined the Wildcat band and played in the drum section along with my classmate Sidney Buskell and high school students Ina Dotson, Don Hurt, Mickey Deel and

Anna Lou Mullins. My parents purchased a deep wooden snare drum for me and I learned the ins and outs of reading drum sheets and playing off beats, flams, paradiddles, etc. I always liked the cadences we could play together, and thus the marching season was more enjoyable to me than the concert music. During concert season, the drum section seemed to stand a lot while doing nothing. It was difficult for us to stay quiet.

The wooden drum seemed to give way to the elements, and wet weather especially had an effect on the cowhide head. The other drummers were getting new and better drums. After two years of complaining, my parents purchased a pearl Ludwig snare drum with a nylon head for me, and that situation improved.

Some of the other band members and I turned out to be future members of our first rock 'n roll group in Pound, called the "Shadows." They were Kennith Ellison, Aaron Ellison, and Donnie Mullins.

Our band director, William Duckworth, was a great woodwind player, musician, and teacher. He was a wonderful music mentor for many Pound students. We did not really appreciate him until many years later. Bill moved on from Pound to Abingdon in the mid-60s and David Barker took over as the band director. When Bill retired, he returned to Pound after his wife Margie passed away. He then lived with Margie's mother. He joined the "Jerome Street Ramblers," a band in Big Stone Gap that was started during the 90s by Dave Tipton. Bill played clarinet as long as he was healthy enough to do so, before finally going to the nursing home to live out his days.

My very first guitar was a little three-quarter size Stella that my dad bought for me from Bill Blevins, a fellow mine worker, when I was 10 years old. I was very interested in the beautiful tones of the strings and the sounds my dad could get when he chorded the little guitar, but my fingers were too small to really start playing. The strings were also far off the frets. But I loved the sound and tone and I showed a lot of interest and kept trying hard. I listened and watched carefully as my dad played the little guitar and sang tunes like "Goin' Down This Road Feelin' Bad" and "Can I Sleep in Your Barn Tonight Mister." These were old mountain songs that my dad had played with his brother. Arthur had played guitar and my dad mostly played banjo. My Aunt Lena told me about this and how they would occasionally play for parties. My grandmother did not like this because of the moonshine that typically accompanied such events.

The only other old time musicians that I have heard were my old friends, Hobart Crabtree from Big Stone Gap and Papa Joe Smiddy. I have been lucky enough to get to jam some with both of them. They are actually the only others I ever heard besides my father that played the true old claw hammer style. Hobart was always especially adamant about the style and how it should be done.

There have been several other guitar and "banjer" pickers on both sides of our family, including my guitar playing grandmother Lavona and her siblings. My mamaw belonged to the local Old Regular Baptist congregation. I have preserved a recording of her voice as she sang some of the old hymns. It is very special!

My father, William Edward Swindall (1908-1974), was a mountain musician from Osborne's Gap, far back in the hills of Dickenson County, Virginia. He was mostly self-taught, played claw-hammer style banjo very well, and also strummed chords on the guitar, and sang. In his day, there was no bluegrass nor country/western. He enjoyed playing and singing at mountain parties and watching folks have a good time. He never had music heroes like kids have today. My dad certainly was my first music hero and guitar teacher. The old mountain style of banjo playing is almost a lost art.

SCHOOL BREAKS AND INDIAN CREEK NEIGHBORS

Most youngsters, especially boys, always love their time off from school. I was no exception. My time away from school was even more precious during the fourth and fifth grades. After school, during holidays, and summer breaks I spent a huge amount of time outside, working in the garden, roaming the forest, fishing, swimming, and numerous other activities.

During a week of the summer break in 1955, I had my first real trip away from home without my parents. I was in 4-H club at school. During our meetings, Mr. Jim McCormick, the county extension agent, described the summer camp to us. I decided I wanted to go. One day all the 4-H kids from surrounding counties and ours climbed aboard a Greyhound Bus. We rode all day to Camp Summers, located just east of Hinton, West Virginia. The week was wonderful. There were tons of 4-H kids from Virginia, West Virginia and Kentucky. We were involved with sports, dancing, arts and crafts and other activities. We were all assigned as members of Indian tribes. I was Cherokee. I became friends with James Ham from Coeburn, but I never saw him again after that week. The good Clintwood athlete, Kelly Sutherland, was there that week and was chief of the Shawnee tribe. I had swimming lessons, and learned the "jellyfish float." I did not become a skilled swimmer on that trip, but any former fears that I had experienced were diminished, and I was starting to learn. Camp Summers had been a very memorable experience. I wondered if I might be able to go again the following summer. The fee was only $50 for the entire week.

Our next-door neighbors across the hill were Newton and Muriel Cantrell and their four boys: Denny, Gerald, Randall and Stacy. I spent many Saturday mornings in their home laying on the living room floor with the boys, watching Saturday westerns and cartoons. Denny and I were closer in age and spent a large amount of time together, mostly in the forest. One of the things we enjoyed was building little square one room cabins. These were built with poles that we cut with axes. We occasionally went camping. Between the two families, we probably had 15-16 acres of property to enjoy.

Another activity that was a little more productive for Denny and me was digging mayapple. We would go together and dig the roots for hours, then each of us would take our sacks of "treasure" home, wash it and lay it out on the roof to dry. One of the pitfalls was the occasional contact with poison ivy. The results were often disappointing because ten pounds of roots dried up into about one pound of saleable product. When we had enough, my mother would load us up and drive us over to Coeburn to sell our stash. The last summer that we dug, we were getting thirty-two cents per pound. We didn't make a lot of money, but it was a worthwhile experience. I learned later that the mayapple was crushed up and a medicine was extracted from it. This extract has tumor inhibiting properties, and it may be used in the treatment of small-cell lung cancer and testicular cancer, among other applications.

With Denny or my family, I often made trips to the Johnny Green Cliffs, which were enormous rocks in the forested hill about one quarter mile down from our property. We played there fairly often, sometimes with other kids, pretending to be early residents or Indians. We climbed all over the rocks, up and down, repelling and exploring. There was some indication that early Indians might have used the area. Our invitation to one another was always, "Let's go to the cliffs today." It's just one of many examples of the richness that I experienced as I was growing up. I feel so lucky!

The Cantrell boys got bikes before I did, but they often allowed me to go up to their house and ride one of their bikes. This was great fun. Newton Cantrell and my dad rode to work together for several years while they worked at Meade Creek, alternating the times when each took a vehicle. Newton loved to entertain his boys and other kids in the neighborhood. He and the boys built a basketball court on the hill behind his home. They labored hard, digging and leveling out a spot large enough for the court. He had been a very good athlete at the old Christopher Gist High School downtown. He was a real model citizen for neighborhood kids. Newton essentially taught and inspired me to play the game of basketball on this old hand dug court.

Another thing that Newton did in the summertime was to load up his boys and other neighborhood kids and take us all to the strip ponds on left hand fork of Bold Camp. The ponds that were left there by stripping coal filled with rainwater and runoff and became clean water holes for swimming. With Newton's help, I honed my swimming skills that I had briefly started to learn at 4H camp. He was the teacher and lifeguard for the kids that he took swimming.

There was a drive-in theatre on Indian Creek for a brief time. It was located across the road from Preacher Francis's home on Conley Mullins' property. He had terraced it and made it suitable for parking cars. The Cantrell boys and I made a few trips to the drive-in to see a movie. We took our blankets and laid on the ground in front of the big screen. The Stanley Brothers did a concert on the small stage in front of the screen. The Stanleys had their best of times in the early fifties. They played all over our area and were also on the Grand Ole Opry. I remember being down town and seeing their Cadillac go through with the big bass fiddle attached to the top of the car.

Newton Cantrell had a large influence on my growing up years. Another point of interest was the proliferation of minnows in most of the strip ponds which Newton spotted and told us about. My dad and I set minnow traps and caught dozens to be used on our occasional lake fishing trips. The ponds were all completely closed off from creeks in the area. Where the minnows originally came from was always a puzzle to us.

We quickly learned that one of the primary vegetations that returned to an abandoned strip mine was blackberry vines, so we also made trips to the Bold Camp/Meade Creek area during berry pickin' time.

The family that lived just below us in the next house were the Freemans, Guy and Francis, along with their three kids: Jimmy, Donna and Gary. Jimmy was a couple of years older than me, Donna was a little older but nearer my age and Gary was about three years younger.

Jimmy taught me to play mumbly peg. <u>Every man should carry a pocketknife.</u> It's handy for cutting open packages, severing twine and of course, eating an apple like a real man. But it can also be a source of instant, anywhere entertainment because it's all you need to play the game of mumbly peg, or as Jim called it, "mumble de peg." The aim is simply to get the knife to stick in the ground. What makes it even more tricky is that it involves progressively more difficult flips and trick tosses. The first man to successfully perform all the trick tosses wins and gets to drive the mumbly peg into the ground with the handle of his pocket knife. The loser has to pull the mumbly peg out of the ground <u>with his teeth</u>. Jim and I played this game fairly often when we were bored and needed something to do. He also taught me a few things that I probably didn't need to know, but I will not reveal them all.

We sometimes had Rook games at Jim's house, either just the two of us, or with other kids in the neighborhood. Jim wanted me to learn to chew tobacco. So, with his encouragement I bit off a chew from a plug of Day's Work while we were playing cards. I was OK for a few minutes, then I probably started turning green. It made me very sick, and I remember him saying, "Well, you're not supposed to swallow it." (And why did he not tell me??)

Since I didn't yet have a bike, Jim would sometimes let me sit on the crossbar of his bike and "double head" me around the neighborhood. We took trips down the old road which ran parallel in places to the newer highway. Occasionally, we rode all the way to Killen Hollow and played baseball with the Meade and Hurt boys. After I got my bike on my twelfth birthday, I rode far and wide, including all the way to town and all the way to the head of Indian Creek. My Huffy was an important addition to my life and it added fun and flexibility at a time when I needed it most. One of my riding partners was Tracy Boggs, a neighborhood friend in my same grade, who was adopted by Leonard and Emma Barnette. They owned the grocery store just down the road about one hundred yards. We explored the neighborhood on our bikes, riding to Newton's to play basketball, and visiting other kids. We even rode to the Pound-Jenkins railroad tunnel a few times in the summer, and walked through the tunnel over to the Jenkins swimming pool. When Tracy and I later got our driver's licenses, we were allowed to drive all the way to the Camp Creek, Caney Creek, Norton, or Jenkins swimming pools where my mother had been taking us earlier. We enjoyed a lot of time together.

Soon after I got my bike, I also got a job as a daily newspaper boy for the neighborhood. Our neighborhood was not thickly populated and I didn't have many customers. I faithfully delivered the Knoxville News Sentinel to about 30-40 customers from Killen Hollow to the curve above the present location of *Robo's* drive-in restaurant. The meager cut that I received, along with the occasional bad weather conditions, made me stop and assess the actual value of the job as opposed to doing something else with my time. I stayed with it about one year.

In addition to being an electrician in the mines, Guy Freeman was a radio repairman and ham radio operator. His family was probably one of the first in the neighborhood to own a TV. I often spent some time on Friday nights and Saturday nights catching the Friday night fights, wrestling, The Big Story, and Dragnet, etc. We finally got a TV when I was a junior in high school. We shared their ribbon signal line with them. It ran to the top of our relatively steep mountain which was about one quarter of a mile away. The antenna was in the top of a tree which had been stripped of its limbs. As might be expected, during storms or heavy snow, there were many obstacles to our reception. Newton Cantrell's family also used this signal line for a while. I climbed the hill along with Jim, Denny, Gerald or my dad many times to raise or repair the line after a storm.

The other Freeman sibling, Gary, was always fascinated by the songs of Elvis. I think he knew them all and he would sometimes come to our house and ask me to play some chords behind him as he sang. Later in life, we even played together professionally for a while in the house band at Club Scotty, a local night spot.

In Jan, 1957, we had a bad flood in the Pound area. It had rained all night and my father had just left for work when the waters of Indian Creek began to raise. The highway in front of our house was soon covered. The water raised into the Freeman's garage. Gary came up to see me and we stood and watched out the window as the water raised up to the top of the Freeman's porch. In Pound, the water ran down the streets. Many of the houses in Pound Bottom had water either running into their attic or they were completely covered. The results were devastating. Our flood made the national news and the area was declared a disaster area. The Stanley Brothers wrote and recorded a song in the springtime. It was simply called "The Flood of '57."

Middle School

SIXTH GRADE

We didn't actually have a middle school when I was in school in the fifties. It was all called elementary school, from first through seventh grade, but it seemed to be a big step for all of us when we made it to the sixth grade. We were, for the first time, actually allowed to write with ink! Mom bought a fountain pen for me along with a bottle of ink, and I began making messes like the rest of the students. The good Scripto brand bottles had "ink wells" in the top of the bottle so we didn't have to dip the pen all the way down to fill it. We tried to be careful, but we did spill ink very often and we smeared it on the desks, on our papers and also on our clothes. Things improved somewhat with the advent of the cartridge pens. The small ink-filled plastic cartridge could be inserted inside the pen and closed with very little or no mess. The problem was that kids (including me) even tried to refill these cartridges, since they were more expensive than just refilling a fountain pen as before. How pleased the teachers must have been when the ball point pen came into existence!

Kennith Ellison and his family were strong republicans. The town of Pound and surrounding area was inhabited mostly by folks that were loyal to the democratic party. Our family did not claim allegiance to either party. When the Ellisons moved to Pound, Dwight D. Eisenhower was our president. Eisenhower was a very highly respected and notable General during the second world war. He had won the election in 1952, and he was running for re-election in 1956 against Adlai Stevenson, the same democrat candidate that he had defeated in 1952. Richard Nixon, a strong anti-communist advocate, was "Ike's" running mate both times.

Our teacher, Ms. Qualls allowed us to have some fun during the election by campaigning with speeches and posters, etc. We also had students that represented the actual candidates. Kennith became Eisenhower and I became Nixon. It was fun, but we were defeated. We felt as if the cards had been already stacked against us.

One of the events that occurred periodically was the arrival of Reverend John Henry to the school to tell kids Bible stories. (It was legal then). He spoke in a strong booming, yet calming and constantly reassuring voice, always so pleasant. Reverend Henry and his assistant, Jack Lloyd brought props for their stories consisting of a large felt board and cutout characters and letters. We always looked forward to his times with us, not just because it got us out of class for a while, but it was always entertaining and informative. All of us loved to see John Henry come to school.

My sixth-grade teacher, Ms. Emily Qualls, was to be the best teacher and person that I would remember during all of my school years. In so many ways, she was my education salvation and inspiration. I am happy to say that I was able to spend some moments of time with this precious old friend through the years. She had been my teacher in 6th grade, and again in high school where she taught geometry. Later she became a colleague and valuable mentor when I was fortunate enough to teach in the same school. She is listed in the top echelons of all teachers that taught in Pound schools through the years. When I last visited her, she was 95 years young and would be 96 within two months. She was happy, alert and full of smiles. Ms. Emily Qualls was a model teacher and wonderful fellow human being. She was never married and thus had no children of her own, yet she had so many! Her disciplinary skills and deep caring for her students left no doubt that she would have made a great mom. She is loved by all.

We talked about several things that day, and her memory as well as her willingness and eagerness to share her thoughts were both refreshing and admirable. I hadn't thought of the following story in many years, but it popped into my mind that day and I was amazed that she too, remembered the story and even added to what I remembered.

A SANTA CLAUS

Visualize if you will, those colder November days, when it's better to be inside than out. The cloak room rack is bulging with the 11 and 12-year old's heavier coats and hats. Lunch kits are lined up neatly across the cloak room floor. The steam radiator hisses and pops as it works to release its warmth. The huge wooden framed, single pane windows leak cold air into the room, but basically just enough for fresh air. The dark wooden floors are slick with the sweeping compound and oils that have been used to clean and preserve them. The smell of the material used on the floors is always present, and it is an everyday constituent of the smells in the room. The sights and sounds in all of the elementary school's rooms were also etched into my memory.

The morning bell sounds and all students scramble to their desks with their books, paper and other materials stowed away in the bottom. The day starts with the Lord's Prayer (it was legal then). The Pledge of Allegiance was next (we stood and respectfully placed our hand over our heart). The morning's opening ceremonies ended with a song like "America," or maybe even a hymn. Then comes the moment everyone has been waiting for. Ms. Qualls reaches to the front of her desk and slides out her copy of the Hardy Boys, "The Disappearing Floor" by Franklin Dixon. A hush falls over the room and everyone gets really quiet while she reads another exciting chapter of the book. At the end of her reading she leaves the children in a gasp as she reads that Joe Hardy has just had a mishap and his life may be threatened.

"That's all today boys and girls. We'll read another chapter tomorrow. Now please get out your arithmetic books and pass in the homework that you were assigned yesterday."

Ms. Qualls leads the children through another important lesson, explains a new concept, then gives an in-class assignment, "Now when you finish this exercise, you may turn in your papers and perhaps work on the Santa Claus if you wish."

The children all began working excitedly on the assignment.

This was a typical late fall day in Ms. Qualls' room. The Santa Claus was an idea for a Christmas project, a bit of artwork and an incentive for study. It was working. Chicken wire had been used to roughly form the shape, followed by papier-mâché to more accurately form the shape of the body. The students worked on the project daily and for several days, even during recess.

Something else often occurred during recess whenever Ms. Qualls needed to leave the room to talk to another teacher or go to the office. Some of the students (including me) would sneak the Hardy Boys book from her desk and read a few lines from the next chapter. When I visited her this year, I told her about this, and I suddenly realized that she probably knew about it then. After all, reading aloud to us from an especially interesting book was a tactic to encourage us to read for ourselves. Like I said, she was a great teacher.

One day Mr. Morris, the principal at the high school, came into the room for a visit. Ms. Qualls was not expecting him and the students were working on the Santa Claus project. The messy white goop of the papier-mâché was all over our hands and arms. She told me when I visited her that Mr. Morris' appearance had worried her, but she told me that he did not call her down for the mess.

Finally, the shape was finished. After it dried a couple of days, Ms. Qualls provided paint for a few of us to finish the job. She was so pleased with the result that she felt that the Santa Claus was worthy of display. She decided that it was good enough to be seen downtown, and the Pound Hardware might be an ideal place. She proceeded to take it over and show it to Mr. Harold Jackson, Eva Mae's father. He agreed, so during the Christmas holidays of 1954, our beloved Santa Claus made an appearance downtown Pound for all to see. The project was not repeated again.

As I was leaving Ms. Qualls after my visit to the Wise Laurels assisted living center that day, I assured her that she was definitely one of the best and most memorable teachers that I had in school, and that I loved her. She told us to please visit again and more often. "You are all my family," she said.

Ms. Emily Qualls passed away May 26, 2012 at the age of 99, leaving a legacy to long be remembered by the many people whose lives she touched.

PICKIN' AND GRINNIN'

I received a brand-new f-hole Kay hollow body guitar from Sears & Roebuck for Christmas when I was 12 years old. I had learned chords (G, C, and D). The very first song I learned to play was, as I realized later, a tribute to A.P. Carter and Maybelle Carter (his sister-in-law). It was A.P.'s idea for Maybelle to use her guitar pick to pick out breaks on the guitar since they had no traditional fiddle. She was the first in history to do this, strumming and picking at the same time. Now I could do it also, with the Carter Family's "Wildwood Flower." I was so proud. At that time in history, I believe that this song had been the first to be learned on guitar by many young beginners.

I loved my new guitar and it made me want to learn more. My dad had taught the simple chords to me, and he inspired me to start playing and loving music. He did the same for my cousin Janice. He even taught her to play banjo first. She later switched to guitar, and she had a sweet voice for vocals.

We loved to listen to the "Grand Ole Opry" and we later learned many of the songs that were played on the show. We were fans of them all. We listened intently to Hank Williams, Kitty Wells, Martha Carson, Hank Snow, Ernest Tubb and many others. Then we were suddenly at the beginning of the 'Rockabilly' era, when Elvis was just beginning to break into the music business. It was a great time to be playing music! Finally, when I was about 13 years old, I recorded for the first time with Janice. We watched with fascination as Alec Tompkins used his equipment to literally cut our records. My first on-radio experience was in 1956 with Janice on WTCW, Whitesburg KY, one of the first radio stations in the area. When Janice was married, she moved away, leaving me to either go it alone or find someone else to pick with. Music is good for the soul and most folks that learn to play an instrument do not stop playing during their life. It is a talent, a blessing and a gift to be shared with others. Musicians generally have a different perspective on life itself. Now in her 70s, Janice still plays and sings today.

My favorite musician "buddy" was Aunt Nora's daughter, my first cousin, Janice Vanover. We made an effort to spend as much time together as possible, pickin' and singin'. Janice was a very good vocalist, and I learned much from her in my efforts to try to keep up and play guitar behind her while singing either unison or harmony. Her brothers and sisters had purchased a really nice jumbo Gibson for her and the sound was so wonderful. We played and sang a lot together at every opportunity. She was always both a great lead vocalist and harmony singer.

Family Life On Indian Creek

LIVING OFF THE LAND

My dad worked hard in the mines and my parents were very frugal. My dad enjoyed hunting a little, fishing occasionally, and he always liked to take a trip somewhere during his two-week vacation period which was around the fourth of July. This might be the time for one of those fishing trips with my Uncle Curtis and me, or maybe a "faraway" family trip to somewhere like the Smoky Mountains in Tennessee.

Our garden was a source of pleasure and pride for my parents and they worked hard to keep it going. They considered it to be a necessity, and I was expected to work in it also. If there was work to be done by me, I tried to be very diligent and complete it promptly. I found out that if I did not do my work, then I might be knocking myself out of a trip to town for a movie, to the swimming hole with the Cantrell's, or to a neighbor's house to watch tv. So, with that as an additional incentive, I helped my mom and dad plant, cultivate and harvest potatoes, sweet corn, beans, tomatoes, beets, carrots, cabbage, okra, mustard, kale, turnips and radishes. We dug potatoes and holed them up for the winter or kept them in a large dry whiskey barrel in the furnace room. We ate potatoes, sweet corn, beans and tomatoes, fresh carrots, radishes, mustard and kale directly from the garden. We canned many quarts of green beans and tomatoes. We made pickled beets, pickled corn and kraut. All of these skills had been passed down by my grandparents.

During a two-year period, we even grew peanuts. I learned that when cultivated and hoed for the final time, the white blooms are always covered. The peanuts develop underground where the flower was covered. We had over a bushel of peanuts during each of those years. We roasted them in the oven and enjoyed them many times during the winter.

If we had an over-abundance of garden vegetables we would give some away. We would also sell them to local retailers, or we would even peddle them to other locations.

Our family owned a large field of about two acres near the top of the ridge. Each summer we went there to pick blackberries. After a couple of trips, we would end up with 4-5 gallons of berries. My mom made blackberry jelly and jam. Just after we picked the berries, she would make fresh blackberry cobbler, then freeze some berries for the winter. I even tried my hand at making a batch of wine a couple of times. The fields and forests offer so many wild edibles for us to enjoy. I know that I haven't scratched the surface in my lifetime, but while growing up I noticed and tasted so many wonderful things. Even now, I love to chew tender teaberry leaves and tender birch twigs. Wild huckleberries grew all over the hill above the house. The chinquapin trees (*Castanea pumila*) were always a little more difficult to locate, but if I found one the payoff was great. In the fall, the nuts inside the burr were always very tasty. The beech tree nuts and hickory nuts, even though delicious, are probably better left for the squirrels, which seem to be much more adept at extracting the nut. My mother loved the taste of the paw-paw fruit in the fall, but I have always been allergic to the fruit. There are many more foods in nature that are common and well worth mentioning but I'll leave those for *Simon and Sheuster*.

Our property was large enough to have a few fruit trees. There was an old June apple tree in the backyard across the ditch. One of my favorite things to do was to sit on a limb in the tree and eat the apples when they were ripe. I did the same in a couple of tart cherry trees in the side yard. There were five total apple trees around the yard and they were all loaded with fruit at different times. I enjoyed horse apples, rusty coats and small striped summer rambos at other times. We had a concord grape arbor up beside the smokehouse and it was always one of my favorite destinations in the early fall. I was also known to pull ripe tomatoes from the garden during late summer, grab a salt shake and take them into the front yard to sit and enjoy. The fresh raw carrots, radishes and cabbage were also a treat for me. We lived good lives in the 50s!

Besides random jobs that I was asked to do, it was my duty to mow the lawn every week or two in the summer months. Dad had bought a Briggs and Stratton rotary mower from Pound Hardware, and it happened to be one of the most cantankerous beasts that I ever tried to operate! I worked a lot at home, and it gave me an appreciation for helping out and being a part of something bigger than me. There were certainly times when it seemed to interfere with my own selfish plans and motives. I carried the work ethic with me into adulthood and was always sure that my children should help with the work in our home and that their incentive should sometimes be cash payment. I feel like more parents could develop this philosophy. It builds character. This good practice, and spending lots of time with your children as they grow up are the most precious gifts that you can give them. I never wanted to be away from my kids as some parents seem to want to do. Keep them busy, work and play with them, and enjoy time together. You will never regret it!

Another activity that I observed, and in which I participated while I was growing up, was butchering hogs. During several years, Dad would purchase a young pig or two and we would fatten them for butchering. He always liked to get Hampshire pigs for this purpose. They were black with a white band around the shoulder area. I had the job of "slopping" the hogs most of the time. We fed them some table scraps (no meat), garden plants, juicy weeds and pig feed purchased at Barnette's store down the road.

When frost came to the mountains, it was time to start thinking about butchering. I always heard or watched the gunshot but never actually did the shooting. A close range shot between the eyes with a 22-caliber rifle did the trick. The pig was then strung up by its hind legs on a homemade rack, the jugulars were cut, and it was allowed to "bleed out." When I was old enough, I had to help carry boiling water and begin washing it down so I could begin to help scrape all the hair off. A large galvanized wash tub was moved into place and I watched as my dad cut a longitudinal line down the belly and began raking and pulling all the entrails down into the tub. Except for the liver, we usually buried these deeply. The carcass was separated with the special saw into two longitudinal halves. The rest seemed fairly simple. The two halves were carried to a table where the limbs were removed, again with a saw. Following this, the front shoulder was cut off and the rear hams were removed. The mid portion was again divided three ways into the belly, the ribs and the back strap. The back strap was the source of the pork chops and tenderloin, the ribs would be cooked, the upper part of the belly became bacon, and the lower portion became fatback which was sliced for seasoning food during cooking or used to render lard. Sometimes we gave the head away.

I was never really fond of any of the butchering process but I must admit that I really enjoyed the "fruits" of our labor later. We usually had fresh pork chops the very next morning, and after curing, the hams and bacon were fantastic. I remember tasting the sweetbreads, the thymus gland in the throat, but never the other with the same name, the pancreas. We ate sweetbreads at my brother-in-law's wedding many years later. The term is sometimes used as a misnomer for brains, which is incorrect. I have tasted pig brains and eggs also, however. That is not one of my favorite foods.

All of the meat had to be kept cold. Soon after the butchering process, Dad would almost immediately begin curing the meat. He used brown Morton's salt/sugar for curing. He thoroughly rubbed the shoulders, ham, fatback and bacon with the compound. He then mixed up a solution of it with water and used a large metal hypodermic syringe to squirt it in around the bone of the hams and shoulders. He sliced up the pork chops and ribs and my mom wrapped them and placed them into our chest freezer. There were a lot of trimmings left when all of this process was over. These trimmings, plus some other meat that had been purposefully cut off, were all ground up and mixed with spices to make sausage which was then frozen or canned. There was very little waste. All of this meat was a very important staple in our winter diet, along with occasional beef, chicken and fish purchased from the market. The obvious savings of money, the satisfaction and pride along with the healthier less worry-free lifestyle is something that very few people enjoy today.

One of the great perks of home butchering and curing was the ham. After each ham was cured, Dad carefully wrapped them in burlap and hung them from a rafter in the smokehouse. We usually had several guests for Christmas dinner and a ham was always at the center of the table. Dad removed a ham, or half of a ham, depending on the size, into the house for my mom to prepare on the day before Christmas. She washed it carefully and dried it. Then she scored all of the top into small squares. She prepared a mixture of molasses and mustard which was rubbed thoroughly over the entire surface. A clove was stuck into each of the squares that had been scored into the top. The ham was wrapped in a couple of layers of aluminum foil and placed on a very large baking sheet. It was then placed into the oven at 325° for several hours overnight. The house filled with the always nostalgic smell of the cooking ham, leaving us all with one of many delightful memories of Christmas during that time.

Any ham that was left over after Christmas dinner was either consumed during the next few days, or it was frozen for future use. The other ham was rarely baked. It was instead periodically sliced and fried for use as a breakfast meat or for another meal with vegetables.

It seems that the work never stopped or even slowed down around our home. When we weren't canning or drying beans, chopping cabbage, canning kraut or making apple butter in the fall, then my mom was always busy preparing meals, packing lunches or cleaning house. I was a participant in all of these things as well. One of my biggest dreads was being required to get down and buff the oak floors in our home after they had been waxed.

BILL ED

My dad was honest, reliable and dedicated to his family and his brothers in the UMWA. He told horror stories of the early days when men that worked for the big companies worked like horses and were treated like animals for very small pay and no benefits while the companies became richer. He was convinced that the younger men never fully understood this. My dad was involved in helping to form the union, and he became the president of the Pound local union in 1955. He worked with the others as they argued, went on strikes and negotiated for better conditions for all the miners. The UMWA was resented by many people, including some of the miners themselves, but even people that worked for the scab mines received many of the benefits for which people like my father fought. He attended the UMWA convention in Cincinnati, Ohio in 1956. There he heard John L. Louis when he addressed the assembly. He was a strong union member all of his life, even after he retired. When I was growing up, we always went to the big UMWA Labor Day celebration.

Dad grew into manhood at the beginning of the Great Depression and he learned how to survive. Out of necessity he learned many skills that he used throughout his life. I was constantly witnessing his practicality and ingenuity. He always felt that he could do anything that was necessary if he just tried.

I gained a real appreciation for his work in the mines when I watched him demonstrate his skill at home one day. We had a huge sandstone boulder that had been sitting at the entrance to our garden since we had lived there. One day he decided "enough was enough." He had chosen, as he said, "to take a stick of dynamite to it." I watched excitedly as he drilled a deep hole in the rock and placed a blasting cap attached to a wire in the bottom of the hole. Then he poured powder into the hole and tamped it. He ran a wire back down to the house where he had a battery waiting. We hovered down behind the wall of our old water well. I was expecting a huge blast. I covered my ears, but when he touched the wire to the battery all I heard was, "Poof." The rock fell apart into hundreds of pieces. Nothing flew through the air. I suppose I was a little disappointed because of the lack of drama. I later realized that this was a much-needed skill inside a mine. I helped shovel it up into the wheelbarrow so we could take it and dump it.

My mom was always interested in baking and catering. She was never in position to actually start a business, but if she had been given the opportunity, it could have been a lucrative sideline (as if she didn't already have enough to do!). Mom signed up for a couple of weeks of training at the Wilton School of Cake Decorating. She packed up and took a train all the way to St. Paul, MN during January, 1956, leaving my dad and I to fend for ourselves for several days.

When she returned, I remember my dad telling her, "Don't you ever leave me for that long again."

It had been difficult for him to maintain the house, cook, pack his and my lunch, and work every day except Sunday.

We both depended on her heavily to keep the household running smoothly. After her training, she was known and sought after for her cake decorating skills.

Margaret Jackson asked mom to start a catering shop with her, but Mom told her, "I just have too many other responsibilities."

My mother baked and decorated many dozens of cakes for various occasions, including parties, wedding receptions, birthdays, etc. She had the skill and the talent for creating some beautiful designs and making sugar flowers that looked real. It was my responsibility to help her deliver the cakes to the parties. What a delicate, nerve-racking task! I remember many times carefully holding one of the most delicate cake layers of a multi-layered cake while she drove over sometimes bumpy roads to get to the client's home or a church. Ah, the good ole days!

SOME WHIPPINS

"Spare the rod and spoil the child." I guess that old philosophy is true to a certain extent.

Out of necessity, my mom spanked me or used a little switch on me occasionally as I was growing up. It was probably all pretty much justified, except for the time that the neighbor girl lied to her about something that I had supposedly said to her. I guess it was because the girl never liked me anyway, but be assured that I have never forgotten that lie.

On the other hand, my dad whipped me two times in my life, so I am not likely to ever forget those times. Here is the first story: I was little more than a toddler. My dad had only returned from the army a year or so before that. I hadn't really gotten to know him very well. We were living on Georges Fork at the time. My dad was building the smokehouse in the backyard. He was nearly finished except for the roofing. He had a ladder leaning against the rafters and he was on the roof. I excitedly climbed the ladder. He saw me coming and told me to get down. I ignored him and continued to climb nearly to the top.

He warned me once more, "I told you to get down, you'll fall!"

Well, it was time for me to express my feelings (oops! bad mistake!).

I just looked up at him in anger and said, "I hope you fall and break your leg."

He told me one final time to get down, and this time he was coming down also. I got to the bottom and ran. He caught me and used his big hand on my butt. I snubbed and pouted for a long time, until I could see that it was all fruitless. I learned a lesson without actually getting injured.

Many little kids are inconsiderate when dealing with adults. Children tend to think they are too special sometimes and it breeds bad behavior, lack of respect, and selfishness. Events that cause a child to realize just how much a parent cares are great learning experiences. I certainly will never forget something that happened to me whereby my father saved me from being electrocuted. He was working in the yard and I was playing under the floor of our home. I was barefooted. We had an outdoor faucet underneath that was used to attach a water hose whenever it was needed. For some unknown reason, I decided to turn the valve. When I gripped it, I received a tremendous electrical shock. I could not move. My arm was paralyzed by the energy. I was able to scream for help. Dad ran to me quickly and accessed the situation. There was a board laying nearby which he used to partially push and actually knock me away from the faucet. He saved my life that day. I remember that it scared him a lot.

I told my daughter this story and she said, "Well, I sure am glad that he saved you!"

I responded, "Yes, or you might not be here."

This incident had been the result of grounding the electrical system into the water pipes. Evidently this was common practice for many years. Codes today do not allow this practice.

I loved to go to the Pound Theatre and see movies, especially on Saturdays when lots of other kids were there. When I was about 12-13 years old and big enough to go alone, my mom or dad would allow me to ride downtown with a neighbor or they would take me. Often, when I was ready to return, I would go to the taxi cab stand and ride back home for a quarter in the old Plymouth of Thurman Baker. During one of my trips to the movies, dad was planning to come back and pick me up at a location that we had decided upon. When the movie was over, I called him and told him I was ready. I waited several minutes and when he didn't show up, I decided to strike out on my own, with the plan of hailing him as he drove by on the road to get me. I had good intentions. Mistake! I walked about a half mile. As he came by I waved, trying to get him to see me and stop. He did not see me. I walked all the way home as I watched for him to come behind me and stop. I arrived at home and he pulled into the driveway shortly thereafter.

He said very little other than, "When you tell me you will be somewhere, you'd better be there."

He pulled off his belt and strapped me with it about six times. Oh, it hurt like h---! I learned something about my father on that day that I would never forget. He said what he meant and he meant what he said (one of his quotes). My dad was a good man, and I always had a great deal of respect for him.

SEVENTH GRADE

At some point during those last couple of elementary school years, I made a few friends that were to become my best friends all the way through high school and even in college. One of them was Ronnie Clark. He had recently transferred down to the Pound school from Riner School on Indian Creek. We enjoyed each other's company and soon became lifetime good friends. The Hubert and Agnes Ellison family moved from Big Stone Gap back to Pound and I quickly became acquainted with Kennith, his parents and his three brothers. The oldest was Curt, Kennith was next and he was my age. The next younger brother was Aaron, and the youngest was Robert.

The main reason that Kennith and I hooked up as friends was the fact that he had recently been a member of the band in Big Stone Gap. He was already experienced in band participation. He played trombone and his brother Curt played tuba in the newly formed Pound band. Kennith and I spent much time together. We could often be seen together in town and at ballgames or other extra-curricular activities. Kennith and I were a couple of clowns and we sometimes entertained our classmates. It remained this way until the fall of our junior year when I became more interested in a girl.

Our school band had been performing at football games and even at the Bristol Band Festival. We had only been wearing Pound Wildcat sweatshirts and jeans because we did not yet have uniforms. That changed in the fall of 1955 during my sixth-grade year. We were proud and sharp looking in our new band uniforms. I have fond memories of traveling to the festival on a Greyhound bus and marching down State Street that day. When I got home I told my mom that I was marching down the street taking alternate steps in Virginia and Tennessee. We performed our show in the Stone Castle at Tennessee High School. The Castle was a multipurpose football field built in 1937 by the PWA. At one point, all of the participating bands from all over the region came together on the field for the purpose of playing a couple of marches together, like "The Thunderer" and "Stars and Stripes" by John Phillip Sousa. When it all came together, it was very impressive, and I was proud to be a part of it. Another exciting part of the festival were the cadences played by all the drummers in all the bands. When we stood at attention for a long period of time, we became bored. Someone would start a marching cadence and soon all the drummers joined in. It was an exciting big sound.

Our seventh-grade teachers were Simon Meade, Kenneth Stallard, Bessie Williams and Tollie Boggs. Mr. Stallard taught English and seemed to be especially fond of Shakespeare. We read "Othello" and even ended up performing it in front of all of the seventh grade rooms. Kennith was Othello.

In seventh grade, when I carried my lunch, I would often have lunch with another one of my friends, Herman Meade. We would sometimes exchange some of the things that our mothers had packed for us. Whenever I had something very special I was known to trade it to Herman for the privilege of wearing his Bulova watch for the remainder of the afternoon. When I told my mother about this, she made plans by Christmas time to provide a watch of my own for me to wear.

We had a candy and snack store in the school. One of my best memories was whenever I had a bit of extra money, I would purchase something called orange aid. It was a fabulous tasty little drink in a four-ounce glass bottle distributed by Clinch Haven Farms, along with milk which was also available at the school. The milk and orange aid were expensive, three cents!

Mr. Duckworth did not teach separate music classes at the

elementary school. Band practice was held in the band room at the high school, which was located upstairs at the back of the building. The elementary school students that were in the band were transported by bus to the high school during the last period of the day. Most of the time that bus was driven by Mr. Simon Meade. We caught our own neighborhood bus from the high school just after practice.

One of my costly conduct mistakes was made that year while riding the bus over to the high school. Sidney Buskell and I had just learned something about the deadly accuracy and devastation that could be wrought with a "pea-shooter." We even found that we could make our own with an oversized milkshake drinking straw. Instead of peas as bullets, we used "spit balls," a wetted small piece of paper wadded into a ball to stick together. This was especially gross when left a little bit wet just before the shot. We practiced on each other until we were very skilled. But what happened on this day was a discouragement for me to ever use the weapon again! I had taken a seat in the back of the bus behind all the other kids. Eva Mae Jackson, Rose Ann Swindall, Lynn Fleming, Patricia Stallard, Ginger Roberts, Mary Ann Hollyfield and others were riding the bus on this day. My friend Sidney was only a couple of seats back from Mr. Meade and occasionally we were "shooting" at each other. I was ducking most of his shots and had been pretty successful in hitting him so I rolled up a nice juicy one and sat quietly, not realizing that he had a sinister plan. He raised up and turned around as if to shoot at me, and I let him have it, or so I thought. He ducked, and oh no! My nice spit ball hit Mr. Simon Meade right in back of the neck. We had just gotten to the intersection in the middle of town. He looked up immediately into the rear-view mirror and he swiped the paper from the back of his neck as if swatting a bug. He was looking straight at me. He gestured with his index finger for me to come forward. When I got to the front of the bus, he pointed toward the steps. He said, Young man you go ahead and get off the bus now. I want you to walk back to the school. Go and sit in the office. I will be back shortly.

My ears started to burn like they always did when I knew I was in trouble. I walked back across the bridge to the school and waited. When he returned, he didn't talk much. He simply asked me to stand and bend over the office desk. Then he unleashed his own weapon with a fury. Others had talked about it and described it and experienced it, but not me, until that day. The weapon consisted of a thin board paddle about twenty inches long and it was wrapped tightly with slick electrical tape. He burned me with seven good swift swings and I could not hold back the tears. I sat in the office with my stinging butt and deflated ego until the end of school. I never told my parents what had happened.

Another lifetime friend that I made in grade school was Donnie Mullins. He was also in the band and played trombone in the lineup with Kennith and a couple of others. Donnie, Kennith, Ronnie Clark and I, all had both sports and music connections throughout our school years and beyond.

Kennith and I loved to walk around town after school or on weekends. We went to the Pound Theatre for a movie or we visited other friends. We popped into Wright's Restaurant or the Pound Drug Store for something to drink. As we got a little older we visited the pool room down behind the taxi stand. Kennith, Donnie, Jay and I loved to go in and play a couple of rounds of pool. It was only ten cents. I never got very good at it, but it was one of those forbidden things that I did. My mom had warned me never to go into Shade Bank's pool room. She had heard that "they gambled in there." I never witnessed any gambling, but I did occasionally observe Blaine Sturgill, Fred Mullins and our principal Mr. Morris, along with a few others in one of the side rooms playing "Rook."

That summer after seventh-grade, I was able to make another 4-H trip to Camp Summers in West Virginia. A sixth-grade student made the trip also, and we sat together on the bus ride. His name was Larry Alderson. He lived on Indian Creek in the New Camp housing area. His father was also a miner. Larry and I became friends and enjoyed our time together in camp that summer. Later, we were also on the J.V. basketball team during the 1958-59 school year. The following year his brother Roger and I were teammates on the varsity team.

Here is a short story that I can only tell by briefly jumping

71

forward in time about 60 years: During the summer of 2014, my wife and I went on vacation to the Pipestem Resort State Park in southern West Virginia. While on this trip, I decided I wanted to see if the old Camp Summers still existed. We drove back down to Hinton and went to the Chamber of Commerce office. There we received directions to the camp. When we got there, I was amazed. It was still there and was still functional. The camp was as beautiful as I remembered from my childhood. It had been well maintained and loved. They were working that day and getting ready for a gaggle of kids to come in the next week. I talked with one of the directors and told him that I had been there to camp about 60 years before. I noticed his Camp Staff T-shirt and asked if I could buy one. He asked me to follow him into the office area. There he reached me a shirt and when I offered to pay, he refused. He said, "You came to camp here 60 years ago, and you're back to visit today. That's payment enough for me."

I treasure my T-shirt plus any and all of my experiences which might allow for such wonderful revisiting, either real or virtual. My wife and I continued our camping/vacation trip that summer as we returned to Pipestem. From here we visited the famous New River Gorge bridge and other interesting sites in the region.

High School

SPORTS AND MORE

After seventh grade at the elementary school, students entered eighth grade in the Pound High School building. 1956-57 was a year of adapting ourselves to the new building and the new methods. All of this was fairly easy because I had already spent some time in parts of the building as a band student. I continued with the band the following year as I started my real high school years as a freshman in the ninth grade. I was beginning to be involved in several other activities however, and my interest in the band was beginning to diminish. We had a concert season in the springtime and we practiced all winter long to get ready for it. I marched in the fall of 1956, and participated in the spring concert for the last time in 1957.

One of the inconsiderate jokes that we played several times on Bill Duckworth was to drift his car down from the high school to the bottom of the hill. He always left the doors unlocked so he was an easy target. This was mostly Kennith's idea but I always went along with it. The first time we did it, we all thought it was funny and Bill even chuckled about it.

The second time was a little less funny to him and two or three times later he finally told us, "OK fellows. It was funny at first, but if you do it again, I am going to report you to Mr. Morris."

He never reported us, but we thought it was odd that he still never locked his car.

To Mr. Duckworth's dismay, he could not seem to keep some of my friends and me interested in the band. I continued with the band until the fall marching season of 1957 was over. My closest friends were starting to play football and basketball and they were encouraging me to do the same. Kennith's brother Curt was playing football and Kennith and Ronnie Clark had already played J.V. basketball as eighth graders. I was beginning to get the itch. They couldn't talk me into playing football yet but I did quit going to band in the fall and went out for J.V. basketball. I made the team and began to discover some things about myself that I had never known. I became a "jumper" and found myself starting at center in many games because I could time my jump and get the tip over all of my teammates and most of my opponents. When the high school principal, Mr. O.M. Morris, first saw me play, he was impressed and gave me and the coach lots of encouragement. I got a lot of playtime even though it was my first year. Kennith, Ronnie Clark and Donnie were all on the J.V. squad, and we were really enjoying the sport.

I loved the game of basketball and I especially loved playing for Coach Varner. He was serious, compassionate and wanted us to have fun. Like us, he wanted to win. Bob Varner is one of my most highly respected and loved teachers and coaches. He was also my geography teacher. In his later years, he became the principal at Adams Combined School in Pound.

My friends and I loved basketball so much that we tried to play as often as possible, wherever we could find a court. We climbed up on the door cover near the bus loading platform and found open windows that we could reach. We "broke in" (without really breaking anything) to the gym at PHS on Saturdays and holidays year-around. We sometimes even turned on the lights, played as long as we wished, swept the floor and "broke out." Nobody ever came to check on us. We felt lucky about that, but the real probability is that the coaches and our principal actually knew that we were there but never said anything about it. It was their way of providing out-of-season practice in a "legal" way. Don't try this today!!! I still love sports and I am an avid fan of college basketball and football, and pro football.

The girls in my neighborhood would sometimes have parties and they tried to always invite an equal number of boys and girls. The major games at these parties were kissing games like "Spin the Bottle" and "Post Office." One of these parties when I was a little older, was at Donna Freeman's invitation. I got a few nonchalant pecks that night, but my first mind blowing kiss came at the hands (or should I say lips) of Delores Baker. I was in love for a while after that French kiss, but I was not really ready to start dating until a lot later. Because of another party after this, I did however, develop an attraction and affection for Linda Bolling for a while.

The following year was my sophomore year at Pound High School and I was under pressure from my friends to also play football. In the fall of 1958 I started the dreaded two-a-days in August. It was the roughest and most difficult time I had ever had in my life. When I first started, I doubted that I could even live, much less stick with it. The coaches were head coach, Marvin Barker and assistant Trig Dotson, and they were tough!

The first task was to get us in good physical condition and season us for toughness. They did it. Running up that steep, long, and loose earth bank on the right on the near side of the football field was a real killer, and the heavier guys sometimes only made one trip before they collapsed. After a few dashes up the hill I was ready to go home, but that was just the beginning. We still ran dashes and sprints and suicides on the field. We had calisthenics, then we butted heads, and I mean that literally. There seemed to not be a lot of discussion, worry, or consideration for the possibility of breaking bones, getting internal injuries, or getting a concussion back then. We were just trying to learn to be tough. It is done very differently today with the same or even better results.

One of the drills that we did was called "bullpen." Everyone was given a number. We stood around in a ring. Whenever someone's number was called, he was required to go to the middle of the ring. Then coach would call out another number at random. That person's job was to immediately run as hard and fast as he could and hit the middle player. If you weren't ready, that's tough. You might get it from the side or back, but if you were lucky and prepared you could lower yourself and take it head-on. It taught us alertness, toughness and resiliency, but there is no doubt that it was dangerous.

My position was end, on both defense and offense. I was never a good football player. I tried hard and I was fairly tough, but two things worked against me constantly. I was almost six feet tall but I only weighed about 155 pounds. I got knocked around a lot and I couldn't tackle hard because I didn't have any weight to throw into it. My worst enemy in football was my nearsightedness. I could run about as fast as anybody on the team, but when I went out for a pass, I rarely saw the ball coming. Kennith was the team quarterback. He and I practiced passing routes as often as possible. I did pretty well when I didn't have sweat or mud blocking my view, but that was not the case during head knocking practice and during games. When playing defense, I had trouble seeing the ball carrier. My mom purchased some sports glasses for me, and I wore them in football and basketball. They consisted of a metal frame coated with rubber around two extremely thick plastic lenses. Contact lenses were also available at the time but they were also thick, uncomfortable and expensive. They also had not yet been proven to be effective nor practical for someone like me. I remember Mickey Cantrell trying to wear them in basketball and having them pop out sometimes during practice or a game. When the glasses I wore became covered with sweat, dirt and grass, it would have sometimes been better not to have had them at all, but I stuck with it.

The glasses were more useful for basketball. It wasn't the best situation that a player could have but I toughed it out, and I played J.V. basketball again during my sophomore year with some degree of success, starting at center and scoring quite often from the key. I loved every moment of it.

Kennith and I decided to take the speech class under Ms. Ruth Ringstaff that year. We were required to do speeches in front of the class as she taught us to gain confidence and overcome our fear of speaking to a group. All students that were taking or had taken speech were automatically in the Speech and Drama club. The club performed three one act plays that year and I had a lead role in one of them, a comedy. We saw a Barter Theatre play that year and had a couple of other field trips, one of which was to Natural Tunnel.

I was also in another club called the Future Teachers of America (FTA). In addition, I had been selected by my good friend and mentor Johnny Wright, to be a member of the school newspaper staff, the *Tomahawk*. I just did what I was told to do. The girls made most of the decisions.

Kennith and I were also together in Mr. Quentin Franklin's biology class. He was humorous and interesting, and I really liked the subject. We did leaf collections in his class, an activity that I continued to do with my classes when I taught biology many years later. We were required to do a science project, and we were allowed to work in pairs. Kennith and I were partners, and we did an unusual project on nightcrawlers, with some pretty interesting looking drawings and information. We won first place in the school fair, but that's as far as it got. I did most of the work.

I loved college and pro sports and tried to listen to the UT games on WNVA Norton radio. Later, when everyone started getting TVs, watching actual basketball and football games was a great joy to me. Kennith had relatives in Baltimore so he was a huge Colts fan. He especially loved Johnny Unitas. We talked about the passing relationship between Unitas and Raymond Berry. Berry was Johnny's favorite receiver, and I related to him because he had poor eyesight. Ray wore contacts and even had one leg shorter than the other, but he was a great player. We also had lots of other favorites on the pro football and basketball teams. We were living through the beginnings of the booming popularity of all professional sports. We loved to watch and discuss such names as Jim Brown, Unitas, Berry, Bart Starr, Paul Hornung, Carroll Dale, or Lou Michaels that played at Kentucky. My favorite team was the Cleveland Browns back in the day when they won championships, and the great Jim Brown played for them. The Browns have struggled for many years now but I still pull for them. Dick Butkus was only one year older than us, and was a great college player at Illinois. We closely followed names like Bob Cousy, Bob Pettit, Wilt Chamberlain, Elgin Baylor, Bob Russell and Jerry West in basketball. We read *Sport* magazine and watched the games on TV at every chance.

My maternal grandparents lived in East Jenkins, Kentucky and I spent lots of time there as a youngster. It was a short walk from their home to Whitaker's music store. He kept both new and used records, and both new and used musical instruments. The used records had been taken from juke boxes around the area that he serviced. Occasionally, I found some real jewels. We were on the cusp of the big transition between 45 and 78 rpm records and players. I had received a record player for Christmas one year which would play either one. I purchased 78 rpm records like Hank Williams' "Your Cheating Heart" and "Kawliga," and the Everly Brothers' "Wake Up Little Susie" for as little as five or ten cents each. I made a big important purchase from Whitaker that year. It was the Higgins electric guitar and Epiphone amplifier that I bought for about 95 dollars. It put me on the road toward learning to become a professional musician.

The year 1958-59 was another wonderful year for me in music. It was rock 'n roll time in the late 50s and my buddies were all interested. Donnie, Kennith and I had gotten together often the previous year and sang some of the hits of the day with me strumming guitar behind them. Kennith's dad had a little Gibson guitar that had a great sound, so I played it sometimes and really loved jamming around. Then when his dad saw Kennith and Aaron's interest in music, he bought them a Les Paul TV Model guitar and a Gibson amplifier. I couldn't believe the quality of sounds from that combination. Roger Boggs was a senior trumpet player in the high school band. In the early spring after basketball season, he asked me to play drums on a trap set with a little group that he had gotten together to play at the prom. The equipment was poor, and I didn't have much to work with but I tried. I decided that I wasn't cut out to be a trap drummer. I was going to be a guitarist.

THE "SHADOWS"

That summer, Mickey Cantrell, a trumpet player in the high school band, had gotten the idea to get some guys together and form a combo. The little group consisted of Kennith, Donnie, Aaron, and Mickey. One night they were playing at a local dive called the Indian Head which was a couple of miles up the road from our home. After the first set, they came to my house and asked if I could go back out and play some music with them. They were feeling like the sound was "a little bit empty." Naturally I wanted to go, but we couldn't tell my mom where I was going. I played with them that night and it was the start of our new band. Mickey decided that his trumpet did not fit into the scheme of things, so he faded out. When we were trying to decide on a name, we used a term that our high school principal had used when referring to Kennith and me as a pair.

When Mr. O.M. Morris saw us together, he would say, "I see you have your shadow with you."

So, we became the "Shadows," the first rock 'n roll band to exist in Pound, Virginia, and maybe even for many more miles around. We played every chance we got. We played at the Pound Theatre, the Norton Theatre, we played sock hops, we played at the clubhouse in Wise, the Copper Kettle, the American Legion in Jenkins, Kentucky, the VFW in Whitesburg, Kentucky on New Year's Eve, etc. We played on the air at WNKY radio, and even opened for a Carl Perkins concert at Fleming/Neon High School in Neon, Kentucky. This gig had been booked for us by our good friend Bobby Joe Pass at the radio station. We were really having a blast.

During the 1950s, I tried to spend a lot of time with Gene, my cool uncle and friend. Sometimes we would just get in his car and ride around. We talked about movies, music, and girls. Talking with him about anything and everything was one of my favorite pastimes. He seemed to enjoy my company as well, and he thought it was special that I was learning to play the guitar. I rode in the front seat and played blues and boogie-woogie licks as we rode along. We put in many hours like that, and I don't regret a single second. He loved Hank Williams and knew most of his songs by heart., but he also kept up closely with the latest rock 'n roll songs of the day.

Gene and I often sat in the car late at night with the radio turned up loud, and we listened to John R on WLAC, Nashville TN, and

Dick Deante on WLS, Chicago. It was an exciting time for me. This was during a time when tons of new music was produced that really appealed to me. We experienced the first releases of many of my first heroes in rock 'n roll; like Chuck Berry, Elvis, Little Richard, Fats Domino, Rick Nelson, Buddy Holly, and so many others. I would often strum the chords to the songs and he would sing as we cruised to Norton, Pound, Jenkins, Neon, Pikeville, etc. We loved listening to country, rock 'n roll and blues. I played "The Long Black Veil" by Lefty Frizzell, "Oh My Soul" by Little Richard, "Hey Boss Man" by Jimmie Reed, "That's Alright Mama" by Elvis, and dozens of popular songs of that time. I was always elated to see him when he visited home intermittently, or even when he was laid off from work from his job in Michigan like he was that summer of '59. He seemed more like a brother to me than an uncle and he treated me that way as well. Gene always offered more support and encouragement for my efforts in music than anyone else on that side of the family. He was proud of me and the fact that I could play guitar. He was only about 5 years older than me. Other than Uncle Gene, most of my motivation in music came from outside the family.

My papaw worked as a custodian at Jenkins High School. He secured jobs as window cleaners for Gene and me at Jenkins High School. The work was to be completed before school started in the fall of '59. We made $1.00/hr.

During that summer, I also worked some for Leonard Barnette whenever he received loads of produce or needed an extra hand to make a delivery. My mother had also been working here for a while as a clerk. I would occasionally accompany my friend Tracy in Barnette's little green pickup truck as we made grocery and farm feed deliveries around the area. I was helping to pay my parents back for the guitar/amp purchase I had made at Whitaker's Music Store.

One of the two trips that I took out of the country happened that summer. Gene had to go back to Detroit to report in and sign up for unemployment. He was driving a 1954 model Chevrolet convertible at the time. We picked up his good friend. Kenneth Burke, and headed off on an adventure. When we arrived in Detroit, Kenneth stated that

80

he had never been to Canada. I quickly chimed in that I had not either. Gene was always ready to please. We headed across the Ambassador Bridge and into Windsor, Ontario. During those days, there were border checks, but it only consisted of a few questions, taking about 2-3 minutes. Passports from the U.S. were not required. We drove into the city, pooled our resources and had lunch in a slightly fancy restaurant under a huge picture of the Queen of England. We walked on the streets, drove around a bit more, and then headed back across the bridge.

Another relative that was very close to me was my Uncle Curt. He was in the army at the time and was due to get out that year. He sent money for Gene to purchase a used car for him. Gene selected a used Hudson Hornet. I remember when we picked Curt up at Tri-Cities airport, he asked, "Well, is this my car?"

I had my driver's license when I was 16, and I sometimes drove our car to school. Later that year, dad bought a beautiful little two-tone blue 54½ model pickup. I sort of adopted it as mine and drove it a lot, but I was still not allowed to take a vehicle to school every day. Ronnie Clark would stop and pick me up most of the time, so I didn't actually have to ride the bus with the "little kids."

My junior year in high school brought about a lot of changes in my life. For one thing, I was actually getting to play more in the football games.

I was still not yet a full-fledged starter, but I was playing on special teams and got in on occasional substitutions on both defense and offense. Things were looking up. The first Friday night of the season, during the game with Pennington Gap, which we won 7-0, I got in the game more than usual, and played on the receiving team. The "hyped up" picture on the left was taken for the annual that year.

FEMALE COMPANIONSHIP

After the Pennington Gap game, as I was walking off the field, someone grabbed my arm and held on. I looked down and saw that it was one of the cute little cheerleaders, Glenda Hayes, a girl in my class. I must say I was pleasantly surprised that I was sort of being "sought after" that evening.

She held my arm and walked with me all the way to the fieldhouse, and when we got there, she said, "Are you going anywhere after the game?"

I told her that I sometimes went to Bucks after the games. She told me that one of her friends, Jo Anne, and she were riding that night with Jo Anne's big brother Foyster. They were going to stop at Bucks.

Bucks was a local drive-in and "night spot" for teens located just up the road from our home on Indian Creek. It sat back from the main highway at the entrance to Cox Hollow, and just above my Uncle Hoshea's gas station. Buck's was owned and operated by the Buchanan family.

I quickly showered and dressed and drove to my destination. When I arrived, the parking lot was nearly full. I found a place off to the side and walked toward the main building. The juke box was going strong and I could hear Little Richard's "Long Tall Sally." The booths were full of kids inside, and there were a lot of people sitting in the cars parked out front. I saw and greeted several of my friends. I tried not to be too conspicuous but I looked around for a short time to see if I could spot Glenda. I was just about to give up.

I saw Glenda in the back of Foyster's car. When she saw me, she waved me over and invited me into the back seat with her. That was the beginning of a romance that lasted several years. We began dating and spending a lot of time together going to the movies, bowling, skating, the fair, and other places for entertainment. When we received our class rings later in 1960, we exchanged rings and committed ourselves to "going steady." We went to Sunday school and church together and I had many Sunday dinners with the Hayes Family.

We attended Sunday School and church at the little Freewill Baptist Church on Indian Creek with several of our other friends. A few of the Indian Creek gang are seen in the photo. Our Sunday School teacher was Ronnie's mother, Violet Clark, one of the finest ladies I have ever known. She was like another mother, and Ronnie was like a brother. I was now trying to juggle my new romance with school and studying, football, basketball, and music gigs with the "Shadows" and later the "Wildcats." In addition, I was trying to keep up and spend time with my best friends.

Some of the "Indian Creek Gang": L to R: Me, Glenda, Fred Gibson Tracy Boggs, Delores Bailey, Ronnie Clark, and Jo Anne Bolling

Some of my friends and teachers had started talking about college during this year. The importance of making good grades in order to enter a good school was being discussed. I hadn't thought much about college before now, but it began to interest me. And when it interested me, then it interested my parents as well. My parents did not finish high school, much less college, and they always wanted the best for me. We all began to think about that possibility. When school started, my dad had a word of advice for me. He had spent most of his working life in the coal mines at the expense of his health. He said, "Ronnie, I want you to get more education. I am not sending you to school just to come back and work in the mines. I want you to do better."

Many years later I wrote a song about these moments of philosophy with my dad, called, "Michael's Song." I have recorded it and still enjoy playing it today, and when I do so, I think of my dad and my life.

My two favorite classes that year were geometry and English (would you believe?) My favorite teacher, Ms. Emily Qualls, had been moved to the high school to teach math. I took her geometry class and loved it. I loved the challenge and the problems, and she responded with the same love. The other teacher that I grew to love was Grace Edwards, the junior English teacher. Her dedication to teaching was phenomenal. It was amazing how we wrote themes in class almost every day and she would take them home, grade them, and hand them back the very next day. Her class was a real learning experience, and my gleanings were extremely valuable to me throughout the rest of my life. I must give her credit for teaching me the correct way to organize my thoughts and to write. She became one of my most beloved teachers. Grace Edwards was inspirational.

The junior class always presented a three act play to the school and community each year. Maybe because I had a speech and drama background or maybe just because she liked me, Ms. Edwards chose me for the lead role in her junior class play. I was "Touchy," a football hero. My  girlfriend in the play was my third-grade sweetheart, Betty Hodges. Kennith and Glenda were a married couple. The play was a comedy called "Cradle Troubadour."

One of Ms. Edwards' assignments during that year was to have her students write poems. She provided the lessons for proper mechanics, line length, etc. Even though I really didn't like the high school history class that I was taking under another teacher, I was struck by one of the stories about a patriot from Virginia during the Revolutionary War. I wrote a poem called "Virginia's Paul Revere." It told the story of Jack Jouett, who warned Virginians about the approaching British army. Ms. Edwards was so impressed by my efforts that she insisted that I enter my poem into a state contest that was taking place. I did not win or place in the contest, but I was encouraged by her confidence in me. She also made other comments which inspired me not only to do well in her writing class, but in future writing efforts as well.

LOVING BASKETBALL

As football season ended and basketball started that fall, I put my heart into my favorite sport. At the same time, I was being chastised by my coach and teammates for spending so much time with my girlfriend. Coach Dotson didn't even know about my 'other love' at that time. Playing music and spending all those late nights at gigs with the band was a joy to me. I was a 6th or 7th man on the team and I lettered that year despite playing second team to some of the best athletes and seniors on our team in many years. Johnny Wright, Lee Moore, Ralph Boggs, Roger Alderson and Roger ("Soc") Mullins were very good athletes. It was hard to get playtime with the big 6'3" senior at center in front of me.

We had a great team that year, and we were Wise County tournament champions. I will never forget the last play of our district championship game. Charlie Janway drove into the key and scored the final two points, winning the game for Thomas Walker in the last 5 seconds. In the process, he totally ran over Kennith, who was standing flat-footed and never moved any part of his body. No foul was called. No personal foul, no charging foul, nothing. Unfortunately, because of a very poorly officiated game, we lost the finals of the district tournament championship game and did not get that coveted trip to state. It was a huge disappointment for us, but we all eventually came around to realizing that it was just another of many human errors. If we had played better from the start, we should have beaten this team, but that's all long-gone speculation.

1959—'60
Wise County Champions
First in District Eight Standing

L to R (front, kneeling): Ralph Boggs, Lee Moore, Roger (Soc) Mullins), Johnny Wright, Kennith Ellison, Roger Alderson. L to R (rear, standing): Managers Jay Corder, Burns Robinson, Newton McCoy, Kent Chapman, Ronnie Swindall, Donnie Mullins, and Coach James (Trig) Dotson.

MUSIC EXCITEMENT INCREASES

One of the gigs for the Shadows band that year was the Holly Ball at Lincoln Memorial University in Harrogate, TN just before Christmas holidays. The trip and the gig were very memorable. We secured this gig through a friend that was attending school there, Helen Dotson. She was the girlfriend of Kennith's brother Curt. There was a huge snowstorm the evening that we left home, and driving there was very tricky in Kennith's old Hudson. Brenda Dotson, Helen's sister accompanied us to the gig.

The picture below was made on the night of the Holly Ball at LMU. Notice my Higgins guitar and big Epiphone amplifier (behind Aaron). Our vocal microphone was routed into the Gibson guitar amp up front. Our drummer, Donnie Mullins, cannot be seen in this picture. He is behind me. L to R: Aaron Ellison - guitar, Ron Swindall -guitar, Kennith Ellison - vocals, and J. Corder - saxophone. This was to be one of our last gigs as the "Shadows."

The "Shadows"

During my junior year in high school, academics and college became more important to me. I didn't know a lot about any of the schools, but my interest was stimulated when I thought about UT,

VPI or University of Richmond. Roger Soc Mullins had graduated and was preparing to go to Richmond to play basketball. Kennith had peaked my interest in VPI because of the ROTC program and military connection, and I identified with UT because of the sports.

MISCHIEF

Since elementary school, "sleeping over" was a common occurrence with my friends, and this continued all through high school. I spent many nights with Ronnie Clark, Donnie, Kennith and others, and they returned the favor. We sometimes "caroused" at night on the streets in town and participated in questionable activities like "corn night" on the night before Halloween, but we never got into a lot of trouble. The worst night was when we were throwing corn at cars in the Killen Hollow curve. The gang consisted of several neighborhood boys. Two of my best friends, Donnie and Jay, were with the group. They were supposed to be spending the night with me, and I was supposedly spending the night with them. Benjamin Dotson, whose broken arm was in a sling, picked up some small gravels either by mistake or on purpose. He threw the handful at a car and the driver stopped, got out of the car and yelled something. A short time later the town police came up with lights flashing. They turned on their spotlight and pointed it toward the top of the bank where we were perched. Benji raised his arms and waved and said, "Here we are!"

We could not believe he was trying to get their attention. The spotlight was immediately on us and we all ran up the hill through the briars and rocks. I was bruised, scratched and bleeding. Eventually, we ended up back down on the small road that ran into Killen Hollow. Brothers David and Jerry Meade told us that we could all sleep in the hay in their barn that night. Unexpectedly, one of the boys pulled out a couple of pints of his homemade moonshine and we, in our "coolness" started passing it around. Jay still tells the story today,

"If someone only took a sip, then they were forced to turn it up again and drink until they made it gurgle or bubble."

Needless to say, we all went to sleep very soon. When I awoke the next morning, I was woozy and my whole world looked yellow. Kennith and Donnie went on their way. I limped home and sneaked into the bathroom to clean up.

It had not been my first partaking of alcohol. Dad and my uncles would give me a little taste of their beer from time to time. Also, I had discovered where my dad hid his pint of Four Roses liquor in the furnace room inside the potato barrel. Actually, it was no big secret except that my mom did not know about it. Dad kept it handy so he could have a swig occasionally or offer a "horn" to one of his friends or relatives. It was partaken by my Uncles Curt, Gene, Roy, Raymond, Arthur, Joe Burke, and others. Sometimes Kennith and I or another friend and I would get into the barrel and take a nip from the bottle.

In the middle of that summer Tracy took his car, and he, Donnie and I made a trip to Knoxville to check out the University of Tennessee. Donnie was dating Eva Mae Jackson, and she had called her cousin Wendell Jackson, a senior at UT, who was working there and attending school. He told us to come on down on Friday and that we could spend the night with him. We set out early Friday morning for a long trip. There were very few four-lane highways at this time. In 1960, there were no GPS satellite devices to program, but we finally found Wendell's apartment. We actually saw very little of him because he had to work on Saturday. We didn't see very much of the campus either because we had no guide and didn't really know what we were doing. We wandered around Knoxville for a while and then decided to head back.

Mrs. Barnette had talked with her Sister Kate Mullins and she had made arrangements with her son Joe Mack for us to spend the night with him on Saturday night in Kingsport. Our night and the next day there were very pleasant. Joe entertained us by taking us out to Patrick Henry Lake where we all learned to water ski. When we got home we did not really know any more about college than we had before, but the trip was a very nice and memorable short vacation for the three of us.

THE "WILDCATS"

In the late winter of 1960, Fred Adkins had dropped out of school at the University of Maryland where he had been on a basketball scholarship. When he got back to Pound, he met Sidney Amburgey and they wanted to start a band. We were invited to jam with them, and they lured Donnie and me away from the "Shadows." They did not include Kennith because Fred was to be the lead singer. They were also not interested in the sax player. Our band, the "Shadows," had no upcoming gigs and these fellows were offering playtime in a new band, which they had named the "Wildcats," in honor of our high school sports mascot.

Aaron continued to play music as a guitarist and piano player with some local groups after that, but Kennith lost interest and did not pursue the hobby any further. Jay played with Virgil Mullins and Gary Freeman until he went to Maryland to work. The new "Wildcats" became very popular in the area during this time. We played concerts at local theatres, night club gigs at the Copper Kettle, and teen dances at the clubhouse in Wise. Our friend Ronnie Clark was Fred's cousin and he loved to go around with the band. He didn't play, but he took some of us to gigs occasionally and helped us carry equipment. He loved to dance and could be seen out on the floor very often, "cuttin' a rug."

Glenda and I were dating almost every weekend, and along with Tracy and Phyllis Hall, we double dated for the spring prom that year. Tracy was always a good friend so we also went together to other entertainment spots like the movies, bowling or skating.

Dad's Aunt, Hattie Mae and her husband E.B. Shockey also lived in Pound. Their two children were Doug and Mary. We visited them often. Doug and Mary are both a little older than me. Like many of the Pound young folks at the time, they had both left the Pound for "greener pastures." Like me, they are both retired. Doug and his wife Judy live in Arizona. Mary (Mahan) has moved back to Pound.

During the summer of 1960, Raymond Roberson, my uncle by

marriage to my Aunt Lena, secured a job for me from the town of Pound as the driver of Hibert Tackett's garbage truck. I would be working for my great-uncle E.B. Shockey that was the mayor of the town of Pound at that time. The job was smelly and dirty but I was making $35 each week that I worked. I was grossed out by the habits of the town of Pound at that time. I drove the big truck down between the railroad tracks and the river toward Bad Creek. About one mile out, I backed the truck toward the river and raised the bed, dumping the filthy garbage over the bank into the river! Today it is hard to believe that people allowed that to happen. Of course, Pound River was filthy and the entire town ran their sewers and drains out into the river. It wasn't actually cleaned up until many years later.

The garbage job lasted most of the summer. Eventually, the regular driver returned, but I made enough money along with some of my gig money, to begin seriously saving toward the purchase of a new and better guitar. Fred Adkins had already traded his f-hole Gretsch to a new Fender Stratocaster and when I played it, I just knew I had to have one. I made other money during the summer by working for the Wise County School Board as a painter in some of the old feeder schools around the county. I worked with my cousin, Doug Shockey and my good friend Tracy Boggs. Our boss was Owen Branham, the county truant officer, that was doubling as the maintenance supervisor for the summer. The money that I saved added to my stash that I was saving for my new guitar. Tracy and I worked well together, but we would occasionally aggravate each other and get into paint fights. It wasn't pretty, and we were actually caught once and almost fired.

SENIOR YEAR

When it was time for our senior year to start at Pound High School, we all worked hard to mix our seriousness with our fun and foolishness.

Two-a-days started in football and we settled into the routine of getting ready for what we hoped would be a winning season. I ended up starting on offense at end for much of the season, and even caught a few short passes, but no touchdowns. So "Touchy" from the junior play was "touchdownless." We had a very good season, going 7-2-1 overall (we did not play overtimes in football back then). Wise had Jimmy Ray Carter this year and they did beat us 13-0. Appalachia beat us 6-0. We did, however, beat Clintwood 6-0. The Coeburn game at the end of the season was played in a drenching downpour. It was a funny feeling when the final whistle was blown after both teams had been in the middle of the field all night and had basically accomplished nothing after pushing, rooting, shoving, and falling in the mud. The game ended in a 0-0 tie.

My dad was laid off from the mines that fall, and he began to seek a job. He traveled to Columbus, Ohio and Detroit looking for work but to no avail. My dad was now 53 years old, and most companies were opposed to hiring someone at his age. They preferred young men that would still be with them 20-30 years. His friend Corbett Mullins from Clintwood was starting a new business in water well drilling in Florida and wanted to sell his coal truck to my dad. Dad saw this as an opportunity to make some money in the trade. He gave him my little pickup truck which I loved, plus a balance of money, for the coal truck. My dad never drove the truck, but he ended up selling it to our neighbor Newton Cantrell.

The only class that I can truthfully say that I enjoyed during this year was Mr. Earl Baker's chemistry class. I loved the science and the lab times. It was a fun class and I learned a lot. It made an impact on my later studies in college and inspired me to take chemistry and more science classes.

BASKETBALL AND MUSIC BUTT HEADS

In basketball that year, I was a starter, and for the first time I felt like a very important player on the team. I was still a jumper, and I ended up getting tips, pulling down a lot of rebounds and scoring often from the key. Everything was going great. I loved the game. I was really enjoying myself. We had started a good season, winning most of the games up until Christmas. We had beaten Clintwood on their home court 64-54, and this was even the year that they had big James Hughes and Raymond Shipp, the leading scorer in the state. This was probably my best game ever. I could do no wrong. Back then, when there was a held ball, it was always jumped at the nearest circle at the top of either key or in the center court. That night I got every tip I tried, plus many rebounds. With feeds from Donnie, I poured in 16 points in jump shots and hooks around the key. What a great feeling! I played well in other games and we were having a winning season.

Then a couple of things happened that pretty much destroyed all of this for me. I was never allowed to feel triumph in basketball again. First, I got sick and still tried to play, which was a bad mistake. I was dragging. Kids should not be allowed to play sports when they are running a fever. I got over the sickness, but a few days later I made another huge mistake. I went with Fred to Cumberland Valley Music Company in Harlan, KY to buy my new Fender Strat. I had been saving my money for a long time to make this purchase. I played hooky from school, and I thought that I would surely get back before basketball practice. I did not. Fred told me that I should tell coach the truth. When I told Coach Dotson the truth about what had happened, he was steaming mad. He made me run 200 laps the next day during practice. I didn't finish until everyone had gone. After that he ignored me. He started another player at center the next game, and I was not even a sub. He did the same thing during practice and during games in the coming weeks. He broke my spirit. It also drained the life from the team, and it caused us to have a losing season. Because of my spat with coach, I was benched and never played in another game, and the team won only one game in the second half of the season that year. Clintwood even beat us on our court 61-50 in the second game. This was a sad year for PHS basketball. With about 2-3 games left in the season, I took my uniform in and carefully laid it on his desk during the day before one of the games. He never spoke to me again that year and not for several years. It is ironic that I returned to

Pound High School as a teacher in 1966 and later became a coach. I coached J.V. basketball, and later I even became an assistant football coach for him. Trig and I then became friends and we were hunting and fishing partners for most of the time that I taught at PHS, from 1966 until 1973.

"WILDCATS" PICK UP STEAM

The Wildcat Band was on a roll, booking at least a couple of nights each week in area night clubs in Virginia and Kentucky. I loved my new guitar and the band kept getting better and better.

Here's a memorable story: We were playing at the Cumberland VFW one night and someone spilled a drink on the floor. After a break, we went back on the stand and I picked up my new Fender Stratocaster guitar. I stepped over into the wet spot and immediately got a terrific electric shock as my leather shoes grounded out. I dropped my guitar. It hit on the butt end and bounced straight back up. Thanks to Fred it was not damaged. He simply caught it in mid-air and saved it!

Fred Adkins and I had become the best of friends. I had been very close to Kennith, Donnie, and Ronnie Clark, and Fred actually was like an older brother. He seemed to want to watch out for me, and we really always enjoyed our time together. He has been a faithful friend for as long as I've known him. He had a Karmann Ghia convertible and we spent a lot of time just running around in it. He would show up at my home sometimes and just say, "Let's go somewhere." We might end up in Jenkins, Pikeville, Kingsport or someplace else. We always seemed to be on an adventure, and always enjoying each other's company.

The Wildcats played a few times on tv at the small WJHL station in Kingsport, which was a branch of the larger station in Johnson City. We played at the Norton High School prom that spring, and Morris Burchette took our picture there. It was enlarged, and Ms.

Burchette toned and painted the black and white photo so that it became a portrait. She even painted Sidney's shoes black like the rest of ours. The black and white picture became a part of our promo package. We made tentative plans to talk to talent agents, managers, promoters and record companies, etc. We were hoping to record a couple of songs as soon as possible. That did finally happen, but not until 1962.

The Wildcats 1961

Ron Swindall   Ken Duncan   Don Mullins   Fred Adkins   Sid Amburgey

"The Wildcats"

POUND HIGH SCHOOL GRADUATION

Later in the year in 1961, Corbett Mullins called my dad and asked him to come to Tampa, Florida and work with him as a partner in the new drilling business. My dad and mom left me alone at home to take care of myself for a few days while they both went to Florida to check things out. They agreed to move there and join the business.

Kennith, Donnie, and Ronnie and I began to hang out with a new friend, Larry Salyers who was to become another one of my closest friends in this life. His family lived on the hill across from the Austin Motel in a little house that had been built by my great-great-Uncle Dave Austin. The Salyers family bought the properties from our cousin Bud Austin. They ran the motel and owned all of the associated buildings there. We spent time with Larry running around, playing Rook, and picking up some bad habits. One of my worst was smoking cigarettes. We were allowed to smoke at school around back and for some reason I thought this was cool. I usually went out back after lunch and joined Larry, Donnie Bowman, Voin Boggs, and others. I will say that my good friend Ronnie Clark never picked up the habit. Kennith did not smoke until later. My music gigs encouraged smoking on breaks also, so we all seemed to more or less have the habit. We have all quit, or died by now, and I often look back with disdain at this habit that we wish we had never started. I smoked for at least 10-12 years after this.

During that year, the Ellison's home on Bold Camp near the bend in the river, burned to the ground. They all escaped unhurt, but the home and most of their possessions were lost. They rented the house beside Roy and Ruby Addington in uptown new Pound near where my cousin G.F. Austin's Stop and Shop Store was located. We were having a mild recession in 1961 and the coal business was bottoming out. Not only were my dad and Newton Cantrell laid off, but Hubert Ellison's hauling business was not making enough money to support them. Kennith's mother Agnes had been going to school to try to get a teaching degree. Hard times had befallen them. Consequently, Hubert found it necessary to move the family to Lanham, Maryland so he could work in a gas station. Agnes secured a job teaching school, and their outlook began to improve.

As I was preparing to graduate from high school, my whole world was again getting ready to change in a huge way. I had mixed feelings about it. I admit that I may have shed a few tears at the thoughts of having to leave the band, all of my good friends and especially my sweetheart, but it was happening. I had not ever been a very serious student, so I did not graduate with special honors. My academic ranking in the class of 60 was eighth. I had always been cordial and friendly with all of my classmates. This, along with my sports, music and participation in several activities earned Betty Hodges and me the distinction of being selected by our peers as Mr. and Miss Senior. This name of the honor was changed to "best all around," as the student editor specified in the annual that year. Glenda was salutatorian, second in line to Jo Anne Bolling, the valedictorian.

We all graduated on May 23, 1961, and bade a final goodbye to good ole PHS. Graduation was a serious affair, not to be taken lightly by anyone. Our senior sponsor, Ms. Trula Qualls, as always, kept everyone in line right up to the moment we left the school for good. We were all required to sing in the Senior Choir. Our songs were "Be Still My Soul" and "Amazing Grace." We were to sing these at graduation, and we also were required to attend and sing these two songs at our baccalaureate service on Sunday. This was not optional. We heard our final sermon from the Methodist preacher Charles Lipps, as he tried to help prepare us to go out into the big world.

After graduation, my mom wanted to have a cake and punch party at our home for the graduates. Mom was like a fireball of energy and activity all of her life, and I know that I had no understanding of how to appreciate all that she did. Besides hosting this party, she molded little open books of hardened sugar for each graduate. Each book had their name and the graduation date. She explained to them that it could be preserved in a freezer for years to come if they so desired, and that's exactly what many of them did.

Big Moves And College

OFF TO FLORIDA

Too much of my final year had been occupied with "courting." I don't recommend that young folks get too serious and too involved at this early age. I had been only 17 years old up until a few days before graduation. The year had gone by quickly and I had spent a lot of time on college preparations, college board tests, applications, plans, etc. That spring passed quickly. Soon it was summer again, and time for me to pack up and leave Pound, Virginia. I didn't know what the future held, or whether or not I would ever be here again. We were renting out our home and property on Indian Creek, with the intention of selling it all later. I was ripping up my roots and limping away to the unknown. I said goodbye to my friends. I promised Glenda that I would return as often as possible to see her, and someday come and take her away with me.

At this point in time, many of our family's possessions had already been carried to Florida. My mom and I had packed up the remaining furniture, clothing and personal items in boxes. We took as much as we could with us and left the rest to be picked up on another trip, which I found out later would be a trip to sign final papers to sell the property.

There were no interstates and four lane highways in our region in 1961. We took off very early one morning in Dad's little '56 Chevy, winding down route 23, to Asheville, North Carolina. We had a late breakfast at the Lazy Susan Restaurant, just south of the city. I even remember my breakfast of ham, grits and eggs that morning. We drove on to Statesboro, GA, where we spent the night and drove on to Florida the next day.

We arrived that evening at the little house at 32 Lake Ellen Lane, and the small lot that my dad had purchased from Mr. R.E. Remines in Tampa. The house was neat, pretty and pleasant. I was happy to see the palmetto trees, and the orange and lemon trees in the yard. It was during the sweltering hot and humid rainy season. There was no air conditioning. I laid in my bed and sweated all night long and got very little sleep. There was little relief from the heat and humidity in Tampa, Florida at that time of year.

The next day, I made it a point to sit down and write to my girlfriend and a couple of my other friends back in Virginia. Then I quickly applied for college at the all new University of South Florida in Tampa. I was accepted within a few days, so I went over and registered. Near the first of September, school started and I attended my first college experience. I went for almost one week and I did not like the classes nor the young people in them. Hillbilly that I was, I felt like I was in a foreign country. Maybe it was because I was just a mountain boy at heart and I missed my girlfriend, my other friends, and my music. I did not like it and I was very unhappy.

Fred Adkins saved me from my misery! He called me toward the end of that week and gave me the news that he had become partners with another fellow, and that they had purchased an old skating rink. They had remodeled it into a nightclub and restaurant. He told me that he wanted me to come back and continue playing guitar in the band. I would be guaranteed $50 each week for playing on Friday and

Saturday nights. Ronnie Clark and Donnie Mullins had chosen to go to school at East Tennessee State College (now the University) that fall. Fred had already made arrangements for me to stay with them in a small house trailer that Ronnie's dad, Elliot, had purchased. He said I could stay with him at his grandparents' home on the weekends. The house band would always be the Wildcats, consisting of Fred and me on guitars, Fred and Sidney on vocals, Donnie on drums, and Kenny Duncan on Tenor Sax.

BACK 'HOME' TO VIRGINIA

It was a done deal. I didn't like being in Florida anyway, so I decided to go back to Virginia. My mom cried when I told her I was leaving, and my dad told me later that she was depressed for a long time. I packed as many clothes as I could carry in my dad's old Samsonite suitcase and I caught a Greyhound bus and made a miserable 32-hour trip back to Indian Creek and Fred's home. I think the bus must have toured the southeast, stopping in every little town along the way. I arrived during the night and knocked on Fred's bedroom door. He was really happy to see me. He let me go to bed immediately. I was exhausted.

The next day I called Glenda and went to her house to see her for the first time in about two months. There was no doubt about it. I just felt like I was home again. I called my parents and told them that everything was going fine. Fred took me to the place that he and Dan Vasvary had bought. They were putting the final touches on the remodeling of the interior. They named the business Club Scotty, in honor of an old friend of Dan's while he was in the service. I was impressed with the appearance and their plans. The restaurant, which they were calling the Wagon Wheel Lounge, had a huge real wagon wheel hanging in the middle of the dining room. It held electric lanterns all around the rim, and it was the primary source of light for the room. The big kitchen was fully modern with all new appliances.

They had already hired Glen Thacker as their cook, and plans were made to open for business in a couple of weeks.

Fred had also taken a job as a coal truck driver for his dad. Part of his route took him down Wise Mountain past the old library and into Esserville. One day his brakes failed near George Barnette's home and property. He described his scary ride down the mountain. He stayed with the truck, gearing it down as much as possible. It was moving far too fast to control. When he got to Esserville, he guided the truck to the left of the road and down between the highway and Guest River. He then turned it to the right just enough toward the embankment to slow it to a stop. It turned over on its side as a result of the angle. Fred climbed up and out of the driver's side window, and an observer yelled to him to see if he was OK. He told them that he was alright and that his brakes had failed. The fellow said, "Well, I believe that was about the best job of wrecking a truck that I've ever seen."

EAST TENNESSEE STATE COLLEGE

I rode down to Johnson City, TN with Ronnie Clark and prepared myself for my first step into higher education. ETSC was one of the schools that had accepted my application, so I was ready to go from the start. The registration process was a beast! We met first with our advisors in whatever curriculum that we had chosen. My first choice of majors was business. We were required to wait in long lines for each class and time period that we wanted. Here we pulled a card for the class, which then had to be taken and put on file. It was a learning process. I often waited in line for a long time before being disappointed to watch them raise a sign that informed us that the class was full. I would choose another class, have it approved by a temporary advisor and then wait again in another line. I finally had my freshman class load lined up. I started with fifteen total quarter hours, four three hour courses (English, college algebra, health, and European history) and three one hour classes. The one hour classes were physical education (soccer), freshman orientation, and ROTC.

Donnie, Ronnie and I were classmates again, as well as brothers and roommates. It all just seemed very natural that we should be living together. We all traveled together, partied together, played together, ate together, had classes together, and studied some. Eating out or in the cafeteria was a choice, but I usually could not afford to eat out, so I scrimped and learned to cook my own food. I learned frugality and ate quite well as I shopped in the Giant Food Market on Walnut Street. I cooked up some rather tasty breakfasts, lunches, and dinners for myself, and occasionally for the other two friends as well.

As to be expected, we had little disagreements from time to time, but we cared about our friendships so much that we made it easily through those times. In fairness, since it was Ronnie's trailer, he always had first dibs on the bedroom. Donnie and I alternated sleeping with him or on the couch. Ronnie's mom, Violet, had provided him with a nice soft and warm, gold colored comforter. He called it his "comfort." His habit at night was to roll up in it, and sleep near the wall. He would sometimes come back to the trailer during the day, roll up inside his comforter and take a nap. Donnie and I could only use the comforter when Ronnie wasn't there, which we did. If he came home and one of us was wrapped up taking a nap, he would say, "Man! Get out of my comfort." We would sometimes hide it from him just to aggravate him. "Alright guys, where's my dang comfort?!" We were like brothers, and sometimes like the Three Stooges. We loved each other and we generated many good memories.

Starting freshman year, we were required to take ROTC classes in warfare, safety, gun handling and shooting, for two years. On

Thursdays, we were required to put on our uniforms that had been issued to us. We left early and went marching with the entire Corps. Our guns, uniforms, shoes, and belt buckles were all inspected to see if they were clean and sharp. Ronnie beat us all in this category. He carried with him the habit learned from his mom of being very organized and particular, into the ROTC. He spent lots of time getting ready for drill. He spit-shined his shoes, polished the brass belt buckle and buttons, pressed his uniform and cleaned his rifle. I don't believe he ever got a single demerit for any of these things. Donnie and I didn't do a poor job at this either, but never as well as Ronnie.

I had not learned to study in high school, and I began to struggle through the academics some in my beginning freshman classes. I was fairly comfortable with Ms. Carson's college algebra class. I actually enjoyed Mrs. Star Wood's English class. Mrs. Wood seemed to like me, and her methods reminded me of my high school English teacher, Grace Edwards. She was the wife of State's football coach. My worst class was Mrs. Hartsock's European history class. She seemed to cater to a few of the front row bunch that could always answer her class questions. She was a poor teacher, and that certainly did not bode well for me because my high school history background was already very weak. I did not even have a single European history class in high school. I always enjoyed any P.E. class that I took, but the freshman orientation was a joke and a waste of time. The ROTC was something totally new and unexpected for me and I did not particularly like it, but it was required, so I did my best. I changed my declared major that year from business to physical education, with thoughts that I might someday be a coach.

A CAR

Back at home in Wise County, I was able to spend time with Glenda and play music at the club. The first weekend that it opened was a grand affair. Prominent businessmen and their wives were invited to join us free of charge for a full evening of food and fun. They were invited to byob (bring your own bottle). Ice and setups were provided. Fred and Dan had already known that this would be a large investment of time, energy, and money, but they were prepared. The kickoff evening was a great success and it turned out to be a rather classy affair as well.

As the club grew in popularity and people began to spread the news, our crowds grew larger and larger. Two African American guys were hired and provided with white suits to wait on tables. They were paid for their work, but they always made much additional money in tips. They went  home with more in their pockets than the band members were getting, but everyone made money, and all went well.

Glenda had started school at Clinch Valley College where she also had a job with the annual staff. As it had been in high school, her academic record was exceptional. She knew how to study, something I had not quite mastered yet. We continued to see each other at least once or twice each weekend. Sundays seemed to provide more free time for us both. I always had to be ready for my ride back to school in Johnson City whenever the driver was ready to go. I rode to school and back to Wise County with Ronnie, or another Wise County student that was headed in that direction for the weekend.

That fall in 1961 while I was in Mrs. Wood's English class, I was called out to the department chairman's office to answer the phone. I thought something might be wrong at home. It was my Uncle Thelmer, dad's brother. He told me about a 1953 Chevy that he had, and that it would be ideal for me. I told him that I was coming in that weekend and if he could bring it to Pound I would take a look at it. He only wanted two hundred dollars. I was excited about the possibility of having my own wheels. When I called my parents, they reluctantly agreed to help me buy it. It was a two-tone green four door sedan with automatic transmission. My uncle told me that it used a little oil. He allowed me to go ahead and keep it until I could pay him. Glenda and I went on a date in the car, and I drove it back to school on Sunday night.

I was pleased to have a car and the independence that it provided, but the car slowly became more of a debit than an asset. That winter my good friend Stewart Judkins and I made a trip to Florida for Christmas with my parents. The car did OK, but it was smoking and using a lot of oil. Donnie and I were riding back to school one night after that, and I noticed the lights getting dimmer and dimmer. Finally, I couldn't see to drive further so I drifted to the shoulder of the road. The engine died and the starter would not even turn it over. I left my car parked beside the road near Speers Ferry, and we began to thumb to Johnson City. We luckily caught a ride very quickly with one of the Cherry Brothers, a NASCAR race driver. He was driving a new Ford Galaxy. It was the fastest trip that I ever made back to school! I glanced at the speedometer occasionally and noticed that during a good portion of the trip that we were cruising smoothly at well over one hundred miles an hour!

I went to Wise County for my weekly music gigs the following weekend. Sidney Amburgey agreed to help me with my car problem, but when I returned a few days later with a new battery, my car was gone! I now understand that if a car is abandoned, the highway patrol is required to have it towed. On investigation, we found that it was impounded in a lot in Gate City. When I went to get it, I was required to pay the towing bill, which was $15. Sid helped me to install the battery, but by the time we got back to Wise County the electrical system was starting to fail again. Sid, being somewhat of a novice mechanic, suggested that it was either the generator or voltage regulator, and he had a way to check it. Luckily, he found out that it was only the voltage regulator. I was able to purchase a rebuilt regulator pretty cheaply and he installed it for me. I was back on the road again.

There were many stories that developed about Sid. He was a little older than us, and we looked up to him. We learned that he was somewhat of a non-conformist, and maybe not always the best model for us.

Just a couple of many stories: Sid had purchased a beautiful '55 Belair Chevy. One night after playing at the club, we all walked outside just as Sid was leaving. He was in a hurry to go meet a girl, but he had locked his keys in the car. He mumbled under his breath as he walked around the car a couple of times with his hands on his hips. Then with no fanfare, he simply picked up a rather large rock. He broke out the driver's side window, reached in, and unlocked the door handle. Then he opened the door, got in, and drove away.

Another night after finishing our gig at the club, Sid practically ran out the door, again in a hurry to meet a girl. I followed him to the door as he sped away (in a different car this time). I noticed that it had started to snow, and the snow was beginning to lay on the road. A few minutes later, as Donnie and I eased down the hill onto the river road, we saw Sid. It looked like he was floating in the air, waving his arms. Actually, he was standing on top of his car, which had slid across the road at the intersection with the main Guest River Road. The car had slid over the bank, and settled into the shallow water of the river.

I must say in his defense, that Sid lived his younger life like the piano rides that he took. He took life either fast and furious, or sometimes slowly with emotion, but always with passion. He has carried that passion into his older age, along with many personal stories of conquest and fame. Many of the stories that he remembers sometimes seem to possess a good amount of elasticity, but Sidney Amburgey was, and still is, a colorful character!

My new old car soon used so much oil that it seemed as if I always had to put almost a quart in it each time that I filled it up with gas. I called and discussed this with my dad. My parents were still not well-off financially at the time. He had gotten out of the drilling business and had taken a menial job with Globe Security for much less pay than he was accustomed to. My mother had taken a job as a clerk at

Eckerd's drug store. They had been consistently sending me money every week to help with school and living expenses, but dad offered to help pay for repairs on the vehicle.

One Saturday I took the car to Witt Motor Company in Norton. I asked Donnie to follow me in his Chevrolet coupe which his parents had also purchased for him that year. I left my car at Witt's that week and they overhauled the engine with new rings. I wrote them a check for ninety-five dollars and left feeling pretty good. It didn't burn any more oil after that, but it was only getting about ten miles per gallon of gas on the highway. Gasoline was cheap at about thirty cents per gallon in the early sixties, so I was able to stand that for a while. Then the power steering mechanism tore up and I had to manhandle the car to make turns. I was hoping there might be a chance in the near future to make some changes in my transportation needs.

I didn't always stay with Fred on the weekends when I went to Wise County to play with the band. Sometimes I would call ahead and let my grandmother know that I was coming, then I would go in late after a gig and go to bed there. My grandparents lived in Burdine, Kentucky at the time. I loved my mamaw and she always treated me very well, cooking for me and asking me if I needed anything. She would always try to give me food to take back.

I was driving too fast toward her house one Saturday morning. I was stopped by a state policeman. He gave me a speeding ticket. I had been in a hurry to get to Mamaw's house and change clothes. I was on my way to the Breaks of the Mountain Interstate Park. We were scheduled to play music for a UMWA fish fry and union convention. When I told Mamaw about the ticket she was upset. She looked at the ticket and sat down beside the telephone and dialed a number. Her side of the conversation went something like this: "Hello, is that you Jess? Well yes, my grandson just got a speeding ticket and the policeman wrote on this paper that he was making 70 mph. Now Jess, you know that he couldn't have been going that fast around these curves between here and Jenkins! You will? Well, you know that I surely thank you. Yes, I will. OK. I'll see you. Ronnie, he said to tell you to slow down and to be more careful."

She had called the county judge, Jess Bates, and he had agreed to tear up the ticket. My mamaw Mullins always treated me like I was her son instead of her grandson. She was such a jewel!

Glenn Smith had started playing with us occasionally when Kenny was not available. On that same day, Glenn stopped at my grandparent's home and picked me up to ride with him to the fish fry gig. While there, Glenn ate lunch with us. I'll never forget how nice Glenn was to my grandmother. He paid her the deserved compliments for the food. She seemed to like him very much as well. I never knew anyone that didn't like Glenn Smith. The day was fun. We set up and played on the trailer of a flatbed truck. We were fed, paid and enjoyed ourselves. That night we played at the club.

I also sometimes stayed with my Aunt Lena Roberson's family in Pound after a night at the club. They lived in the first house on the right just past Horse Gap in Pound. She was always so good to me. There was always a bed ready for me when I came in so late, and she always made a nice breakfast for me the next morning. I was probably taking a bed from one of the kids that had to sleep on a couch or elsewhere.

Jack Scott, a friend of Dan Vasvary, had been instrumental in helping to remodel the club and get it ready to open as a business. He also assisted Dan and Fred in opening up the attic, and in building a bedroom on the top floor above the lounge. Dan and Fred felt that someone should stand guard over the club at night, so Jack was chosen to do that. I stayed with Jack at night sometimes. It was very convenient after the gig to just go upstairs and go to bed without having to drive several miles.

My next trip to see my parents in Florida was during the spring break of 1962. I was accompanied on that trip by a new friend that I had made, Haskel Phipps from Rogersville, Tennessee. We had a great time touring around the Tampa Bay area and visiting my parents. Haskel was very personable and we enjoyed being together. I saw him a few more times at school that spring and then he left school. I didn't see Haskel again until almost 50 years later when he drove by our lake house in Tennessee one day.

"WILDCAT" EXCITEMENT

Sometime during the spring of 1962, the "Wildcats" went to McKinney's little studio in Johnson City and recorded two songs. The songs were "Harlem Nocturne," an old big band jazz sax tune that Kenny had taught us, and "Fannie Mae," a cover song instrumental on which Sidney played harmonica. Electronic reverberation had become available to the public, and McKinney was one of the first to have it. "Harlem Nocturne," written in 1939 by Earle Hagen, has a wonderful melody, and Kenny's interpretation of it on tenor sax was superb. Our music was good and tight, and when McKinney added the reverb effect it was transformed into something that almost sounded unworldly to us. It was hauntingly beautiful.

The recordings had been done on a 7.5 ips reel to reel machine. Fred had one at home that he brought to the club so we, and others could listen to our recording. Kenny was exceptionally proud and excited about the tracks, and we all actually thought it could become a hit. We knew nothing about the music industry, but Fred and Kenny packed up that week and left for Nashville to try and push our music. Fred called one night while we were at the club, and told us to turn on the radio. He wanted us to tune in to WLAC radio, and listen for our songs to be played. John R. played them both a few times that night. We were all so excited to have everyone within range of this powerful blues station to hear our music and begin to know about the Wildcat band. We thought we were on our way to the big time. It was not to be. That's the last we heard about our recording from the outside world even though it was played a lot on local radio stations. Most folks that heard it said emphatically that our version of "Harlem Nocturne," was much better than the Viscounts' version. I'm not sure that was true, but we were indeed very proud of our recording.

During this time, Patsy Cline's promoters released her recording of "Crazy," which was written by Willie Nelson. Her producer was Owen Bradley. Owen played piano on many of Patsy's recordings and wrote the arrangements for the studio orchestration. I'll always remember Kenny's response to Patsy Cline's "Crazy." We always loved it, but anytime it was played on the jukebox, Kenny would stop whatever he was doing and bow his head, just moving it back and forth.

Many years later, and during one of our recording sessions to Bradley's barn in Nashville in 1979, Thomas Countiss and I met Owen, who was Harold Bradley's brother.

RONNIE CLARK FALLS IN LOVE

Ronnie Clark wandered into Wright's Restaurant for his usual hotdog with mayonnaise and no mustard. Our high school classmate, Ginger Roberts, introduced him to her cousin Ginny from Akron, Ohio. Ronnie Clark had met the girl of his dreams.

Ginny was the daughter of Glenn Roberts, who was a member of the original Roberts Brothers basketball team from Pound. They won two state high school basketball championships, and Glenn is many times given credit for "inventing" the jump shot.

Ginny was immediately impressed with Ronnie's neat, clean cut appearance. He obviously made a positive first impression. She even remembers the clothes he wore on that day over 50 years ago, including the black nylon jacket.

Ronnie later asked Roger "Soc" Mullins to accompany him. He had made an excuse to drive all the way to her home in Akron, Ohio to see her. They stayed with the Roberts family 3 days. We kidded with Ronnie and told him it was a fruitless effort, and that he would never be able to "woo" her. The Glenn Roberts family soon moved to Wise, and Ronnie and Ginny started dating in the early 60s.

KENNITH SHOWS UP AGAIN

After graduation from high school, my good buddy, Kennith Ellison had joined his family in Maryland. He got a job in construction on the campus of the University of Maryland during that summer in 1961. Kennith decided to go to Virginia Tech that fall. It was called V.P.I, or Virginia Polytechnic Institute at that time. While in high school, we had talked a lot about the military schools like West Point, the Air Force and Naval Academies, as well as V.M.I. and V.P.I. He only lasted one semester before being placed on probation. After that semester, Kennith went back to Maryland for a few months. His study habits in high school had been even worse than mine, and it quickly became a problem.

Just before the spring quarter in 1962, I heard from my friend Kennith. He did not want to try to go back to V.P.I. He had been accepted at ETSC, and he was looking for a place to live. We met at the Apex on Market Street for a cold mug of beer and a burger one day. I thought it might be a good idea for us to room together. I was happy at the thought of getting to room with my good old buddy from high school. Also, the living space in the trailer was cramped for three people, and I thought that it might be a relief for all of us to have more space. We found a two-room efficiency apartment with two beds on Maple Street, within easy walking distance of the campus. Kennith didn't study much at all and we were probably even bad influences on each other. It is fortunate that I didn't pick up all of his bad habits, however. He spent a lot of time in the Sportsmen's Billiard Parlor downtown trying to win money on the pinball machine, and he drank more beer than I could afford. I wasn't earning flying colors but I was learning to study enough to get by. With Kennith around, my music, and trips in to Wise County to play music, and see Glenda on the weekends, my studies were taking a beating. At least I was passing the courses and earning credits.

One Friday night in late spring when Kennith went with me to

Club Scotty, Jack Scott greeted us at the door of the club. He said, "Guess who made a reservation and is coming here tonight?"

I shrugged, and he said, "Pat Panel called and said Johnny Unitas is speaking for the sports awards banquet at J.J. Kelly High School, and he wants some night life afterwards."

Long story shortened, he did actually show up with Pat later that evening. Kennith and I were able to meet and talk to one of our sports idols, the man himself, Johnny Unitas.

I was speechless when he first shook my hand and he said, "Glad to meet you."

I could not believe the size of Johnny U's huge hand. It wrapped around my hand like it was a rabbit's foot. We were thrilled and very emotional to have the opportunity to talk with him for a short time, but we were warned not to dominate his playtime. He stayed and danced and enjoyed himself for a couple of sets. After the third set started, I looked over to see him waving goodbye to me and others. What a memorable experience! Needless to say, Kennith was elated.

Back at school, the little apartment was airy and not very nice. We made plans to move. We moved into a larger basement apartment out on West Walnut Street, which was further out from school. Kennith tried to walk onto the ETSC football team. He started practice with them that spring and he kept telling everyone that he was going to make it. He said that Coach Star Wood liked him. I went to a couple of practice sessions to watch him work with the team. It didn't work out for him, probably because of his grades. Kennith flunked a couple of classes and made low grades in the others. They placed him on probation after that quarter. He left after spring quarter and went back to his parent's home in Lanham, Maryland. Then he went to Lincoln Memorial University where we had played for the Christmas gig a couple of years before. After a lack of success there he joined the Air Force in the winter of 1962-63. I lost communication and I didn't see Kennith again for over ten years.

That fall, I was again looking for a place to stay. Donnie had gotten married. He and his new wife, Eva Jackson, were living in a trailer in the student housing lots behind the college. I decided that I would move back in with Ronnie in the trailer on Wilson Avenue that fall. I spent my sophomore year with Ronnie in the trailer.

WORK, STUDY AND MUSIC

Dan Vasvary was a really good friend to me and Jack Scott. He even allowed us to cruise around in Norton in his new car. It had air conditioning and a stereo system with a 45-rpm record player mounted under the dash. Very cool! Dan agreed to accompany me on my next trip to Florida. After school was out, we drove down in his nearly new Grand Prix Pontiac. We stayed almost a week. Dan enjoyed the trip and my parents' hospitality.

During the summer, I looked for work. One of the jobs that Donnie and I got through Fred was a cleanup of the rubble created by the burning of a local restaurant, The Golden Pine, in Pound. After it burned, Fred's uncle Carl McAfee purchased the property as an investment. That job only lasted a few days. Glenda's relative, Lester Baker, was a contractor and a preacher in the Old Regular Baptist church where we sometimes went with her family. He offered me a job at $1.00 an hour as a "gopher" for the skilled masons and carpenters. I had no skills to offer, but I was happy to be making some summer money. This was when I first met and worked with my good friend Coy Boggs. He was also working for Mr. Baker. Coy became a lifetime friend and musician buddy.

I started my second year of college in a little better financial shape, and with a slight bit more confidence in my academic progress. After declaring a change in my major to P.E, I was required to change curriculums into education. I was still unsure about what I wanted for my future. I found out pretty quickly that the P.E. courses were fairly easy, and I always felt that the education courses were a waste of time. I decided to start working toward satisfying my science requirements, so I signed up for physical science survey under Dean Thomas. The subject matter seemed to come easy to me and I enjoyed the class, making my first "A" in college.

Glenda and I, along with Tracy and Phyllis Hall, saw and heard our first big concert in Brooks' Gym. It was one of our idols, Ray Charles. His very popular songs of the time were "What'd I Say," I Can't Stop Loving You," and "You Are My Sunshine." We all loved the concert, and it spurred me to learn more Ray Charles songs.

That fall, I was walking down the street in Johnson City and I saw a bass guitar in the window of Uncle Sam's Pawn Shop. I went in and asked to see it. It was a Fender Precision bass, and it seemed to be in excellent condition. We had never used a bass in our band but we had noticed that it was pretty common in most groups of the day. I inquired about the price and the fellow told me it was $150. I put a little money down to hold it until the weekend when I could talk to Fred. I discussed it with Fred on Friday evening and we went down to Sam's on Saturday morning and he made the purchase. Naturally, we needed an amplifier. We stopped by Joseph's Music Center in Kingsport on the way back and Fred decided to purchase a top of the line amplifier. He got the latest and best thing available in bass amps which was the piggy back Fender Bassman. We were all set with some very fine high quality equipment, but we did not have a player for it. I told Fred about Coy Boggs, the worker and musician that I had met the preceding summer. When Fred asked him to play with the band, he agreed. We became a five, and sometimes six-piece band (with sax) on stage at Club Scotty, and we were hotter than ever. We did still book the band out in other places occasionally. One such gig was the Holly Ball in the Jefferson Lounge at Clinch Valley College.

The "Wildcats" playing for the Holly Ball at Clinch Valley College in December, 1962. L-R: Coy Boggs, Glenn Smith, Ron Swindall, Fred Adkins, Donnie Mullins, Sidney Amburgey

UH OH!

Glenda and I also went to a couple of Pound High football games on a couple of Friday nights when business at the club was low. On one of these outings, I got a shock.

When we arrived at the game and started to get out of the car, she touched my arm, "wait, I want to tell you something," she said.

I asked, "what?"

She told me that she had met a guy at CVC where she was going to school. They worked together on the annual staff and had become really close friends.

Of course, my question was, "how close?"

She told me that they really liked each other and he wanted to date her. She admitted that they had spent a lot of time together, walking and talking on campus, and always having lunch together. Obviously, I was heartbroken. How could this be happening? We had even already talked about being married.

I asked her, "what do you want, and what can I do?"

She did not answer. She gave my class ring back, and she just said, "I'm sorry. I'm just confused. I don't know what I want."

Then she cried a little, "I still want to see you," she said, "but I don't want to go steady anymore."

"Please take the ring back," I begged, "I'll do anything you ask me to do."

She said, "it would be best if I don't wear the ring."

I was numb for a few days after going back to school. I attended my classes, went to R.O.T.C. drill, attended football and basketball games and tried to feel more like a college student than ever before. I looked at girls and thought about asking someone out, but I did not. When the quarter was over, I went to see Glenda a couple of times, but things were just not quite right.

My high school classmate and friend, Bill Bolling showed up at Club Scotty a couple of times. He and another friend, Newton McCoy, had been going to Emory and Henry College, hoping to play football. I invited Bill to go home to Florida with me during the holidays and he accepted. It was really nice to leave the cold weather in Virginia and spend a few days in the tropical warmth of Florida. I was hoping the trip might ease some of the pain of my romantic woes.

My little '53 Chevy was beginning to have on-going problems and was becoming more and more undependable. My dad had purchased a Nash Rambler and he liked it a lot. He felt like it was a very economical car. He had not traded in the '56 Chevy that he had purchased in Virginia a few years back. On my trip to Florida that winter I asked Dad if I might be able to take the '56 Chevy back with me and leave him the '53. He was reluctant, but with mom's help I was able to convince him that I needed it. It would be just another addition to my life to help me forget my problems.

In the meantime, I had decided to buy Glenda an engagement ring. I thought something big like that might solve the problem and that things would then be OK. I went in debt and purchased a nice ½ caret diamond ring and presented it to her the next time we were together. She seemed happy, and we talked more seriously about marriage after we finished school. I continued to see her on weekends, but somehow things were still not quite the same as before. Something was standing in the way, and I was pretty sure I knew what it was. This whole scenario was changing my ego. I was beginning to feel these changes in my thought processes and in my body.

During the winter quarter, I signed up for the second course in physical science survey. I was succeeding in the science curriculum. I didn't go home to Florida during spring break this time, for obvious reasons. I was staying close to hopefully try and protect my interests.

In addition to the required courses in education, I enrolled in biological science survey for spring quarter. I was in my last required R.O.T.C. class, and I would soon be a college junior.

Then it happened again. One weekend, Glenda wanted to give the engagement ring back. I was desperate. I couldn't think straight. She was the only girl I had ever dated, and I was losing out.

I immediately made a hasty decision, "we can get married now."

She hesitated, but I didn't take the hint. I insisted, and so we began to discuss how this could take place. I told her that Fred would help us and we could go to Clintwood or Lebanon and get married. It was agreed. Looking back, I really believe that she made the decision because her home life had not been pleasant. I talked to Fred, and plans were made to go the following Saturday.

MARRIED!

I played at the club on Friday night and Glenda went with me. The next morning, Fred and I picked her up at her home. We went by and picked up Fred's girlfriend, Joyce Kanode, in Norton. We drove to Lebanon, went by a lab and had blood tests, got a license, and stopped at the big First Baptist Church in Lebanon. We were married there by the pastor with Fred and Joyce as witnesses, on Saturday, May 4, 1963. I was only 19 years old.

That night I played at the club as usual. My friend Coy Boggs and his wife Anna Ruth had previously invited us to spend that night with them on South Fork in Pound. We didn't really have any other place to go. They provided a nice private upstairs bedroom for us. This became Glenda's room during the week while I was at school. She rode to CVC with a friend. We settled into the idea of being married, but I was still gone away far too much of the time.

During spring quarter, I looked into the requirements for majoring in general science, and I decided to change majors again. I also decided that I would move into curriculum D, which was a non-teaching curriculum. I had all of my required education courses except for two or three, but I had not planned for student teaching which would cost me an extra fall quarter to graduate. The state of Virginia, at that time however, did not require student teaching for a certificate, so that became my route. I had it worked out, starting with the fall quarter, so I could graduate in eight quarters.

I completed R.O.T.C. that spring and made high grades on the final tests. I was called into Captain Lamas' office and asked to enter into the advanced program that fall. This could have led directly into Officer Candidate School and resulted in my becoming a second lieutenant. I politely told him that I had no interest in the military service.

I was back in Wise County for the summer. We looked for a reasonable place to rent for the summer. Dan Vasvary had been renting a one room brick cottage in West Norton behind Bertha's Grill. He had moved and suggested that we might want to live there. It was only one room, but it had everything we needed, including bed, stove, and bathroom. We rented it. It was furnished with all utilities at only $30/month. Glenda had finished all of the courses that the two-year school, Clinch Valley College, offered at that time. She took a job as a clerk at the Federated Store in Pound. I went back to work with Lester Baker's crew, restoring the Hibbitt's house in Wise and doing some painting at other places. We also helped in building the new Bold Camp church in Gilliam Hollow. I was making $1.00 an hour and Coy was only getting $1.25, even though he was much more skilled. He deserved to make a higher hourly wage. He asked if I wanted to just join him and do some free-lancing. I told him that

I would. We worked together for the rest of the summer. We laid bathroom tile in the Collin's home on Indian Creek, which later was purchased by my Aunt Lena Roberson and her husband, Raymond. We did painting and remodeling for Jack Bolling in Pound, and we painted Ms. Bertha Maxwell's home on Mill Creek a nice soft green color. Coy soon left Pound for greener pastures.

Jim Dockery became our bass player for a while when Coy left to work in Defiance, Ohio. Then Jim left soon to join with Coy in a group that was first called the "Cousins," then later became the "Originals." They had all moved to Defiance, Ohio.

I met and became friends with Danny Green at the end of that summer. We had played some music together, and he took over on bass in the band to replace Jim. Danny had just made a purchase of a newfangled device that connected to the guitar amplifier, called a reverberation unit. I loved the new sound. Danny allowed me to use it when we played, and it really inspired me. I eventually talked Fred into buying one to be used onstage at the club.

By the end of that summer, Glenda and I had saved enough money to rent an efficiency apartment in Johnson City on Maple Street for only $25/mo. I learned that year why people in Tennessee loved TVA so much. Electricity was as cheap as dirt. We had electric heat in the apartment and the highest bill that winter was about $1.50. Obviously, this is one of the reasons why Tennessee and the other TVA states did not vote for Barry Goldwater, who announced that he thought TVA should be sold to private industry. Oh well, it happened later anyway, but the statement damaged Barry's political career.

With the money that we had saved from the summer we could buy some groceries and look ahead a little bit. Glenda wanted to find work. With her clerk's background at the Federated Store she was able to secure a job at Dosser's Department Store in downtown Johnson City. She worked on the bottom floor in the costume jewelry department. She didn't like this as much as selling clothing, but it was a job. Her salary, along with my music gig money, was earning us enough to get by. We enjoyed time visiting and playing cards with our high school friends, Donnie and Eva Mullins.

In November, 1963, while still living in the efficiency apartment on Maple Street, we and the rest of the nation experienced one of the great tragedies of our time. I was in Dr. Eliason's Principles of Education class when we got the news that our President Kennedy had been shot. We were all stunned. All classes at the college were dismissed and we all went home, or to our rooms. Dosser's was closed and Glenda went home. I had just secured a used tv from my grandmother, and we were able to watch the entire drama as it all unfolded in front of us. The country and the world were changed permanently as a result of the assassination.

We began looking for a larger and a little bit nicer apartment. What we found was a three-room apartment with bedroom, bath, separate kitchen and separate living room. Even though it was located all the way out on north Roan Street near Steed College, we took it.

Glenda had to work on Saturdays, so her chances to go back to Wise County with me on the weekends were minimal. It was becoming a problem. We only had one vehicle. I either had to ride in with someone else to play music for the weekend, or she had to find a way to get to work when I was gone. She worked on Saturdays, had very little free time, and I was gone entirely too much. To add to this, I had taken up fishing again, and would sometimes even spend time away from her for this activity. Not smart! It was not a good situation to start with, but I wasn't helping it in any way. Sometimes I don't think I really began to grow up until I was about 30 years old, but I have no real excuses for my immaturity.

During the junior year at college, I had begun to find myself even more interested in academics. I began to take chemistry and biology courses to meet my general science requirements in that major. In my first biology lab course, I enrolled in Dr. Robert Creek's class. He was a fabulous and inspiring teacher, and he is another one that I would consider to be in my top five group. I took another course under him, then I started taking advanced courses in biology. I made flying colors in all of them. I even enrolled and did well in a couple of graduate and pre-med courses.

Many of the East Tennessee legislators had been pushing for a change in status for ETSC. During this year, they approved the legislation and ETSC became East Tennessee State University, another reason for students like me to be proud of the school.

Things were changing pretty drastically once again at the club. Fred had decided to go back to school. He took some classes at Clinch Valley College. Then he attended E.T.S.U. for a couple more needed courses while he stayed in the trailer with Ronnie Clark. The romance between Ronnie and Ginny had gotten serious, and they made the decision to get married in June, 1965. Fred moved out of the trailer. With the financial backing of his Uncle Carl, he entered law school at the University of Tennessee. Ronnie and Ginny attended school at ETSU one more quarter. After graduation, they moved the trailer back to Wise County, and they both took teaching jobs at Pound High School. After teaching, Ronnie went into the coal mining business with his father and worked until he retired.

When Danny Green left to go to work in the D.C. area, our bass player became Larry Bolling from Pound. Larry ("Labo") became a quick friend, and he has been a good friend for many years. We enjoyed playing and spending time together. All of the original "Wildcats" were gone except me. The house band consisted of Gary Freeman, Leland Maggard, Labo and me. We had many musicians that sat in and substituted for regular members over the years. Some of them were Jay Corder, Bob Baker on drums, Stewart Judkins on keyboards and/or drums, and Tracy Boggs on organ.

During my senior year, it was looking more and more like I was really going to get a college degree. I was looking ahead and I could see the light at the end of the tunnel. Glenda was able to move to the top floor of Dosser's and work in the lady's clothing department. She liked this much better because it was easier to stand on the carpet rather than the hard floor of the jewelry department. We were both glad about that.

WORKING AT DOSSER'S

I was getting some extra fill-in work at Dosser's. The manager, Mr. Hobson, had asked Glenda if I might be interested in filling in occasionally. The older handy man, Ralph, wanted to take a day off fairly often. If he called in sick or wanted to be off for another reason, I was called in. I became an overall "gopher" for the store, but the main two jobs that I had were elevator operator and delivery boy.

Mr. Dosser's son, Bobby, had been stricken by polio as a child, but he could still drive. His legs were of no use to him, but he had a special car which allowed for full operation with his hands only. We loaded up the station wagon with packages containing dresses, shoes and other items that had been ordered for trial by some of the old reliable customers. Bobby drove around the neighborhoods in Johnson City, and I took the packages to the door of some of the finest homes in the area. I also picked up items that had been tried and rejected, and these were returned to the store.

My other main task was to operate the old Otis elevator in the store. It was not automatic and could not be operated by customers.

My main conversation with the clientele consisted of, "hello. Step to the rear please." Or, "Step up please." Or "Step down please."

The elevator had to be stopped with a handle that was placed in a middle position. It was then raised or lowered by lifting or pressing down on the handle. After closing the front gate, one could actually still see which level that was being approached. This was always a little bit tricky. I sometimes got it perfect, but many times I would stop a few inches high or too low. If I missed badly, then I had to try to line up with the floor, sometimes resulting in an uncomfortable bounce and abrupt stop. Even for a young man, this activity was tiring, and I occasionally got some disapproving glares. I rode up and down all day between the first floor, mezzanine, second floor and third floor. I <u>was</u> making extra money, and that was a good thing.

We decided that we might be able to afford a new little car. The Chevy had developed a gear shift problem. We ordered a new Volkswagen when we went to Florida on winter break. During spring break, we went to Florida and traded the '56 Chevy for the new white VW "bug.

A New Job

MOVING BACK TO POUND

I finished my last course at ETSU and received my B.S. degree in General Science and Psychology in August, 1965. It was a great feeling of relief and accomplishment to walk across the stage in Brooks gymnasium and be handed a diploma by Dr. D. P. Culp, the president of ETSU. My dad and mom drove up from Florida and attended the  graduation ceremonies. They were so proud. I was the first on either side of our family to receive a four-year college degree.

I had applied for a job as a teacher in Wise County Schools. I went for an interview with Mr. W.D. Richmond during the summer. He was impressed with my science credentials and hired me immediately. He placed me at Appalachia high school, and I was assigned to teach biology and general science. I was a replacement for Mr. Jack Sizemore, who had gone back to school to get a master's degree.

Glenda and I packed up our few household belongings and moved back to Wise County. Unfortunately, we had to stay with her parents for a few days before getting squared away. We had no other place to go.

Mr. Reasor, the principal at Appalachia High School, tried to help us find an apartment or house for rent in Appalachia. Nothing was suitable.

We began to look for an apartment or house to rent in Pound. Glenda had already been told that she could go back to work at the Federated Store if she wished. We were hoping to find a residence close to town so that she could walk to work at the Federated Store. Emma Gray Large was my former friend, Billy Moore's relative. She and her husband had built a new house in Pound Bottom and had only lived there a short time. The house was for rent. We decided to take it at $100/ month, which was a little steep for someone that had just signed a teaching contract for $3900/year, but we saw it as an opportunity. We had no furniture. We went to Pound Hardware and talked to our friend Tracy Boggs, who was working there at the time. He helped us to select living room furniture and bedroom furniture, but we had no way to pay for it. When we asked for credit, Mr. Earl Jackson told us that we would need a cosigner. I thought that would be no problem. We asked Mr. Hayes, Glenda's father, to cosign. That was a mistake. He refused. We didn't really know what to do next. We decided to go to the Federated Store and talk with Mr. Orby Cantrell, Glenda's boss and also a member of the board at Peoples Bank where the money would be borrowed.

When we asked Orby for help, his comment was, "Stay right there. I will call Mr. Jackson."

The conversation on his end went something like this: "Earl, this is Orby. About this furniture that Ronnie Swindall wants to charge. Now I've known Ronnie since he was a little boy and I have known that family to be honest and to always pay their bills. I don't think we would have a thing to worry about. They mentioned that you had asked them to have a cosigner. I really doubt that is necessary. Now Earl, if need be I'll be glad to sign the note myself. Well, ok, thank you. Goodbye."

It was that easy. They delivered our furniture to the house the next day and we were all set, but we didn't get to stay long. The owners decided to sell the house, and we had to move again in the late fall.

Luckily, a couple of inquiries led to our locating another relatively nice new house. Bud Austin had nearly completed the building of a house for his mother-in-law and she had passed away. His wife, Eva Johnson Austin, had been our high school librarian. Even though I had probably aggravated her during study hall much more that I should, she really liked Glenda. Ms. Austin talked Bud into renting the house to us for $60/month. He even told us that each rental payment would go toward the purchase price later if we wished to buy.

The new dwelling in Austin Bottom in Pound had been built with the same style of tile that my dad had used to build our house on Indian Creek. Bud had filled the holes in the tile block with ashes as an insulator and stuffed insulation all inside the ceiling. Even though this helped, we had electric heat, and the inefficiency of the resistance heaters caused the electric bill to mount quickly when the weather turned colder. We were still driving the VW, and it had already started having mechanical problems. It was supposed to have more traction on snow than the average car, but even that was in question.

LARRY LESLIE SALYERS

Our high school classmates, Larry Salyers and Brenda Dotson had gotten married while I was in college. They had moved to Tampa, Florida where Brenda's mother lived. This was the same city where my parents had settled. Larry had been working in a fertilizer plant there. His parents owned the Austin Motel and the Pound Market and they needed Larry's help. Larry and Brenda had moved back into the little house on the hill across from the motel. It was nice to have them within walking distance of our new abode. We spent lots of time with them, playing cards and enjoying other games and their company.

Larry had grown up in a serious fishing family, and I soon became his new fishing partner. One of the first destinations was Cherokee Lake. I loved the lake, and I especially loved being able to take advantage of Larry's expertise. One of the first trips I made with him in their family boat resulted in dozens of bass, crappie and white bass. I got the itch, and it made me want to go as often as possible. There were three main spots where we launched the boat in Cherokee. The first was the Cherokee Marina or Cherokee Boat Dock. Sometimes we launched at Church House Point, just above the marina. The third place was out on Lakemont Drive in what we called Beauty Rest Hollow, so called because there was once a motel with that name out on the entrance road.

On my first trip to the lake, the leaves had turned color and were just starting to gradually fall. It was a beautiful warm day with bright sunshine glimmering on the water. We spotted an old fellow wading on the old road bed at the mouth of Beauty Rest Hollow. We stopped the boat and watched a while. He was catching a fish on every cast, and loading up on crappie, bass or stripes. He saw us looking and waved us on in. He smiled with a snaggle-toothed bearded look. We eased the boat up close so we could talk to him. During our conversation with him, we learned that his nickname was "Popeye." He was an old timer that lived nearby and often fished by wading a few spots up and down the lake.

We cautiously asked him how he was catching all of those fish and he said, "Oh I use my little fly (he held it up) with a floater tied about 2-3 feet above it."

We watched as he caught a few more, then we popped the question, "Well, where do you get those little flies?"

"Oh, I make 'em," he said.

"Do you have any more with you? We'd be willing to buy some."

Then the surprise. He flung his short waisted coat open and revealed dozens of popeye flies in all colors. We bought several cards of flies from him. We tied the flies on as he had taught us to do. We caught a bunch of fish that day. For years after that, we continued to use the popeye method, and we landed many fish.

In the very late fall or early spring, we sometimes put the boat in at Caney Creek by sliding the boat out over the frozen mud. We waited until it re-froze in the evening before bringing it in again. We fished the Holston River all the way to Rogersville (about 10 miles upstream) in the springtime. The white bass were spawning in the river during

April. In the summertime, we trolled and caught many of the white bass that were often found hovering above a covered island at the mouth of Poor Valley Creek. We had names to describe our favorite spots, like the House Seat, Three Springs, Poor Valley Island, Point 25, Stump Island, Under the Power Lines, etc. On almost every trip, we passed by the homes and several boathouses lining the bank on Lakemont Drive, and we coveted the idea of being able to keep a boat in one.

One of the exciting events that occurred during warm weather on the lake was stripe breaks. The white bass (stripes) schooled up a couple of times during the day and declared war on the large schools of shad minnows. They would swim under them and then swim up and trap them between their school and the surface. They then began voraciously killing the shad by snapping at them to kill them. They might stay up near the top like this for 5-10 minutes or more each time. When their killing foray was over, they fed on the dead and dying minnows underneath the surface that floated downward all the way to the bottom. Our thrill was to cast a top water (floating) plug into the massacre during the top-water break and just pull it along until a fish struck it. This rarely failed. Afterwards, we still caught the stripes below the surface with shysters or deep running plugs. When they weren't schooled, and feeding, we caught them in deeper water by trolling deep running plugs.

We were anchored over Poor Valley Island one day, waiting and hoping for a break to start. There was another fellow in a boat just a few feet away. It was a hot day, and the sun was beating down. The water was like glass, with not a ripple anywhere. Suddenly we saw some movement in the water about fifty feet away. At first, we thought it might be the beginning of some feeding activity. Whatever it was, came straight toward our boat. As it came closer, we realized that it was a snake, a big one! It came close enough to our boat that we could see the rattle at the end with about 6-8 buttons. The rattlesnake was between 3 and 4 feet long. It swam past us and straight toward the other boat.

When the other fellow saw it, he said, "If he comes close enough to me, I'm gonna catch it. That would make a nice hat band."

It swam very close beside his boat, and Larry and I watched in disbelief as the man used his fishing net and dipped it under the snake. He lifted it into his boat and immediately grabbed his paddle and began hammering the snake, which was now laying on the seat of his aluminum boat.

When he stopped hammering, he held the snake up by the tail and told us again, "See, this will make a good-looking band for my hat."

We agreed, then we returned to our business of casting over the island for stripes. Everything returned to normal for a little while, until we heard a commotion in the other boat. The guy was hurrying toward one end of his boat with his paddle in his hand. The snake had suddenly revived and was crawling and wriggling around in his boat. He had another battle on his hands as he tried to aim his paddle toward the head of the snake once more. He was finally able to quiet the struggling snake. He cut off the head this time and tossed it into the water.

This was just another one of so many memorable experiences that Larry and I had as we fished, hunted, built things and just had fun together.

It probably should be against the law to have as much fun as we had during these times!

When it was not reasonable for Larry and I to make a trip to Cherokee, we enjoyed our little North Fork Lake in Pound.

Sometimes we fished in Flannagan Lake in Dickenson County. One of the summertime trips we loved was to go to Flannagan and catch the big nesting male bluegills with a flyrod and a popping bug. I learned early on that the large bluegills can be easily filleted. I think they are wonderful table fare when fried in a skillet, and after rolling them in egg, beer and meal batter.

Larry and I tried rabbit hunting a few times with not much success, maybe because we were not using dogs to sniff them out for us. One day he got wind that someone was giving beagles away. He talked me into taking two of them, with the argument that I had more room and a safer place to keep them. I agreed. We were going to share the beagles, and we hoped that we could train them to hunt for us. It was soon time for their worm shots and rabies vaccinations. Instead of going to the local vet, Foy Meade, for these, I decided that I would order the supplies and do it myself (this is probably illegal now). I ordered and received the vials and needles. I called Larry to come and help me when I was ready. I had read about the proper method of vaccinating animals and I was confident that I could do it correctly. I loaded up. Larry held Sebastion (one of the beagles) and I pulled the hide up on the dog's back as I had read. I stuck the needle into the skin and pressed the plunger.

Larry yelled, "Woah Swindall! You just shot that stuff all over my shoe!"

I had plunged the needle all the way through both layers of loose skin, and all of the medicine hit Larry's shoe and the ground. None of it benefited the dog.

APPALACHIA HIGH SCHOOL

I had not been overly excited about driving to Appalachia every day, and I was not totally happy with my placement in that particular high school. As it turned out, it was probably the best thing that could have happened for me. The school had a six-period day. My teaching assignments included an eighth-grade homeroom, three biology classes, two physical science classes and a study hall. I had absolutely no teaching experience, and curriculum D at ETSU did not include student teaching (now called intern teaching). I learned quickly that I could not afford to walk into the class unprepared. I started my classes by having my students read aloud from the text, with the pretense that I was testing their reading ability. This was only partially true. I was shooting from the hip.

To my advantage, I did know the material very well, and thus began lecturing on day 2 by sharing my knowledge and additional information related to the text material. By the end of the first week, it was surprising to me how easy it was becoming to expound upon the subject matter. The students seemed eager to listen to my information, which was infused with my own experiences. Making maximum use of the meager supplies and equipment that was available, we had lab sessions. Assignments were made, homework was checked, and discussions ensued. Even though I often gave quizzes and tests, the students seemed to like me and enjoy the classes.

There were almost no laboratory materials in stock in my lab at Appalachia High School in 1961. I couldn't imagine how anyone had taught the classes without a few of the bare essentials needed for demonstrations and hands-on experiences for the students. I scrimped the tiny budget that I was given and also bought a few things with my own personal funds. I asked the students to bring some basic items from home. I asked them to also be involved in money-making schemes like bake sales, etc. With all of this, along with other items that I begged from the chemistry teacher and others, I was able to put together some memorable labs and demos.

The microscopes were of poor quality and in disrepair. I pieced the best of them together and used them mainly for demo purposes. There was no chance that all of the students would have a chance to actually learn to use the instrument.

I enjoyed teaching, and it seemed that there was always something memorable happening in my classes. One time in science class, I was demonstrating the properties of hydrogen gas. I had constructed a simple hydrogen generator with an Erlenmeyer flask, and a two-hole stopper. I inserted the stem of a small glass funnel in one hole and a piece of glass tubing was secured in the other. I had bent the tubing into a right angle and had drawn the end of it into an open jet tip. I opened the stopper and placed several pieces of mossy zinc into the bottom of the flask. I then added some dilute hydrochloric acid and quickly replaced the stopper. My intention was to show the students how the hydrogen coming from the tip would burn with a colorless flame. I struck a match and lit the hydrogen at the end of the tip, and BOOM! The generator exploded, and luckily it did not break. The stopper, funnel, and tubing blew out and hit the ceiling. The students were all very excited because they had been watching closely and had seen it all. I surprised myself at my own coolness as I proceeded to calm them. I explained the chemical reaction that produced the gas as well as the one that had produced the explosion. This led to a discussion of the tragedy of the Hindenburg in 1937, and everything was cool. The county even had a 16mm film in the library that few teachers had ever shown. I checked the film out and showed it to the students. Later, I was able to fill a small balloon with hydrogen, and suspend it in the air because of the lighter than air qualities of the gas. Then, from a distance, I lit the balloon which POOFED in a sizable blue flame. The original hydrogen generator had exploded because I had not been patient enough to allow the generated hydrogen enough time to replace all of the air in the flask before igniting it. There had been a sizable amount of oxygen left in the flask to mix with the hydrogen and this had created the explosive mixture. I repeated this demonstration in the proper way. After I lit the hydrogen at the tip to create the colorless flame, I showed the students that there was, in fact, a flame there. I did this by igniting a piece of paper from the invisible flame. Also, by holding a beaker upside down over the burning hydrogen, I demonstrated that the product of burning hydrogen was water. This could be seen by the moisture condensing inside the beaker. There were many demonstrations during my career that always gave me pleasure as I watched and heard the students proclaim their wonder and excitement. My experiences, both expected and unexpected, mounted as time went on.

When the first deep snow came in the winter of 1965-66, the snow plow from the highway department piled up a ridge of snow so deep that it almost blocked our driveway outlet to the main road. Our little VW got hung up on the ridge and just teetered there. I had to dig it out. In the early springtime, I decided to trade the VW for a 1965 Fairlane Ford. It was a sport model with the shift in the floor and a 289 hp engine that was very powerful.

JOSEPH DELMAS FLANARY

As I made several new friends I began to enjoy teaching at Appalachia. Among them were James ("Teddy Bear") Clark, a physics teacher that was an older mentor for me that year. I met and immediately liked, and became friends with Coach Jim Riggs. I also can't forget the friendship and help of Bob Taylor and Jackie Robinette. Joe Flanary, the band director, was perhaps my most important new acquaintance. He was to have a huge influence on the future of my music. He became my music mentor and good friend for many years.

Joe had already earned a reputation as an important and significant music educator in Southwest Virginia. He was fun to be around, and playing music with him was always enjoyable.

Joe was born in Swan Pond, KY near Barbourville, into a traditional mountain music family. After a few moves, the family ended up in the Cumberland-Benham-Lynch area of KY. He became interested in music at an early age. He started on a French horn-like instrument called the peck horn at Benham Elementary School. He later played trombone at Cumberland High School. At this early point, he also began to play dance music in a band under the direction of his teacher, Cecil Karrick. He graduated from high school in 1939 and began playing with the "Grumpy Takus Orchestra." This group played throughout Kentucky. This was a successful and popular group with a big band sound, and it influenced Joe's preference of musical style. He attended school at Eastern Kentucky College for two years, where he was a lead singer in the college men's chorus.

At this point in Joe's life, as he told it, "I was patriotic, I didn't wait to be volunteered, I went ahead and drafted."

Everyone that knew Joe, was very well familiar with his neat sense of humor. He entered the army in 1942, and he served in Germany as a Tech Sergeant where he received a bronze star.

In 1951, Joe was working at Stonega Coal and Coke Company in Glenbrook, KY as a lamp house attendant. He was asked by the nearby Keokee principal to start a band. He agreed, and he became a part time member of their faculty. Soon his students were a full-fledged band with uniforms, and they began marching in parades and they played concerts. He continued to work on the night shift at Stonega Coal Co. Other schools began to take notice. At this time, Mrs. McChestney (another very significant music educator) had started as director at Big Stone Gap. She was spread thin in trying to teach at three schools, which were Big Stone Gap, East Stone Gap and Appalachia. She obviously needed help, and Joe filled the bill. The Wise County School Board and W.D. Richmond offered him a position as the head of the small band program at Appalachia High School. They allowed him to still work on the "Hoot Owl" shift at Glenbrook. He took the job at Appalachia. He was soon laid off at Glenbrook, after which he was given a full-time teaching position.

Joe was never really that fond of marching band. He called it, "a prostitution of the arts."

However, for those that remember the Appalachia High School Tricky Sixty Band, it was known that they played extremely well. In addition, they always looked sharp, and marched like a well-oiled machine. He wrote all of his half-time shows, and he arranged parts from scratch each week. He took a great deal of pride in his work and in the band. The band raised money and traveled a lot. One of the highlights was a trip to the World's Fair in Flushing Meadows Park in the Borough of Queens, New York in 1965.

Joe moved on to Jonesville in 1971 and headed the music program there. He took over a virtually dead program and brought it to full flower. He treated these students to the New Orleans Mardi Gras in 1975. He continued to work at Jonesville until 1978, when he took early retirement.

Joe loved music, and he was an active musician all of his life. He played his trombone or upright bass in groups like "The Townsmen,"

"Hal Salmon Septet," the "Virginians," "Southwinds," and the "Jerome Street Ramblers." He loved to spend his time in the company of other good musicians, such as Rod Tate, Mrs. Mac, Kenny Duncan, Lucian Priode, Steve King, Jim Hurt, Dave Tipton, Bill Duckworth and of course, Glenn Smith.

My association with Joe was in the "Virginians." This group was Joe's baby, and it was the longest lasting band for him and for most of the rest of us. Joe had a broad taste in music. He loved all of the good sounds from classical, jazz, big band, and rock 'n roll. He had grown weary of the traditional dance band sound, and he wanted something different and more fully entertaining with a lot of variety. Other than the variety of music, the high quality of the musicians, and the sound of this group, there was a main reason for its success. It was Joe himself. He was always complimentary and helpful toward any and all musicians, especially those in his band.

The original "Wildcat" band was losing steam in the fall of 1965. I was the last original member to leave Club Scotty and the "Wildcats." During the last months of the band, I was hanging on at Club Scotty, mostly for the pay, but I had enjoyed playing with Larry (Labo) Bolling, Bob Baker, Gary Freeman, Leland Maggard and Mickey Mullins. Fred and Donnie rarely ever showed up to play. Labo had left for the army, and Bob Baker moved away. I was planning my exit. Before long, Joe Flanary knew of my guitar playing ability. In an effort to expand the horizons of his variety group, the "Virginians," he invited me to join them and become an important part of the rock 'n roll branch of the band. I left the "Wildcats" and Club Scotty in Jan. 1966, and for the first time since 1961, I began to expand my own musical horizons.

Joe affectionately called me "Swin" and he always made me feel like I was nothing less than a professional musician. Since I was in his band, to him, I was one of the best! Joe said that music was like an addictive drug to him. He just simply couldn't get enough. I'm sure that if you are a musician reading these biographies, you must know that feeling. Joe Flanary was always dedicated to any group in which he was performing. I feel fortunate to have known this man, to have had him as my friend and mentor, and to have played music professionally with him. He was such an asset to musical entertainment and music education.

THE "VIRGINIANS"

The "Virginians" band was a variety group. We did not cull any type of music, and we became popular for that reason and for the high-quality sound. The main fingerprint of our group was the big band sound. When our clients hired us for a gig, they knew that we could meet their requests for Glenn Miller and Tommy Dorsey and all big band tunes. The surprise for any audience that had not heard us before was not only the quality productions of modern jazz tunes, but the rock 'n roll, country-western, polka, Latin and other styles. The first "Virginians" crew consisted of: Joe Flanary - trombone, Merle Dockery - bass, Danny Collier - drums, Glenn Smith - alto saxophone, Ron Flanary - trumpet and vocals, William (Buddy) Stewart - trumpet, and me (Ron Swindall) on guitar. I remained with the "Virginians" until the group totally disbanded in 1975.

Glenn Smith wrote most of the arrangements, and in the early days we featured Ronnie Flanary (Joe's son) and Buddy Stewart on trumpets. We played many of the Herp Albert "Tijuana Brass" tunes. It was also a part of our i.d. during 1965-1967. We played all over East Tennessee, Southwest Virginia and Eastern Kentucky. We played for the country clubs, Moose Clubs, Elks Clubs, high school proms, night clubs, etc. The money was good and we enjoyed ourselves. During the coming years, the face of the band changed many times. School, the army, and a quest for work carried members away. I stayed with the group for ten years, as did Joe and Glenn.

The promo picture below shows everyone that has been mentioned except Merle, who was replaced by Carl Hoag on bass the next year. Carl was from Kentucky and was in Norton, where he was a DJ for WNVA radio. In 1970, he left the group to become "Jack Lasalle," his alias on a Bristol radio station. Carl is currently working at a large AM/FM station in Beckley, West Virginia. He was later replaced on bass by Mark Wooten. By this time, I had been through a couple more guitars. I traded the Strat for a Tennessean model (a mistake, considering the Strat is now worth thousands as a vintage pre-CBS Fender). I traded again later for another Gretsch Chet Atkins model.

In the promo photo above, in front L-R: Ron Flanary, William Stewart, Glenn Smith, Joe Flanary. Back: Ron Swindall, J.D. Collier, Carl Hoag.

Through the years, temporary substitutes and permanent replacements brought many new faces and talents to the "Virginians." With all of this, the basic styles did not change, and our sound remained very identifiable. In the middle years, we found ourselves traveling further distances more often, but we still enjoyed playing locally, and we played for several high school proms. Our versatility allowed for many top 40 pop and rock tunes as well. We entertained several times at the Fine Arts Center in Kingsport, TN where we met Bill Gamble, a lawyer that played great Dixieland clarinet. Bill made recordings of our concerts, which we still have today. We also met Charles Goodwin, a notable piano player that formed a big band called the "Charles Goodwin Orchestra." Buddy played with them occasionally through the years, and he also performed with many other musicians around the area.

When Buddy Stewart returned from his stint in the army, he became the band director at Elizabethton High School. He later returned to Wise County and became band director at J.I. Burton High School where Dave Tipton had retired. Buddy remained in this position until he retired in 2015.

MARK WOOTEN

Mark Wooten was still in high school when he replaced Merle Dockery on bass in the "Virginians." Mark and I had a lot in common and we became immediate friends. He was always a lot of fun to be around. I especially enjoyed playing music with him. We enjoyed the same kinds of rock music and had a common interest in other diversions. One of Mark's important assets was his ability to sight read music. He had played trumpet in the J.I. Burton high school band, but he could also read notes from the bass cleft.

He was, and still is a complete musician. He compliments any group when he joins them on bass. Mark was in school at Virginia Tech when our "High Country Band" started, and he was still there when "Spectrum" came into existence. He was, however, the third and final bass player in the "Spectrum" band before it disbanded. After this, he was one of the members of "Blue Sky." He later played bass for some recordings and performances by the "Kennedy Brothers." He has shared his expertise in the orchestra for the very classy "Nine O'clock" productions which were produced each year by Jan Thompson, first at J. J. Kelly High School, and later at the new consolidated Central High School. He currently also plays with Richie Kennedy occasionally in a duo.

Mark and I had the original idea for the Glenn Smith album, "The Genius of Glenn Smith," and his bass is heard on all of the tracks except one played by Jimmy Baird.

Anytime Mark and I can pick a little and share old memories, it is always a pleasure. We performed together in two "Virginians" reunion concerts. The concerts were done with other remaining members of the band, including Dave Tipton, John D. Collier, Buddy Stewart, and Ron Flanary. Richie Kennedy sat in and played during the second concert.

GLENN CARSON SMITH

One of the first notable jazz performers and big band musicians in Norton was Glenn Smith. His band, the "Glenn Smith Orchestra" played in the 40s for high school proms and other events. They also gigged in some of the night spots like the Copper Kettle. Glenn grew up in Norton and attended high school there. He was in the high school band, and he was also a very good athlete. Glenn was in the army band overseas. He returned to Norton and worked in the post office until he retired. He is most remembered for his great sound on alto sax. He played piano and wrote creative band arrangements. His style is rooted in jazz, stage music and big band. I remember Glenn fondly as one of my best friends. He was my mentor and teacher, always encouraging and helping me to grow musically. Glenn was one of the finest human beings I have ever known! His life story is both sad and happy. He loved his family, and was very proud of all of his children. Music was one of his greatest joys. He loved to listen, play, share, teach, arrange, and talk about music. His appreciation for the talents of Benny Goodman, Woody Herman, Charlie Byrd, Paul Desmond, Dizzy Gillespie, Glenn Miller, Tommy Dorsey, Les Brown, Lionel Hampton, Maynard Ferguson, Guy Lombardo, Quincy Jones, Doc Severinsen, Billie Holiday, Louis Armstrong and countless others, was a love and respect rarely found.

Glenn Smith was my most important music teacher. I met Glenn for the first time in 1960 when he sat in with the "Wildcat" band as a sub for Kenny Duncan. I was immediately taken by his manner and his unique style on sax. He struck me as a very easy going fellow with a great deal of consideration for others. He was so cool! I was still 16 years old and didn't fully appreciate his musical talents for what they were at the time. I didn't really understand jazz and the big band sound. Glenn was definitely not a rock 'n roller, but over the years he became proficient in all types of popular music, and exceptional in jazz. He was a writer, an arranger, a teacher, a performer and a functional musician extraordinaire. Kenneth Duncan had been playing tenor sax with us and needed to be off occasionally. Glenn and Kenneth were old friends. They had gone to school together at Norton High School and had played music together for a long time. Kenny recommended Glenn to us as a replacement when he was unavailable. Everything worked out fine since he was easily familiar with most of the standard tunes that we had in our repertoire. These old tunes took up the slack in our early rock 'n roll set lists. We only saw Glenn occasionally in those days but everyone knew and respected him. I didn't realize how lucky I was to have the privilege of playing music with him.

Glenn's musical career began long before I knew him. He was born in Norton, VA in September, 1927 and grew up on 11th Street. He attended elementary school and high school in Norton. Glenn was asked one time to tell about his earliest recollections of music in his life. As is many times the case, he said that his fascination with music began at home and in church. He remembered listening intently to his father sing in the choir at the First Baptist Church in Norton and he was particularly drawn to the big sound of the pipe organ. He listened closely to the sounds of Duke Ellington, Benny Goodman, Count Basie, Glen Miller and others of that era on the radio.

Glenn actually began learning to play on a $30 second-hand saxophone at age eleven. By the age of fourteen, he had his own band. They were playing on WNVA every week, as well as traveling to Jenkins, Pikeville and Bristol to perform. He often talked about some of those early musicians that were in the band. This included C.B. Porter, Jack Barton, Neil Barton, Marilyn Barton Browning, Paris Barton, Lee Shelton, Joe Cooch, his brother Herman Smith (who he nicknamed 'Pete'), and his good friend Kenny Duncan. Kenny was one of the last musicians with which he played. His bands at that time used some stock arrangements for their music. Glenn was re-writing intros and endings and arranging whole tunes for the band even then. When he was fifteen, Glenn went to New York City to visit his brother, Bruce, who was in the service at that time. He had the opportunity to hear Doris Day, singing at the Hotel Pennsylvania with the "Les Brown Band." He spoke with Doris that night and got her autograph. Glenn also saw and heard Duke Ellington, Don Byas, and Ben Webster. This is where Glenn began to have an insight into the expression of jazz, and to see the possibility of conversation between musicians, not in words, but through music. At this moment, he realized that he someday wanted to try to be right in the middle of all of the happenings in the "big apple."

I remember one of Glenn's expressions on the set while playing with others when someone was taking a ride, "Yeah, talk to me now. Mmmmhmmm, I hear you."

Glenn was elected "King" at his high school senior prom. His band was hired to play for the prom. The only dance he had that evening was the one which was dedicated to him and the young lady who was selected as "Queen."

He enlisted in the army when he was nineteen. He played drums in an army marching band and sax in a smaller combo. After the war in Germany, he was placed in charge of the dance band, a job which he dearly loved. In addition to other places, he had the great experience of playing in Frankfurt. He even gigged on Hitler's captured yacht as it sailed the Rhineland.

He returned to Norton after he was discharged and worked in the post office until 1949. He took advantage of the GI Bill and was accepted into the Brooklyn Conservatory of Music. His dream was to become an arranger and composer for movies and TV. He studied under Pete Mondello, one of the veteran members of the

"Woody Herman Band." Glenn respected Pete a great deal and gave him credit for "straightening out" his horn playing and for having an influence on his style. The "Woody Herman Band" was one of Glenn's favorites. I remember with great fondness playing Glenn's lively arrangement of "The Preacher" when I played with him in the 60's and 70's.

While in New York he got an 802 card, which gave him membership in the very selective New York Federation of Musicians. He played in a band led by Joe Barone from the Conservatory. He told me about playing all over Long Island, in resorts in the Poconos, and all the way to Oklahoma.

Glenn's father became ill in 1951 and family responsibilities brought Glenn back home to Norton. He again got a job at the post office. He never complained, but his dreams faded as he was obligated to care for his family. He continued to love music and was involved in any way possible.

A few years later, he was called by Charles Goodwin with the news that the "Glen Miller Band" was touring the South and that they needed a sax player. He was able to play with one of the bands of his dreams, but was unable to stay on the road because of personal health problems. The rigorous schedule was too much for his diabetes. Glenn said jokingly of some of Glen Miller's handwritten arrangements that it looked like "chicken scratching across the page."

To all who knew him, he was an intelligent, patient, kind, gentle and considerate man, and one of the finest musicians to hail from Southwest Virginia. He did not play the music of the mountains but of the world and the stage. Because of this, Glenn Smith was not well known among many folks in our area. He had an immense love for music, sought no fame for himself, and had a passion for sharing what he knew with others.

When I first joined the "Virginians," Glenn was playing occasionally with this group, and sharing his time with the "Hal Salmon Band." He gave Hal his notice and began playing full time with the "Virginians" in the spring of 1966. I once again had the luck of being associated with Glenn Smith! In this band, he mostly played alto sax, which was definitely his best instrument. He also contributed greatly with his own style on tenor sax, clarinet, piano, vibes and marimbas. This band lasted longer than most such groups ever stay together. The "Virginians" functioned as a professional band well into the '70's. The success was due, in large part, to the hard work of Joe Flanary as he both played and managed the bookings for the group.

Glenn's priceless contributions to the "Virginians" were his untiring music instruction to us all, his wonderful musical performance, and his never-ending flow of unique written scores and arrangements. He tirelessly wrote out complete scores for everything from Glen Miller's "Moonlight Serenade" to Chicago's "25 or 6 To 4." The versatility of the group made it a choice of country clubs throughout the area. Due to the shortage of night spots in Southwest Virginia, the "Virginians" traveled into Kentucky and Tennessee for most gigs.

Glenn's comment about the "Virginians" was, "We were not as schooled as some of the big city bands, but we were an all-around good band."

After the "Virginians" finally disbanded, we all went our separate ways. Glenn continued to play music and help others learn the joy of playing. There was a brief appearance of a group called "Jazz Virginia," consisting of Glenn, Ron Flanary, Joe Flanary, Dave Tipton, Noel Collins and others.

In the 80's he traveled and played with a group called "Southwinds." This band was composed of several excellent musicians. It was led by trumpet player, Jim Hurt. Jim was a tremendous trumpet player and was well respected in the area for his professionalism. Southwinds also had members, Kenny Duncan from the old "Wildcats" band, Joe Flanary from the "Virginians" and Noel Collins. Noel is an excellent trombone player who was the band director at Powell Valley High School at that time. The last group that Glenn had the opportunity to play with was the "Jerome Street Ramblers." This was another long lasting local group that had been going strong since 1990. Band leader Dave Tipton told me that Glenn reluctantly joined the group in 1991, after telling Dave that they didn't really need him.

At first, he didn't care for the style of the newly formed group, which concentrated mostly on the Dixieland style. Glenn's interest began to peak when he noticed that Dave and the others were interested in expanding their horizons to include some big band arrangements and more jazz tunes. This band is another that was relatively popular because of the variety of music that they played.

One of Glenn's goals was to help youngsters realize their potential in music. He always said that when he finished at the post office he wanted to work with the band kids. He said there was no reason why a large number of local kids shouldn't be all-state, with the benefit of private instruction.

Glenn reported to his last music practice session in Ted Thompson's basement on Dec. 17, 1992. He was responsible and dedicated as usual, even though he was feeling poorly and reported to the members of the band that he was probably coming down with something. On that evening, Ted's little two-year old granddaughter, Rachael, crawled into Glenn's lap and sat for two hours as he played piano for the last time. She was the last person to be mesmerized and captured by the magic of watching and listening to him play. Bill Duckworth drove Glenn to his home on Spruce Avenue in Norton after practice. Glenn passed away that night, leaving a host of sad friends and a wonderful and proud music legacy.

SETTLING IN

By the summer of 1966, I had a year of teaching experience under my belt at Appalachia. Two things then happened which worked in my favor. My cousin Hazel Carico, had been teaching science at Pound High School. She was retiring, and they needed a science teacher. At the same time, Jack Sizemore was finishing up his Master's Degree and wanted to return to Appalachia High School. I went to talk to the new principal at PHS, Marvin ("Buddy") Barker. He had been my high school football coach. He asked me several questions during the interview, then he asked me if I could teach science. My answer was obvious, and I got the job.

In the fall of 1966, I made a career move to Pound High School. A few of my high school teachers were still there, and they all helped me to quickly settle in. I enjoyed teaching physical science, but my first love was biology. When Earl Baker, my high school chemistry teacher, became the assistant principal the following year, I then became the biology teacher.

COACHING

One of the teachers that helped me to adjust at PHS was Gary D. Bolling, the older brother of Pete Bolling, that had played guard on my high school football team. Gary was helping out in the basketball program by coaching the eighth-grade team. I still loved basketball. Gary had seen me play some in high school and he asked me to come and help him to work with the eighth graders. Even though I already knew the basics, Gary told me what the kids needed to learn, and I began helping him. The following year, Gary decided that he did not want to commit his time to coaching anymore, so I took over as eighth grade coach. Wayne Leftwich had been coaching the junior varsity team, and he had been very successful with them. The varsity coach at that time was Morgan Bolling.

Morgan retired from coaching the following year, and Wayne became the head coach. I was asked to be the new J.V. basketball coach. I was elated with this new responsibility. I was also the coach of the J.V. football team and an assistant football coach to Wayne and Trig Dotson.

I had a memorable and slightly embarrassing experience when I walked onto the field during our game with Appalachia that first year of coaching football. Many of my former students at Appalachia were seniors that year.

They greeted me with a cheer and unison yell from the stands, "Hey Mr. Swindall. Hey Mr. Swindall. Hey Mr. Swindall."

Francis Williams took over the duties as eighth grade basketball coach. He did a fine job of working with them, and feeding new players into our program. Francis also picked up the science classes that I had been teaching before I became the biology teacher.

My new coaching mentors, Wayne Leftwich and Trig Dotson, taught me a lot of basics about dealing with the boys that I coached. I fully enjoyed teaching basics and helping my teams win as often as possible. Coaching was always a joy for me, and I took it very seriously. I was lucky to have the respect of many young gentlemen. They listened, learned, and played hard. We were all successful. I have fond memories of many of the members of my teams. The triumphs, the wins and losses, the mistakes, and good times now come rolling into my memory as I remember details. Skip Lawson, Jerry Dorton, Rex Boggs, Jerry Hollyfield, Robert Meade, Deckie Dotson, Tim Morgan, Ricky Mullins, Jerry Cox, and James ("Chainsaw") Cox are just a few of the many special players that I fondly recall. Some of these fellows have become lifetime friends.

The camaraderie of coaches is unique. Trig, Wayne and I were close. We attended county and district coach's meetings, and we were always together on the sidelines during varsity basketball and football games. Trig invited me to go to a Pound Lions Club meeting, where I joined. The Pound businessmen and others in our community took me under their wing. Some of my favorite and most memorable associations there were with Marvin Barker, Blaine Sturgill, Simon Meade, Jim Robinson, Bill O'Dell, Earl Baker, and Woodrow Adams.

MORE FISHING

I loved coaching, and other than music, fishing was my favorite pastime. I was becoming pretty good at it. I had purchased a 14-foot aluminum jon boat from "Preacher" Francis on Indian Creek. At first, I had borrowed a small 3 hp motor from Bud Austin. Later I purchased a 9.5 hp Johnson motor. I carried the boat on a wooden rack on top of my Fairlane Ford. I was able to make some pretty quick runs up and down Cherokee, Flannagan, and North Fork Lakes with the light aluminum boat. I was keeping our freezer well stocked with fish and we loved eating them.

My dad loved to fish as well, but he had never caught a large number of fish in his lifetime until one summer day in 1966. On this particular September day, we put the boat in at the Skeetrock bridge at the head of Flannagan Lake. Almost immediately, we saw fish breaking and feeding on something around the bridge pylons. I had seen similar action many times on Cherokee Lake so I knew what to do from my experiences there. I used a popeye fly and attached a floater about three feet above it. To make sure, I tested my theory. I threw against the pylon and immediately hooked a fish. As I suspected, it was white bass and they were there in very large numbers. I quickly tied a rig on my dad's line and told him to throw against the pylon. He did, and he caught one. We continued the tactic and we were catching a fish almost every cast. My dad had a blast. He had never had such an experience before. It made me proud and happy to be able to provide and share this memorable and precious time with him. We threw the fly/floater combination against the concrete so many times that we eventually broke the floaters and had to replace them. When I ran out of floaters, we used pieces of sticks for a float and still continued to catch fish. We caught them until we were both worn out. When we got home, we counted 72 fish, and yes, we had a big fish fry the next day. I placed many packs into the freezer for future enjoyment.

Trig and I hunted and fished together a great deal during the late 60s. Larry Salyers and I still had occasional trips to Cherokee Lake.

I made contact with another old diehard fisherman from Pound named Chalmer Bolling. It is well worth noting a couple of the things that my old friend Chalmer taught me. I noticed that he was in possession of some strange looking plugs. I found out that he had actually made them himself from bodies made of cedar wood. The hardware had been purchased from an old company called Herter's Sporting Supplies. He gave me a copy of the catalog and loaned me his wood lathe for making the bodies. I learned by trial and error, as I did many things in those days. I was able to make and paint some pretty fancy top-water lures.

One day Larry and I were fishing with Chalmer near the "Goat Hole" on Cherokee Lake. We were all in Chalmer's small boat. We were easing down the bank and we came to one of Chalmer's favorite spots, an indentation in the bank. This was during the winter and the water was low. There was likely some degree of underwater cover for the fish. All three of us started casting into the spot, being careful that we didn't cross lines. I caught a nice bass. I was using a small black top-water skipjack, one that I had made. No comment was made until I caught another, and they asked what bait I was using. I told them and they both asked at the same time if I had any more of them. I did not. I caught another fish, and they had still not hooked one. They tried plugs that were as close as possible to what I was using, with no luck. It was evident that I was somehow fooling the fish into thinking that my bait was the same as the food they had been eating. I caught eight keeper fish that day to their zero. We all remembered the trip for years.

Chalmer taught me the proper way to fillet a fish. This is a valuable skill, and I have always continued to use the technique to obtain boneless fillets for our enjoyment. I have taught my sons this method, and they practice it as well, especially Reuben. Another bit of knowledge, with reference to preparing and storing fish, is Chalmer's freezer method. It is simple. All that's needed is a good quality Ziplock freezer bag that does not leak when filled with water and zipped up. I use quarts. Place the filets into the bag and fill the bag with clean water until it covers the fish. Leave a little air in the bag for expansion. Zip the bag together and lay it flat in the freezer. With this method, it is possible to keep fish for up to 6 years or more without them suffering freezer burn. The fish can be expected to taste as fresh as the day they were caught when they are stored this way.

I rarely turn down an opportunity to go fishing. I was always ready on opening day of trout season, and I caught my limit most of the time. I fished in Flannagan Lake, Bark Camp Lake, and the area trout streams. I always enjoyed fishing for trout. It is quite a different sport from lake fishing. The taste of freshly prepared trout is unique and special. I do not fillet them. This is done after serving them at the table.

Trig and I made fishing trips with Howard Deel, the former basketball coach and principal at Clintwood High School. We traveled to Douglas Lake in the wintertime and caught many dozens of crappie. At night in the motel, Howard always wanted to play poker. He always sat very still with a Camel cigarette hanging from his lips while he played. Sometimes the ash would grow two inches long before falling in his lap. Howard was a colorful and interesting character. I always enjoyed my time with him. He had been the basketball coach at Clintwood when we beat them on their home court in December, 1960.

One time we walked through a hollow and down to the lake at a spot called the "Ponderosa." I have no idea why it had that name. We tried our usual technique of catching crappie with a green fly and a minnow, moving it very slowly in the eddies of the river. It wasn't working. On one of the casts Trig just jerked his line when he felt some movement and he snagged a nice channel catfish. A little later it happened again and he snagged a bass. We decided that there must be a lot of fish there, but they were not interested in hitting our bait. We then tied on some plain treble hooks and started casting and jerking (illegal, I think). We snagged several nice crappie, bass and catfish that day, so we did not go home empty-handed. The catch of the day was when Trig struggled for about half an hour to drag in about a 30-pound carp. When he lifted it up, it was long enough for its tail fin to reach the ground when the head was at his waist. It had been fun, but of course he just turned it back into the river. Most folks know a carp is not good to eat.

On one trip to Douglas Lake in January, we had to walk through thick mud under the bridge near Nina Creek. The mud came halfway up on our boots with each step. It was very cold that day. I remember clearing the eyes of my rod from ice several times.

But we caught fish there, a lot of them! We counted nearly one hundred crappie. We had so many fish that we had a problem about how we would get them back to the car. We strapped the stringers across a small log found nearby, and carried the pole on our shoulders. Both of us struggled for an hour to walk back over the mud flats and back to the car. It was so cold that we didn't even need to ice them down.

Needless to say, we were exhausted, but we had some fine fish to add to our home freezers. One of the interesting things that we noticed when we arrived home about 3-4 hours later was that most of the fish that we had dumped into the trunk of the car were still alive. It had been like keeping them in a refrigerator. We divided up the fish and both of us filleted for hours the next day. If you enjoy eating fish, there's nothing better that fried crappie fillets with fried potatoes and onions.

On another winter trip to Douglas, Trig and I took my boat and 9.5 hp motor and launched it about one mile below the dam. Our goal was to try and catch some of the sauger that we had heard about below the dam. We went up to the wall of the dam, drove a spike into the concrete, and tied up. We soon learned that the wind was picking up and the wind chill was very uncomfortable. We had a mushroom heater but it seemed of little use at this temperature.

A fellow in a boat beside us had a bucket of sand which he had wetted down with kerosene and lit to produce a nice flame. I thought that we probably needed something like that. Well, I thought it was a good idea, until he clumsily turned the bucket over, spilling the sandy fuel into his boat and creating a boat fire that could have really been dangerous. He was lucky to have been able to smother it out with his coat.

We were fishing with a fly and minnow combination. We were having no luck. About an hour later it started snowing, and this soon changed to heavy sleet. We waited a few minutes and I convinced

Trig that we needed to go back to the car. The wind was blowing toward the dam, so along with the ice storm, we had near white-out conditions. It was all I could do to keep the boat headed in a straight direction. The wind was blowing so hard that not only was I chilled to the bone, but it took almost an hour to move back down the river. That was the coldest time in my life. When we got to the take-out, my face, ears and hands were numb. I thought they were frostbitten because I could not move my fingers. Crazy? Yes! But we survived, Trig better than me because he didn't have to drive the boat. He had pulled his heavy coat over his body and shielded himself from the weather.

In addition to teaching and coaching at Pound, playing music, and fishing, I squirrel hunted every fall with Larry. I also went rabbit hunting with Trig in the fall/winter season, and bird hunting a couple of times with Tom Sturgill.

When we fished on Pound Lake, we sometimes came in to the dock after dark. During these times, we started lending more attention to the sounds on the lake. It was easy to tell that there was a proliferation of bullfrogs. This spurred the idea that maybe we should go gigging for frogs, since neither of us had ever eaten frog legs. We ordered a couple of frog gigging forks and mounted them on long straight poles.

On our frog hunting trips, one of us steered the boat with the electric motor while the other lined up ready to take a stab. Whichever one of us was in the front of the boat held a strong floodlight and a gigging pole. The driver eased up the bank until we heard a big frog. We sneaked up, and while shining the light in his eyes to hypnotize him, he would be taken for dinner. We gigged as many as a dozen or more on a good night. After putting the frog to 'permanent sleep', we took the legs.

These were taken home, washed and skinned, and then rolled in a meal/flour mixture. It was interesting to watch the movement of the frog legs in a frying pan. My first taste of frog legs was a pleasant and tasty experience. We both decided that we should follow up with this activity occasionally.

Larry and I continued to hunt frogs on Pound Lake for a few years. I also hunted frogs there and on other lakes and rivers with Trig and others, like my friends, Terry Collier and Kent Roberson.

THE DRAFT

As a senior in high school I had been required to register for the draft. Such registration had been a requirement since before WW II (1940). Conscription started during the Civil War, and it has been used for all other major conflicts. The draft ended in 1973, but young men are still required to register. While I was a student at ETSU, I had been classified as 2 S. Now that I was out of school I was eligible for the draft. Several of my friends had already been drafted. I dreaded the day when I would be called. I did not like the idea of going into the service. I did receive a draft notice during my second year of teaching at Pound. The letter instructed me to report to a certain location where a bus would pick me up and take me to Roanoke for a physical. If I passed, I would be inducted into the army. My good friend and assistant principal at the time, Woodrow Adams, was on the Board of Supervisors for the county. Woodrow had been drafted, but it was during peacetime and he had used the G.I. bill for education afterwards. He told me that he would try to get me re-classified. He wrote a letter to the draft board. He appealed to them that I was an important teacher in the county, and that I was needed to continue teaching science to young people. I received a letter before the report-in date informing me that I had been reclassified. I breathed a sigh of relief. The Vietnam War was in full swing and many Americans had already been killed. I did not want to participate in the war. The more I learned about the war, the less I respected our nation's leaders for making the decision for our troops to be involved. I was always worried and concerned about my friends that either volunteered or were sent to fight in this ugly war. Many never returned. My football teammates Scott

Dotson and Danny Mullins were killed in the war. My teammate Pete Bolling was left with lifetime scars and injuries. My musician friend Larry ("Labo") Bolling received a Purple Heart for service related injuries. My musician friend Jerry Miller would never talk about his experiences in Vietnam and I'm sure there were very good reasons. This was a useless, senseless war. It basically accomplished nothing after more than 50,000 of our young men were killed there.

BUYING A HOUSE

Neither Glenda nor I seemed to be satisfied with our married life. We had married too young and too hurriedly. Glenda had missed out on finishing college, and other aspects of her life, by being tied down to me and working instead of studying. I felt guilty about this, and I also felt that I was selfish and that I did not want to try to spend more time with her.

Glenda and I made a decision to have a child. This turned out to be the most wonderful decision that we ever made. Michelle Lee Swindall was born June 18, 1968, at the Appalachian Regional Hospital in Wise. I love my sweet baby girl so much. She was, and still is, precious beyond belief. I was beginning to learn what life is all about. Our individual love as a couple was now focused on her, but still not on each other.

My teaching and coaching job went well, and I continued to tackle it with fervor. I also continued to spend too much time with all of my other diversions.

Glenda got a job as a teacher's aide at the Pound elementary school. Our financial situation was improving, but other things were not going so well.

Mr. Bud Austin passed away in March, 1967, and Ms. Austin decided to move back to her hometown in Norton. Russell Hamner in Norton assisted her in selling all of Austin bottom. The Austin home was sold to the Don Stallard family, and we decided that the property would be a good investment for the future. We purchased our home and lot in Austin bottom by borrowing the money from People's Bank of Pound.

MY PARENTS MOVE BACK

In 1969, the country was in turmoil about the war in Viet Nam. This was the year of many protests and rallies, including the peaceful gathering at Woodstock, NY. The tragedy at Kent State, which involved a non-peaceful reaction by police, took place only a year later.

We deeded almost an acre of property beside our house in Austin Bottom to my parents. They bought a trailer and moved back from Florida. My dad's health had begun to deteriorate, and it seemed to do so at an even faster rate when they moved back. He was diagnosed with black lung and pulmonary fibrosis. After that, he never recovered, nor did he improve in any way. Sadly, after a couple of years, he became bedfast, and he finally received the deserved Black Lung benefits, but not in time to enjoy the money. While he had still been able, he had loved to work outside as much as his health would allow. He spent as much time as possible with his new little granddaughter, whom he loved so very much. His garden was his pride and joy. He had a large garden in front of the trailer where he raised lots of beautiful, delicious fruits and vegetables.

One day Dad was checking on his garden and he noticed that some of his cornstalks were ridden down. Something had been chewing into the corn and also eating his beans. He deducted that it was a groundhog, so he decided to waylay it. He had already spotted the groundhog's hole across the driveway, and down beside the river. He got up one morning and loaded my little 20-gauge shotgun. He sat quietly on my porch, waiting for the groundhog to show itself. Before long, the culprit crawled up and stuck his head above the bank to survey the situation. Dad let him have it. We went down to investigate. Surprise! There were two groundhogs laying over the bank. He had killed them both with one shot. Needless to say, his garden fared much better after that day.

A NEW TEACHING CHALLENGE

My principal, Mr. Barker, called me into the office one day at school. He told me that the last visiting committee was very strongly suggesting that each high school offer physics. It was becoming just one of the many requirements for full certification by the Southern Association of high schools and colleges. He needed a physics teacher, so he told me I would be teaching physics the following year. I bucked on the idea, and explained that I did not have a background in physics. My concentration was in biology. The only courses that I had taken that even resembled physics were the two physical science survey courses that I had taken at ETSU. He simply said that I was the closest to being certified than any other teacher, and that he trusted that I would do a good job.

Either because of being prodded by the guidance counselor or because they had an interest, several students signed up for the class that fall. When the class started, I tried to help my students understand the reasons for my being there. I told them about my meager background. I told them that we would all be studying and learning physics together, including me.

I struggled through teaching physics the following year. I studied much more than most of my students. I felt like it was not fair to me nor them that this requirement had fallen on me. I tried my best to muddle through the many complicated problems, some of which required advanced math. I made it through the first year, but I simply skipped over those topics that I did not fully grasp myself. I had nobody to teach me the concepts. I lucked out the following year when Charlie Greene came to PHS to teach advanced math. His apple orchard in the Hurricane section of Wise had not done well, and he decided to try teaching. He helped me tremendously with the electrical circuit and vector problems that I had struggled with so much. Charlie became a very good friend to me and other teachers at PHS. Remembering him is always pleasant.

MY COACHING 'CAREER' ENDS

I had been helping the other coaches raise money for us to go to a week-long coaching clinic. I was eager to learn more, and I wanted to get some new ideas and tips. We raised money for travel to the clinic. Among other things, we sold some commodities and even played a basketball game against a traveling girls team. This all ended in disappointment for me when I found out that I would not be allowed to make the trip. I stewed over this for a while, and one day I made a pretty drastic decision. I walked into the principal's office and asked him what he had hired me to do. He simply said that he had hired me to teach science. I asked him if he had also hired me to coach, and whether or not it would be required for me to continue coaching in order to keep my job.

Mr. Barker simply said, "Of course not."

I told him that I had reached retirement in that field. He was not upset.

He said, "Have you told Trig and Wayne?"

My answer was, "No, I have not, but I will talk to them both about this later today.

I told the other coaches. We all parted as friends.

My friend Bill Bolling, from high school days, was willing to take over my coaching duties at that time. The coaching salary had not been very much. I had been doing it mostly because I loved it. However, in order to continue to help supplement my income a bit, I decided to take on some guitar students. Several young folks and parents had been asking me to do this, so I set up times and prices. I charged $5 for each half-hour lesson. I started with about ten students. I was now spending more time at home without the coaching duties. Also, the lessons were in my living room so I did not have to leave home to do this.

Big Changes

MY MARRIAGE ENDS

By 1970, Glenda and I had both agreed upon terms of non-reconcilable differences and decided to separate for a while. Fred Adkins drew up some preliminary separation papers for us to sign. She decided that she and Michelle would move back in with her parents. Glenda registered for school at Clinch Valley College and started taking classes. This was something that she had really wanted to do but had never really pressed the point. I had reasonable rights of visitation so that I could see my daughter very often. One year later, we signed divorce papers, and we were both free from marriage after almost eight years together.

We both agreed for Glenda to keep the little '65 Fairlane Ford, and I kept a Ford pickup truck that I had purchased the year before. Shortly after I got the truck, I was hauling large rocks to try to build a more solid base under the driveway. It had not yet been paved, and we were sinking up in mud and getting stuck trying to get out of the driveway. While unloading the rocks, I somehow managed to drop one on the middle finger of my right hand. The pain was intense. I did all I knew to try to stop the pain. I had an important gig that night with the "Virginians" at Ridgefield Country Club in Kingsport. I talked Mark into driving me to Kingsport. I then struggled through the first set. All of the guys in the band knew that I was suffering with finger pain. It had swollen up so much that the fingernail was flat and the finger looked fake. I thought maybe a drink might help me to cope with my situation better. I went to the bar downstairs, ordered a martini and drank it straight down. The alcohol didn't seem to help much. I played through the second set and bought another martini during the break. A band member was feeling compassion for me, and he told me that he had some Percocet pain medication with him. He said that I was welcome to try it if I wished. I did. The combination of the alcohol and the Percocet was probably pretty dangerous. By midway in the third set I could not play at all. I leaned against the back wall, slid down to the floor and went to sleep. That's about all I remember until we pulled into Mark's driveway in Norton. I was finally awake enough to drive on to Pound. I was glad that the next day was a non-teaching day. I slept until evening before getting up.

Even though the truck was very handy for hauling gig equipment, I soon decided that I needed a car instead. I traded for a soft yellow two door sport 1973 Ford Gran Torino, a very nice car with a great stereo, AC, and a 302 HP engine. Even with the new and exciting car, I struggled a bit to adjust to my new situation. I continued to see my daughter as often as possible and we shared good times.

My grandparents had retired in Michigan and wanted to move back to the mountains. I consulted with Glenda about the house that we still owned in Austin bottom, and we agreed to sell it. We sold the house and land to my grandparents in November, 1972.

Glenda had been dating a guy named Phil that she met at the college. When we talked, she did not hesitate to tell me about him. He was a biker, and she said she loved riding the bike with him. That lasted a few months, and then she met Ron McMurray. They began dating, and before very long he had asked her to marry him. She accepted.

NEW FEMALE COMPANIONSHIPS

One night while I was playing with the "Virginians" for a gig at the Lonesome Pine Country Club, a crowd came in from the IHRA at Bristol. One of the girls, a good-looking blond, tip-toed up and wanted to sing. Fred was there, and he had known her through a previous girlfriend. He introduced her to me. Her name was Susan. We began to talk at the break about her joining us to sing a song. I found out pretty quick that she couldn't really sing, and I told her that it might be a bit too complicated for us to try that at that time. She then complimented my guitar playing and told me she had always wanted to play. She asked me if I might be willing to teach her. She lived in Bristol, but she had peeked my interest. I told her that we could get together sometime. She set a date for the next Saturday night at her house.

It was the start of an affair that lasted about 6 months. We went out to listen to music, and she accompanied me on some of my gigs. We went to the movies, out to eat, and on trips to local attractions. She loved Gatlinburg, and we went there two or three times. It was a little bit of a twist for me when she told me later that she had been married, and that she had a little three-year old boy. She also said that she had gone to Gate City High School, and that she had dated Ron McMurray. I never discussed this with Ron at any time, even though I saw him and had brief conversations with him through the years. The information that I had gleaned put a damper on our relationship, so I just stopped going to Bristol.

ANOTHER SCIENCE FAIR WINNER

During 1973, I asked my principal if I could teach a course in advanced biology. All of my students were seniors with good science backgrounds. I was free to write my own curriculum for the course, and I decided to spend lots of class time in preparation for the spring science fair. It paid off.

One of my students, Joe Pilkenton, won the fair at C.V.C. in May. During my first year of teaching, one of my students at Appalachia, David Fraley had won the C.V.C. fair and I was allowed to accompany him to the regional fair in Roanoke. As a result of Joe's win, we both got an all-expense paid trip to San Diego to enter the International Science Fair. His project had actually won on the basis of art instead of scientific merit, but it was a treat for us both to make the trip. We flew from Tri-Cities to Atlanta on a Piedmont prop plane, then went on to the west via Delta airlines. We landed briefly in Los Angeles, then flew on to San Diego. We were served a great steak dinner on the plane.

The hotel in San Diego was nice, and it was within walking distance of the convention center and the edge of downtown. The next day we went out to eat and explored the town. We went on an excursion to Mission Bay, the Scripps Institution of Oceanography, and the San Diego Zoo. The following day, Joe's project arrived by freight, and we set it up in the center. I stayed with him until he finished. That afternoon and the next day, he was required to stay with the project. He talked with the judges and the public, answering questions and explaining his ideas. I chose not to stay in the center all day. I roamed around some on my own, and bought gifts for Michelle and my mom. Joe did not place in the competition, but the experience was very worthwhile for us both. I am grateful to Roy Wells and the C.V.C. science faculty for making this trip possible for us.

During the spring of 1973, I had decided that it was time for me to make further changes in my life. I took the Graduate Record Exam, a requirement for being accepted into graduate school by most colleges and universities. One Saturday in early spring, Earl Baker, my high school chemistry teacher and mentor, and I rode together to ETSU to take the general and subject area tests. My score on the general part was average but I made very high scores on the advanced test in biology. I asked that my scores be sent to ETSU where I had also applied for graduate studies in biology. I was called in for an interview by Dr. Copeland, the department head at that time. He had a conference with other members of the department and informed me that I had been accepted. I was awarded a teaching assistantship.

Back at PHS, I was excited and making preparations to leave for graduate school at the end of the year. Jerry Wolfe, who had recently finished his Master's Degree at ETSU was to be my replacement. He would be teaching biology. My friend, Bill Bolling, was leaving PHS and would not be teaching and coaching there. Jerry also took over his duties as the assistant coach to Trig and Wayne.

Dawn Kiser had graduated from PHS the year before. We had always had a good rapport, and we always seemed to enjoy talking to each other. She was a good looking young lady. I decided, 'What the heck, I believe I'll ask her out.' Somewhat to my surprise, she accepted. We ended up going to the drive-in movie in Blackwood. We mostly just talked. It was prom time at good ole PHS, and I decided that night to ask her to go to the prom with me and help me to be a chaperone. She gave me a positive answer. We danced almost every song, we talked, we laughed, and I think we both had a great time. That was the last time we had a date with each other. It was really a different kind of experience to have a date with a former student. She left town soon after that to live in Knoxville and I didn't see her until many years later.

GRADUATE SCHOOL

In the spring of 1973, my father's health had deteriorated to the point that he needed permanent hospitalization. He was admitted to the Veteran's Administration Hospital in Johnson City, TN. I was able to rent the same trailer that my friend Jay Corder had rented while attending school there. It was located on West Walnut Street, about two miles from the university. My mom moved into the trailer that spring. When school was over at Pound High School that year, I moved in with her.

In early June, I started back to school after eight years of taking no classes. I knew it would be a struggle at first, but I was determined. I drove to the college the first day and attended TA orientation. I was surprised to find out that I had been offered an assistantship. I would actually be teaching freshman biology laboratory sessions. I was also required to sit in with a professor as an assistant during one of his classes.

I had known that Vickie Sturgill had applied to the nursing program. She had been accepted at ETSU, and had chosen to start her education early, thinking that she could finish in three years. I found out that she was staying in Yoakley Hall, a girl's dorm, that summer.

She yelled, "Hey Swindall," from the window of her room on the top floor while I was walking to the library one day.

She came down to the street level and we sat on a bench and talked. We decided to go out to dinner together that evening. I went to get Vickie at the dorm, we walked to my car, and I drove up Roan Street, just north of town. We decided to stop at Ponderosa Steak House. As I pulled into the parking area, I realized that I had a flat. I got out and analyzed the situation. It's never fun to have a flat, but even worse if you have a lady passenger, and you are wearing a nice clean yellow shirt and white pants. To make it even worse, it was about 90 degrees in the shade. I swallowed my pride. I got the tire out, and I removed the jack and wrench from the trunk. Of course, I got dirty and sweaty! We went into the restaurant a little later and had supper. I offered to buy her meal, but she insisted that we go Dutch. Afterwards, I took Vickie back to the campus and walked her back to the dorm.

She had just graduated from the high school from which I was taking leave, and had been one of my guitar students a few years back. She had been in my regular biology class, and also in my advanced biology class when she was a senior. There was no doubt that we had spent a lot of time together before this day, and that we had always enjoyed each other's company. Whenever there was a field trip planned or a special concert trip, she was usually along.

We had been sitting together during lunch and talking at school one day. She looked at me intently and said, "I just admire you so much." I had thanked her.

More of my classes would be starting on the following Monday, and I had to go back to the county that weekend for a music gig on Saturday night with the "Virginians." On Friday night, I went to the home of Glenda and her new husband and picked up Michelle. I took her over to my mom and dad's home where we opened up the trailer and spent the night. I kept Michelle most of the following day, then I took her back to her mom. I told my daughter that I could not see her the following day, but that I would return the following weekend. Similar scenarios took place during the following year, but occasionally I would take her back to Johnson City with me for a few days. Glenda was very cooperative and considerate about my visitations with my precious daughter. We were not the typical divorced couple. There was no animosity. We both had respect and cared for each other, and we both loved our daughter and wanted only the best for her.

Back at school on Monday, I began to get into the grind in earnest. I was determined to study hard, make good grades and receive my master's degree.

VICKIE

Vickie and I had another meal together that week, this time at Long John Silver's. I asked her if she might like to go catch a movie together sometime. We both seemed to fully enjoy spending time together. It wasn't long before we began to see each other almost every day. We expressed our feelings for one another.

One evening after dinner we got back in the car, and I reached for a pack of cigarettes above the visor. I had been smoking occasionally while we were together. She grabbed the pack and twisted it, breaking the pack and all the cigarettes inside. "What thuh??!!"

She simply said, "If you are going to be with me, you will have to stop doing this. I'm allergic to tobacco. It stinks, and I don't like it. I like you, but I don't like cigarette smoke, and I don't like you doing it."

That's when I stopped smoking, in the fall of 1973. It was difficult. Oh, I'll admit that I had an occasional cigarette, and that I smoked a pipe a little bit during the 70s, but essentially, tobacco was no longer a desire for me. Even at that, heavy smoking for most of the time during my early twenties took a large toll on me later in life. I would encourage anyone that is now smoking to stop immediately.

During that fall, Vickie started riding to Wise County with me during my trips for music gigs or other purposes. She invited me to have meals at her parent's home. Vickie's father was the pharmacist at Pound Drug Store, and the family lived in an apartment above the store. Her mother ran the Western Auto Store just beside the drug store. Mr. Sturgill did not seem to cater to me very much when he learned that I was dating his daughter, but he never said anything derogatory. I had known Blaine Sturgill since I was a child. Her brother Tom was a graduating senior at Pound high school when I first started teaching. I had known her other brother Don when I was going to school at Pound. I vaguely remembered that Vickie had been the little redheaded girl behind the drug store counter when I was a teenager and lived in Pound. She had made grape and lime freezes for me and others when we stopped by after high school football and basketball practice. Later, she had been my student in high school. Now I was dating her and we cared for each other. I was 12 years older than her, but none of that seemed to matter to either of us.

Vickie and I just always wanted to be together. We included Michelle in our times together as much as possible. Vickie really began to love her very much, and she would ask if we could include her in our outings. We all went out to eat, we went to the drive-in movies together, and went fishing, etc. I took Michelle back to Johnson City with me when she was on break from school. It was a little harder to entertain her during these times, but I loved spending time with her. I was thankful that Michelle and Vickie got along with each other so well, and that they liked each other.

Gigs with the "Virginians" were slowing somewhat in 1973-74. We were not playing as often, and I even heard Joe Flanary tell his son that he was getting tired. Part of the reason Joe was slowing down was obvious. He was getting older, and Mark Wooten and I were restless and wanting to play more rock music than we were at that time.

During the 1973 Arab-Israeli War, Arab members of the Organization of Petroleum Exporting Countries (O. P. E. C.) imposed an embargo against the United States. It was in retaliation for the U. S. decision to resupply the Israeli military, and to gain leverage in the post-war peace negotiations. After October, we found ourselves waiting in line for gasoline. Gas stations weren't receiving as much gas as before and they started rationing the amount that could be purchased. For many stations the limit was 10 gallons. The cost went up drastically from around 35 cents per gallon to almost double that amount. My Ford Torino with the big 302 hp engine would barely make it home on that amount, and then I had to make sure to buy enough fuel to get back to school. It put the clamps on going out in the evenings very often for fear of running out of gas. It had a very dismal effect on the overall economy. I must admit that I panicked a little bit. I went out looking for a smaller and more fuel-efficient car. That led to a mistake that I will never forget. I went to Sherwood Chevrolet in Johnson City and ended up trading my big nice car for a little Chevrolet Vega station wagon. What an absolute piece of junk! Yeah, the Vega got about 30-32 miles per gallon, but it had no power, and about three years later, the aluminum block engine burned up. Michelle tells me she remembers the Vega, and especially the trips to the drive-in that she, Vickie and I took in it.

THESIS

Back at school in 1973, the graduate students had gone to seminars by all of the professors. The purpose of the seminars was to inform us about their major interests. This would allow us to decide on the topic for our own research as we worked with a designated major professor.

I listened very carefully to Dr. Roy Ikenberry as he told us about his interest in marijuana research. I had already been around the drug some, and I was very interested in being able to work with it. My desire was that I might discover something totally new. Dr. Ikenberry told us that many of the studies of the effects of marijuana on the body and mind were probably invalid, because there had been no way to dose it properly. The amount given could not correctly be correlated to the observed effect. This was the area of study that I chose. ETSU had a new gas chromatograph. After some extra training beyond the course in instrumentation that I took that fall, I was assigned to use it for my study.

I started my research in September, 1973. I sat in the instrumentation laboratory for hours, days, and months analyzing and reanalyzing dozens of different samples of marijuana, marijuana smoke extract, and crude marijuana extract. Tetrahydrocannabinol (THC) is the active ingredient in marijuana that is responsible for most of the notorious effects. The previous studies had not actually been correlated to the quantity of THC in the sample. My goal was to suggest a valid method for determining the "strength" of a sample before its administration. My months of work resulted in a successful thesis on this topic. I entitled it *Marijuana Dosage Quantitation by Gas Chromatographic Analysis.*

It took a long time to set up and to occasionally calibrate the equipment by injecting microliters of a standard sample of known concentration. A test sample was then run for a comparison of THC between the sample and the standard.

I was more than pleased to have Vickie's company as I ran

the many samples through the chromatograph. It was very time consuming and somewhat boring in between results. I continued gathering information for my thesis research in the lab, and we used the room for reading and studying during this time.

By the Christmas holidays, Vickie was wearing my engagement ring. She told me that I must ask her father if I could marry her.

While sitting together with the family in the living room one day, I said something very awkward like, "Blaine, Vickie and I would like to get married if it's OK with you."

He did not answer, and he actually never really gave me permission. We made plans to be married anyway because he didn't actually object, at least not to us. Our hopes and plans continued as we went back to ETSU and both continued our studies.

During the winter and spring quarters, Vickie helped me to study. She poured through my lecture and laboratory notes before a test, and she asked me to repeat the information that I had recorded. She skimmed the textbooks and asked me questions from the reading material there. My life consisted of graduate classes and labs, intense research time, performing my duties as a TA, and traveling to play music at least once each week. I didn't have time for much else, but I made some time to return the favor, as I also helped Vickie to study for some of her tests in chemistry and biology. On weekends, we made trips back to Wise County for music, visiting, and seeing Michelle.

My dad wanted to move back home from the V. A. hospital, so in May we moved him back to the trailer in Austin Bottom. He was in bad condition, and it was a really difficult time for my mother. She needed to stay with him constantly, or have someone else come and stay while she went out for a short time to run errands. The church where they were members would come and hold prayer meetings and sing a couple of times each week.

ANOTHER GRADUATION AND MARRIAGE

When the spring quarter was over, Vickie, her mother, and her sister-in-law Anne began to really get busy. They were planning for our wedding, which was to take place on June 8.

We went to my mother and asked her to bake our wedding cake, but she declined, saying that she did not really have the time. We understood. We traveled to Kentucky to ask my Aunt Carol to bake our wedding cake. She agreed to do it but when my mom got wind of this, she immediately told us that she would do it.

Emily and Trula Qualls gave Vickie a bridal shower in the old Copper Kettle building in Norton. We received lots of nice things from many Pound friends and relatives to help us set up housekeeping.

My best man was my long-time friend, Jay Corder. We asked our mutual friend, Terry Collier, to play piano. Glenn Smith played "Let It Be Me" on sax, and Delores Baker Stone sang a song for us. The three ushers were Mark Wooten, Tom Sturgill, and Ron Flanary. Vickie's maid of honor was Eileen Cantrell. The others in her court were Lynette Tunnel, Kathy Mullins, and Debbie Maggard. My beautiful daughter Michelle was our flower girl.

The wedding took place at the Methodist church on the hill in Pound with Reverend Julian Walton officiating.

The reception was in the fellowship hall of the church. It was mainly a social gathering with neither dancing nor music. We had the beautiful wedding cake that my mom had made, and the ladies served finger foods. Vickie's mom, Nannie, was nervous, and she fussed over the punch, constantly asking if we had enough. We cut the cake and stayed a few more minutes. We left shortly thereafter in our little Vega, but only to deliver Michelle out to my mother before we left on our honeymoon. We were headed to Disney World in Florida. Michelle cried to go with us, and it broke our hearts to tell her she could not go. We did, however, promise to go back again later, especially for her, and we did. Blaine was wary of us making such a long trip in our little Vega, and he insisted that we take his Cadillac on the trip. The embargo had been lifted, and there was plenty of gas by that time. The big car was a luxury for us during our honeymoon.

The wedding Party. L-R front: Kathy Mullins (Helton), Lynette Tunnel (Mullins), my daughter Michelle, Vickie, Me, Eileen Bolling (Cantrell), Debbie Maggard (Hartsock). L-R rear: Ron Flanary, Mark Wooten, Reverend Julian Walton, Jay Corder, and Thomas Sturgill

I had correctly estimated that it would be late before we could leave Pound. Reservations had been made for us to stay in Kingsport overnight. At my request, the motel had a bottle of champagne on ice for us when we arrived. We drove to Statesboro, GA, the next day, where we stayed at a Best Western Motel.

The next morning in Statesboro, we had breakfast at a restaurant before leaving. Vickie had a very traditional breakfast, and she was surprised when I ordered steak and eggs. We drove on to Orlando the next day, and spent the night there before driving on to Disney World the next day. After another night in Orlando and a very memorable and fun visit to Disney World, we drove to Tampa. I showed Vickie where mom and dad had lived for ten years. We enjoyed the entertainment and our visits to St. Petersburg Beach, Silver Springs, and Cypress Gardens before heading back to Pound. When we arrived back home, we collected our new treasures from the shower, loaded up the Vega, and headed back to school.

We spent the summer in the little trailer in the Beard's backyard on Walnut Street. We were so happy to be together. Life was good! We were busy though. Vickie signed up for a full class load and more. She had been taking extra classes and would end up with almost enough hours to be classified as a junior at the end of the term.

During the summer of 1974, I worked hard to finish writing my thesis. I borrowed a typewriter from Vickie's brother, Don Sturgill. I sat for many hours typing the document, by using my hunt and peck method on the old analog machine (I didn't take typing in high school). I finished in mid-summer, and I asked my major professor to proofread it. He made a couple of suggestions, and I was ready to type the final draft. When I finished, I took it, along with my pictures, to the printer. They called me a couple of days later and told me there was a problem. The old keys of the typewriter were caked up with dried ink, and some of the letters were almost illegible.

I cleaned the keys thoroughly with a toothbrush and solvent. I retyped the entire thesis. I'll admit that it still looked a little bit questionable in places to me, but I took it back to the printer anyway. Time was running short. They called me again and told me that some of the letters were incomplete. Ouch!

In desperation, we went to Sears and purchased a new electric typewriter. I started retyping my thesis for the fourth time. By now, even though I was hunting and pecking, my speed had increased dramatically. Ha! The final typing was successful. I received my hardbound copies of my thesis a couple of weeks later.

It was a great relief to be able to remove the stress of the thesis from my table, but now I was looking at two more big requirements. Before I would receive a degree, I was required to pass the comprehensive exams in the field of biology. The test was a summation of all of the coursework taken during the five quarters (from the beginning of the summer in 1973 until the end of the summer in 1974). I prepared by studying through my texts and notes as much as I could, after which I went in for the tests with about twenty other graduate students. I sweated through the tests for hours. I watched as one dejected young man got up after a few minutes, wadded the entire test up, threw it into the trash, and walked out. I was pretty well prepared, and I passed the test with flying colors. Whew!

The final test was the oral defense of the thesis. It was held a few days before graduation. It was one of the most intimidating experiences of my life. I was in the conference room with my major professor and four other professors. Dr. Ikenberry sat at one end of the long table with the four professors near him. I was all the way down at the other end of the table.

The first question came from Dr. Moore, "Which did you like best, the dried samples or the C.M.E?"

I was caught off guard and for a moment I couldn't even think and remember what CME was! My quick confusion got the best of me. I posed it as a question, but it was taken as an answer.

I quickly said, "the C.M.E??"

Quick witted Dr. Moore said, "Oh, that's interesting. You liked the crude marijuana extract better than the raw marijuana."

He made notes and then the floor was turned over to Dr. Ikenberry. I almost panicked. Luckily, my major professor did not try to throw me. He asked me a very legitimate question about the use of the gas chromatograph. Then each of the other professors in turn asked me several questions about my research and its significance. There was a discussion as they also contributed their thoughts on the matter. Then I was excused. I left feeling tired and mentally drained. I thought again about Dr. Moore's question and my response. I'm sure that my professors must have had a good laugh at my expense.

A couple of days later, Dr, Ikenberry called me into his office for a consultation.

As I walked in he extended his hand. "Congratulations," he said, "your scores on the comprehensive exams were notable, and we have all decided that your thesis was fully acceptable."

I breathed a sigh of relief.

After a short discussion of my lifetime events and my future plans, he rose and extended his hand once more. "Best of luck," he said, and I left.

I had given one of my thesis copies to my major professor, Dr. Ikenberry. The second copy was presented to the school library. I had two more copies. I presented one of these to J.J. Kelly High School. I hope my local copy was transferred and still resides in the library of the new Central High School. It is a consolidated school that was formed by combining Pound High School with J.J. Kelly. I kept the final copy for my own files.

Graduation was held in Brooks' Gymnasium on August 25, 1974. It was a relief and a joy. My dad had been present when I received my B.S. degree in 1965, but he was not well enough to attend this time to see me receive my M.S. degree. Since my mom was taking care of him 24-7, she could not be there either.

ANOTHER NEW JOB

After attending church at the Methodist Church in Pound one Sunday, my friend Woodrow Adams told me that I would likely be transferred to J.J. Kelly High School if I wanted to continue to teach in the county. This was due to the fact that Jerry Wolfe had not only replaced me as a biology teacher at Pound, but also because he was filling the needed position as assistant coach. When Woodrow told me this, he also told me that he had an opening at the elementary school in Pound where he was the principal. He said that I was welcome to come and teach 7th grade science if I still wanted to stay in Pound. I turned him down and decided to take the position of science and chemistry teacher at J.J. Kelly High School. By this time, I had taught one year at Appalachia High School, seven years at PHS, and one year as lab instructor at ETSU.

During the summer, I had decided on a whim to try growing a

beard. Two of my professors had facial hair, and when I started my own growth, Dr. Moore said to me, "Those ye adulate, ye emulate."

He was always so witty and funny. Moore was my favorite professor at ETSU that year.

Back at home in Pound, when Blaine first saw my beard his comment was, "What does it mean?"

I told him that it didn't really mean anything and that it was just a beard.

I have kept facial hair as a part of my "look" through all of these years except for one year. I shaved it all off one time. When I did, my mom said, "What in the world has happened to your face? Do you have poison ivy or something?"

Michelle's comment was, "Where's my daddy?"

Before that final weekend in Johnson City, Maurice (Chuck) Wooten, Mark's dad, had made arrangements for us to rent an apartment that he had found for us on 12th Street in Norton. We packed all of our goods in the Vega and headed back to our new home in Norton.

We moved into the apartment and got settled. I was attending the first mass teacher's meeting at J.J. Kelly High School on August 22, 1974, when my new principal, Ron Cates, called me out of the meeting. The message was from my mother. She had asked the office to tell me to come to the Appalachian Regional Hospital immediately. I drove to Norton and got Vickie. I was filled with dread as we drove to the hospital. When I arrived, my parent's good friend Jack Goff, met me in the hall. "Your father has just passed away."

Naturally I was very distraught. Even though he had been very ill for many months, and we always knew that his time was short, it was a sharp blow to my mother and me. He was only 66 years old when he died.

My friend, Mr. Bill O'Dell, the funeral director in Pound at that time, was in charge of arrangements. My father was laid to rest in the M.T. Swindall cemetery in Osborne's Gap.

My mother struggled with the loss more than anyone. She had been by my father's side through the many months of his illness. She was upset that we had purchased a home in Norton. Her wish was that we settle in Pound near her. It took her many months to finally come to grips with my father's death. She left and went to Florida, where she spent the winter with the Frank Martin family.

Vickie started school once more in the fall of 1974, this time at Clinch Valley College in Wise, which was now a four-year college. She attended all sessions, including summers. She majored in elementary education and received a B.S. degree on May 23, 1976, just three years after she had graduated from high school. That fall, she got a teaching position at Norton Elementary School, where she remained until she retired. She jokes to our friends that just as soon as she got a job, I ran out and bought a new boat. That is true, but she wanted it also. I didn't even have anything to pull the trailer. Until I finally got a Ford van the following year, we borrowed Blaine's little Chevrolet pickup when we wanted to go fishing. We caught a large number of fish in the MFG bass boat.

The first spring after we got our MFG bass boat and 85 hp motor, I took Papaw Mullins and my uncle Richard (my Aunt Rebecca's husband) to Cherokee during the spring stripe run. We trolled in the river below Rogersville with no luck and decided to go back down the lake and troll for the rockfish. I caught a ten-pounder and a twelve-pounder! They are mounted above my mantel in the lakehouse. My papaw caught a four-pound smallmouth and I also mounted it for him. He kept it on his wall until he passed away. Also on this trip, we observed the white bass breaking at the mouth of Beauty Rest Hollow near our current lakehouse. We began to cast top water plugs, catching a fish on almost every throw. The total on that trip was fifty-five (this was before a limit was placed on the number).

The next spring season, my Uncle Curt came down from Michigan and we went in search of crappie in Cherokee Lake. We took my papaw, who always loved to fish. We went into Poor Valley Creek, and all the way to the edge of the first bridge across the backwaters. The lake had risen pretty quickly that spring due to runoff, and the water had covered up the small willow trees in front of the bridge.

We eased into a spot between two willow trees and used the old proven method of a popeye fly and minnow, this time without the usual floater. Just as soon as the combination hit the water, we started catching fish. It was about noontime. The action didn't slow to a stop until about 5:00 that evening. We  counted 44 nice big "slabs." Needless to say, my papaw was elated, Uncle Curt had a great time, and we had a feast the next day when we got home, with more left for the freezer.

GUEST RIVER

The apartment in Norton was small. There was a living room, a kitchen, a tiny bedroom just big enough for a double bed, and a bathroom. We had very little money to spare and actually didn't want to waste any on a Christmas tree. Our tree that we decorated that year was a microphone stand with a branch of a fresh pine tree stuck into the top end. While we were there we had visits from many of our friends. My good friend Fred Adkins visited after we were settled in. Terry Collier, our friend and pianist for our wedding, and his wife, Teresa came to have dinner with us one evening. The apartment was cramped and it was not very nice, but we were happy to just have a place to live. When I had gotten a few paychecks, we were soon looking for a larger and nicer abode.

Aaron Ellison and his wife Linda visited a couple of times. They had moved back to the area, and Aaron was looking for a job. I got him a job playing with the "Virginians" for a while, then in the spring of 1975 he formed his own group. He called his band "Sour Suite," with Aaron on piano/bass, his wife Linda doing most of the vocals, Randy Adams played drums, and Claude Bolling on guitar.

It was about this time that I began looking for new horizons in music once more. I had been with the "Virginians" for almost 10 years, and I wanted to play more rock 'n roll. Mark Wooten was in school at Virginia Tech, working on an engineering degree, and it was really difficult for him to travel home and play with the "Virginians." During that time period, we tried several bass players. I do remember that Gary Freeman played a few gigs with us, and Mark Jackson played occasionally. Dave Correll, the band director at Norton, played a few times. C.G. Yeary and Greg Still sat in on drums for Danny occasionally. We had other subs such as Paul Dotson on trumpet and Jack Edwards on sax. We even tried a couple of lead singers to replace Ron while he was in the army. Dickie Ward, "Little Willie" Sturgill, George Reynolds, Aaron Ellison and Sam Broach had all taken trial periods on vocals. Whenever a trombone replacement was needed, Lucian Priode was the go to man. Bud Stewart was drafted into the army, and Dave Tipton subbed on trumpet for a while.

In the spring of 1975 Vickie and I made a big move. I used part of the money that I had in savings from the sale of the Pound house. I paid a down payment on a house and property on Guest River. On the moving day, Uncle Curt helped. We moved into the house in April.

The house that we purchased had three bedrooms with a kitchen, living room, den and bathroom. There was also a large back porch that had been converted into another room. I immediately claimed it as a music studio.

We had a fireplace in the Guest River home. Even though it was very sturdy and the chimney was solid, the chimney did not extend through the roof. It had only been used for gas logs which vented through a metal pipe. We decided that we wanted to convert it into a fully functional wood burning fireplace. We hired Royce Sturgill to cut the hole in the roof and lay up the fire tile and outer brick. He did the work quickly in just one day. Vickie always kidded that he built a complete chimney through the roof during the time that it took her to peel a bushel of apples and put them away for the winter.

We were constantly on the lookout for wood, so we cut trees and chunked them up into fireplace size pieces. I split the wood and stacked it on our back porch. I made sure that we never ran out in the winter, during which time we had a fire going almost constantly in the evenings. I had purchased a used Homelite chainsaw from Don Stallard in Pound, and it really made fast work of the wood.

One warm November day my Uncle Curt was down from Michigan, and he and I decided to take Papaw and go to South Fork and get a load or two of wood from a small forest there. A strip mining company had pushed the overburden onto the trees. It was easy cutting and we were doing very well until... I had been getting a little bit cocky with the chainsaw! I sawed almost halfway through a small tree, and I decided to finish pushing it over with my hand. The problem was that I didn't lay the saw down first, and it was still running. Just as the tree snapped and started to fall, I lost my balance. The saw blade fell straight toward my thigh. It ripped through my jeans and continued gnawing at my flesh underneath before I could get control. Blood was gushing from the wound, and I became nauseous, but I still did not panic and I did not pass out. We quickly climbed into my pickup truck and Curt drove me to the hospital. In the emergency room alcove, Dr. Miranda began to work immediately. I watched as he just numbed my leg. He trimmed some of the flesh so he could pull it together and begin sewing it up. It took 13 stitches. When the feeling returned, I needed pain medication for a couple of days. Eventually the pain subsided and it healed well, but it left a permanent scar.

I worked hard through the 14 years that we resided in the house on Guest River. I purchased a radial saw, cut pine boards and made a "fence" around the inside walls of the fireplace room. I fashioned a large thick wooden door with big black metal hinges and metal handle, which gave the entrance to that room a medieval appearance.

Vickie came home from work one day to find Michelle and me sitting in the kitchen floor, staring at a huge hole in the wall. I had a saw in my hand. Vickie was naturally astounded! I explained my vision to her, but she was skeptical. I had cut a huge semi-circle hole in the wall between the kitchen and the prior living room. I had plans to construct a built-in table in the opening.

I worked for several weeks making an oak lazy-susan table to lay between the two rooms. It was eight feet in diameter, and we were able to seat eight people around it. That project had been successful. The table became a functional conversation piece in our home.

I remodeled the music room by covering the walls with carpet. I built a drummer's booth in the corner of the room. New egg crates from Sears were stapled all over the ceiling.

Our master bedroom became much different than any other room in the house. I built a half bath into one side of the original closet. Later, in 1983, I ordered Vickie a king size bed to celebrate her first year of motherhood. The bed was placed in the center of the room and I built closets on either side of the head of the bed. As a final touch, I built a slanted shake roof that extended out over the top of the bed. It was pretty cool and she loved it.

We made many improvements in the house and property before moving away in 1989.

MOVING ON IN MUSIC

I finally left the Virginians. I had stayed with the band longer than with any other group. It had been successful, but I became restless and needed fresh ideas. I was always a rock 'n' roller at heart. I had grown bored of strumming jazz chords behind a horn section most of the time. I rarely got to turn loose with either a beautiful instrumental ballad or a ripping lead. Ron Flanary or one of his subs always did the singing. I will always be especially grateful to Glenn Smith for his patience with me, and to Joe Flanary for the opportunity to play with the "Virginians." I used what I learned about improvisation, jazz chords and patterns as I applied the techniques to improve my leads and my rock music. In the fall of 1975, while still playing with the Virginians, a few friends and I were already jamming up a new sound in that music room in the back of our house on Guest River. My wife, Vickie, loved my involvement in music and was (and always has been) extremely supportive. That year Mark and I both split from the "Virginians." The group dissolved completely a few months later.

Now I was able to spend more time with my precious little daughter. I felt so lucky that my relationship with Glenda was respectful. She was always my good friend. She had guided Michelle extremely well. My daughter was growing and progressing, and I was very proud of her. I was always amazed at her intelligence and her knowledge of so many academic topics. She made straight "As" in school and she was always busy with tasks that would improve her mind. We all had high hopes that she would become a high level professional person, and live a happy and comfortable life as an adult.

HOWIE REX BOGGS

I first met Rex Boggs when I started teaching in 1966. He was in the 9th grade. He was in my science class. Rex was an intelligent and responsible student. His grades were among the top in his class. My next interaction with him was as his coach on the Pound jv basketball team. He was an excellent athlete. He had natural abilities for ball handling that few high school kids ever attain. He and Jerry Dorton played defense in the back court for our little team. The quickness of these two allowed for many steals. Whenever the ball was turned over to us for whatever reason, we worked tirelessly on moving the ball to the goal as fast as possible. Most of our points were scored on fast break layups by Rex or Jerry, resulting from picks by them, bad passes by the other team, rebounds by our bigs followed by quick passes. Rex also had a wonderful hang time, as he vaulted into the air and quickly made a decision to shoot or pass. He was an excellent outside shooter. The quarters in the jv games were only 6 minutes each, but we managed to score as many as 100 points a couple of times and we usually defeated all teams by several points.

Rex was offered a baseball scholarship to Marshall University in West Virginia. Even though his transition to the University did not work out due to personal reasons, he is remembered in our area for his ability in this sport.

One of Vickie's best friends, Debbie Maggard, and Rex were married in the summer of 1974, shortly after our own wedding. Whenever we were in Pound, we spent time with them. This is when Rex and I began developing a music connection. His dad, Rex Senior, had taught him three or four chords on guitar. When we were together, we listened to a lot of music that we both enjoyed, and Rex enjoyed listening to me play. We "discovered" Roy Buchanan as we listened to Austin City Limits one evening. We listened and marveled at Santana's latest music, especially the albums "Abraxus" and "Barboletta." We both loved the music of the "Eagles." He became my musical protégé, and I taught him a few more chords and rhythm licks. I was interested in his vocal ability. We started learning a few songs together, on which I played lead guitar and backup, while he sang and played rhythm. I was amazed at his ability to catch on so fast.

During the fall of 1974, during the time that I felt the need to break away from the "Virginians," Rex and I had the idea to perform together. We accepted an offer to play for a reunion in Pound. It was during October that we decided to actually try and form a band.

Rex and I remained as close friends for many years, tied by our mutual love of music and performing, as well as other interests. Essentially, as of today, this friendship began over 50 years ago.

We are no longer involved in a band together, but he continues to play and perform mostly blues in the tri-cities area. He is now married to Teresa McGuire Boggs. They live in the tri-cities area, and they are both employed by the Wellmont Health Care System.

THE "HIGH COUNTRY" BAND

 Rex and I decided to try and form a band. My friend, Danny Green, who had filled in at Club Scotty a few years before, played bass. With Jack Tolbert on drums, we formed a band called "High Country." The name was about where we lived. We were not playing country music. We did, however, concentrate on playing c/w - rock crossover songs by the "Eagles," "Allman Brothers," and the "Marshall Tucker" band, as well as some pure rock 'n roll.

Even though Rex did the majority of the vocals, I was now finally able to do a few vocals as well. I had purchased a high quality (consumer line) TC-77 Sony tape deck, and I learned to ping-pong tracks as I over-layered covers and a few original songs. Before the band was started, I had even laid down some background tracks and performed a couple of gigs by myself.

We used the Sony recorder for practice and for making a demo. I ended up with a few pretty clean tracks that I still have today. This band stayed together until the summer of 1975 when Jack Tolbert left the band. As the band was reforming, I discovered a fantastic drummer. Patrick Winters was the new band director at Norton High School. He had just graduated from Elon College with a degree in music, and a major in percussion! I also met Richard Kennedy that fall. He became our new keyboard player. Like many other musicians that I met and worked with through the years, Richie became a quick and loyal friend. Danny left the band. He had a hard time enjoying the more progressive styles that we were trying. He was actually a C/W and bluegrass style player.

TOM DAVIS

When the new band, "Spectrum" was forming, and Danny Green was no longer the bass player, we put out the word that we were in search of a rock bass player.

Tom Davis had been an original member of the "Nite Beats," a very popular band that played around southwest Virginia in the 60s. Other members included Thomas Countiss, Jerry Miller, Jack Passmore, Johnny Messer, Greg Edwards, and manager Ernie Benko. The complete story of this band's experiences is a long and interesting one. They opened a teen club called The Morgue on main street in Wise and played there for many months. Funded by Ernie's father, the band even traveled to Memphis and recorded some songs in Phillips' Studio. Most anyone from Wise and the surrounding area in their age group remembers hearing the band and can relate to stories from that era.

From the moment that Tom Davis came to audition for the bass player job in my little Guest River music room, we all knew that he would be the one. All musicians have a different style, but Tom's style on bass was unique. I've never known another player that could make as much out of a whole note as Tom Davis. I'll use the term "splatter." When Tom wanted to emphasize a note, it seemed to just splatter and hold. Some bass players are too busy. Bass is not a lead instrument, with the exception of a few times when the bass player is given solo rides during a jam. A good bass player provides all of the necessary bottom, with tasty fill-ins that provide the support that is needed. Tom always had this talent. He was never fancy, but always completely involved. I loved playing with Tom Davis. His style was always soothing and lifting. Tom and I soon became fast friends.

Our new bass player fit the bill exactly. We practiced hard, and Patrick used his knowledge of booking a band to help us with gigs. We were booking about as often as we could stand to do so. He suggested that we change the name. I wasn't really taken with the idea at first, but learned later that it was a great idea. And then the fun really began.

We had a funny incident to happen on one of our road trips. The agency had sent us to Blacksburg to play for a Virginia Tech fraternity party at the Red Roof Inn. The band was hot that night. The large crowd was into us and we were into them. It was during the time when the "Eagles" had just released their "Hotel California" album. We had immediately learned a few songs from the album and had them worked up to almost perfection. When we played these and the title cut, the crowd went wild. The feeling that zapped between the crowd and the band that night was electric. We all agreed later that we had never had that much fun at a gig.

Tom was a diabetic. His insulin shots were, of course, critical. One of the concerns he had about making the trip was taking his insulin shot early in the morning. His wife had always given him the injection, but she was not making the trip. Vickie had been giving me weekly injections for allergies, so she had volunteered to help Tom with his insulin. In order to save money, some of us shared a room. I heard Tom rise from his bed before daylight. I told him I would wake Vickie. He insisted that I should not wake her, and that he could probably do it himself. I roused Vickie and told her she needed to get up and give Tom his shot. She got up. Tom filled the needle and handed it to Vickie. When she tried to push the needle in his muscular arm, it would not go in. She tried again and failed. On the third try, it went in slightly, and she just passed out, leaving the needle stuck in Tom's arm.

He probably said something else, but all I heard was, "Ron, come and get her."

She had fainted and fallen into the floor. Her head went into one side of an open suitcase and the other side closed on her head. When she came to and I found out that she was OK, I was relieved and we were very amused. We have now laughed for many years about this incident.

Tom eventually had to leave the group for family reasons, but we remained friends. We spent much time together, especially with him and his second wife, Debbie. We have attended concerts, had many meals together, and visited a lot with each other through the years.

Tom worked several years for the TV cable company in Norton. Afterwards, he got a job with Humphries' Enterprises, and worked as a technician. He retired from Humphries about 5 years ago.

"SPECTRUM"

More guitar history: It was sometime during the development of the "Spectrum" band that Richie convinced me that the Gretsch was not as good for pickin' out the lead parts in rock 'n roll. He sold me a 1970 Fender Thinline Telecaster that I still have today. It has been a great guitar! It's considered a vintage guitar at this time.

"Spectrum" was a popular group. We billed ourselves as a top forty band and we booked through Ted Hall's HIT ATTRACTIONS in Charlotte, NC. Ted Hall had one of the largest booking agencies for bands in the south at that time. The agency required a photo and a tape to illustrate our appearance and talent to prospective clients.

"Spectrum" played night clubs, high school proms, concerts, and college functions. We traveled a lot on a circuit that took us from the Quality Inn Tower south of Cincinnati to the south side of Virginia near the coast. We played the clubs in Kingsport, Roanoke, Staunton, and near the Greenbrier in West Virginia. We played fraternity and sorority dances at Virginia Tech, CVC, plus a lot of high school proms and occasional concerts. We were having the time of our lives, loving every minute.

We changed bass players twice. Bobby Blanton played with us for a few months. Mark Wooten, fresh from VA Tech, joined us for the first time at the King's Inn in Roanoke. Mark stayed with the band, as we all did, until Patrick moved away and the band split up in the spring-summer of 1976. Patrick had made a career move to Redlands, CA and became the new band director there. In later years, he moved to Eastern Washington University in Spokane where he became the director of bands. We made an honest effort to try and re-form the band, but without Patrick it seemed impossible. We had reached a pinnacle in our music that we felt might not be topped. Richie started a group called "Blue Sky," with Mark on bass, Tommy Miller on guitar, Sutton Riggs on drums and Frank Amburn on sax. Richie's brother, Brent, also played with them for a while. When forming the group, they had asked me to play guitar, and I decided against it. In the next year, I played alone, recording, overdubbing, and writing. The time was actually fairly productive, but a little crazy, too.

GARY SLEMP

We went to Gary Slemp's four-track studio in the fall of 1975 and made our demo tape. We recorded "Best of My Love," "Still The One," "Devil Woman," Manhattan Island Serenade," "Wisdom," "Taking It To The Streets," and "Can I Change My Mind." Gary did a great job in recording and mixing our tape, and it proved to be sufficient for the big *HIT ATTRACTIONS* agency. We began traveling quite a bit.

Gary Slemp loved music, and he became important to all of us in our circle of friends. Gary was also noted for his radio voice. He worked for local companies like Piggly Wiggly and Witt Motor Company as their very familiar radio voice. He thoroughly enjoyed picking and singing with his friends, and he wrote lyrics for a few songs. His daughters Allison and Molly are both vocalists, and Molly is currently (2017) going to school in Nashville, and hoping for a big break.

Gary was born January 9, 1947, the son of Evelyn and Bill Slemp. He attended J.J. Kelly High School and graduated with the class of 1964. He was married twice, first to Nancy Helbert, and they had one child, Allison Slemp Bartlett. His second wife was Mary Macon. Their two children were Will and Molly. Gary had 2 brothers, Craig and Scott.

Gary's University training was in communications, and he spent a large part of his working life in advertising. He owned a business that he called G. D. S. Productions, that operated out of his small studio located in Scott-Roberson Hollow between Pound and Wise. He recorded local musicians in the studio, and he helped in the production and duplication process for tapes and records. I assisted him a few times by adding guitar chords and solos on some of the tracks.

Gary was an actor, and he was well known for his part with the theatre group that performed "Red Fox Second Hanging." He performed as a guest actor in some of the college productions under the direction of Charles Lewis. He assisted the drama department at the local college, UVA - Wise.

He thoroughly enjoyed jam sessions where he could participate or just listen. All of his friends knew about his garden and were able to partake of its bounty during these sessions or whenever they were just visiting with him. Gary's death was sudden and unexpected on October 21, 2005. We all miss him very much.

SNAKES

I have always been fascinated with snakes. I have never been bitten by a snake, uh, well, there was this one time. I was teaching at Pound. One of the boys had caught a big black snake one morning. It was about 4 feet long, and he had actually brought it into the school. In his excitement, he came straight to my biology lab and showed me the snake. He asked if we could keep it. I thought about it for a moment and told him that maybe we could keep it for one day to show all of the students in my classes. I let him place it into our big terrarium. I quickly covered it with the screen top.

I allotted a few minutes at the beginning of each period to show the snake to the students and to talk about the species and its habits. Each time I started my lecture, I carefully removed the lid and waited a few moments. I then carefully eased my hand into the terrarium from behind the direction in which the snake's head was pointed. I quickly grasped the snake just behind the head. When I did this, it coiled its body around my arm. I held the snake like this, and I walked around the room as I talked. I allowed students to touch it if they wished. After a couple of periods the word was out. Students and teachers came to see the snake.

By 6th period, I was getting cocky. I went to the terrarium, lifted the lid, and reached for the snake. The front of its body was slightly coiled. Before I could think or move, the snake struck me hard in the loose skin between my thumb and forefinger. A blacksnake does not have fangs but it does have teeth. It broke the skin and it hurt. I was a little bit embarrassed and my feelings and pride were certainly hurt more than my hand.

My statement to my students was, "Well this is the way we learn, isn't it?"

I have picked up other snakes during my life, but never a poisonous one. I was at Gary Slemp's home one day. We had been out to the edge of his property looking at his garden. When we came back into the yard, the dogs were excited and barking at something. Upon investigation, we saw a sizable copperhead coiled up beside a fence post. It was ready to strike. I told Gary that I wanted it for my classroom. My plan was to put it into a gallon jar of formaldehyde and keep it as a display. I could then use it with my other specimens as I taught my unit on reptiles.

Gary's question was, "How in the world are you going to catch it?"

I asked him for a couple of items, and he produced a 3-4 ft. length of 2 inch diameter black pvc pipe and a ball of heavy twine. I doubled a piece of twine and dropped it through the pipe, allowing the loop to fall out the other end. My design would allow me to slip the loop over the snake's head, and by pulling the doubled string on the top end, I would trap the snake against the end of the pipe. I thought it was curious that the snake was so patient with us. I thought that it probably would just crawl away. It did not.

Gary was beside himself. He couldn't believe that I was getting so close to the snake. He was holding a garden hoe in his grip as I eased up on the snake. I knew from trusted reading (not by experience) that a snake such as this could only strike a distance of roughly one-half of its body length. By my estimate, the copperhead was about 2 feet long. I speculated that even if the snake could strike for a distance of its entire body length, it still could not reach me. I eased my device down toward the snake. I miss-judged in laying the loop over the head. It tucked its head back and it struck the pipe. When it fell, it immediately coiled again. That's when Gary could wait no longer. He brought the hoe down and partially severed the head of the snake. It was still alive but in no shape to strike again. Fussing about it, I urged Gary to wait as I slipped the loop over the snake, put the snake into the gallon jar, and replaced the lid. I took the specimen to school the next day and filled the jar with formaldehyde solution.

Stories about encounters with snakes abound when the subject is brought up in a crowd. My friend Larry Salyers and I were fishing one night at Flannagan Lake. A water snake kept trying again and again to crawl into the boat with us, even though we kept trying to shoo it off. Larry told me that snakes had always tried to follow him. He told me a story about a black racer that followed him out of the forest one time. Every time he turned around the snake was there. Then of course, there was the interesting story that I related about the rattlesnake which swam toward us in Cherokee Lake. My friend Charlene Edwards seems to attract snakes. She has many stories to tell about her encounters.

CRABS

Any biology teacher worth their salt will make an effort to teach at least a smattering of taxonomy and invertebrate anatomy. It was probably one of my strong points. For example, I always spent some time on the phylum Arthropoda, so unique because of its exoskeleton. Most adults that have had a biology class will remember an experience involving the dissection of a crayfish (we called 'em "crawdads" when I was a kid). During my growing up years, we caught crawdads a number of different ways. Sometimes I would get a bite on a nightcrawler while fishing for bluegill only to raise the line and find a crawdad hanging on. My dad and I unintentionally caught crawdads in our minnow traps. I used to sneak up on crawdads in a clear creek or brook and reach down and quickly place my thumb and forefinger around their thorax from behind. Small crawdads make excellent bait for catching smallmouth bass. The pincers on a large crawdad are very strong and can cause a good deal of pain if they clamp down on a finger. They cannot reach back and clamp you if you pick them up by the thorax as described.

Many arthropods are wonderful table fare. Even the old crawdad, or "mudbug" as it's sometimes called in the south) is considered a delicacy, especially in Louisiana where the bayou is home to millions of them. Shrimp from the east coast and Gulf of Mexico long ago became the basis for dozens of fabulous tasty recipes. The cold-water Maine Lobster is known the world over as a gourmet food. Snow Crab, Dungeness Crab, King Crab and Blue Crab are sought after in restaurants all over.

One of my favorite edible arthropods is the Blue Crab. Three favorite recipes are crab cakes, soft crab sandwiches, and pick and eat. During one of my trips to Edisto Island in South Carolina, I learned to catch and prepare the crabs. Mark Wooten had done it before. He had learned this as a child when his family made trips to the island almost every summer. He was responsible for suggesting

Edisto as a place of treasured family memories. Mark and his family were with us on this particular trip, so he was our instructor. Richie was dating our daughter, Michelle, at the time, and he was with us as well.

We bought chicken necks at the Piggly Wiggly store on the island and let them rot in the hot sun for 2-3 days. We tied strong twine to them and left the line about 10-12 feet long. The bait was thrown out into the water under the bridges just off the island. We stood ankle deep in the mud under the bridge. As we slowly pulled the bait in, we could feel something pulling back. We gradually lowered a long-handled net into the water in preparation for a catch. When the crab came into sight, we rolled the net over it and caught it. We carefully placed our catch of over a dozen nice crabs into a cooler and went back to the house to cook them.

Then came the fun. We got out the large crab pot provided by the unit. We heated water to boiling and poured in our crab boiling spices. Then it was time to drop the crabs into the water and cook them alive. "Mr. Biologist" reached for one. I was sure that I could handle a live crab in my bare hands in the same manner that I had learned to hold a crawdad. Mistake! I started to pick it up. I was warned by Mark and told to use tongs, but no, I was showing off my "biological skills." I picked up a large crab by the carapace behind the head. I immediately got an unpleasant surprise, similar to my snake handling experience in my classroom. But this time, it really hurt. That bad boy swung a big pincer back and clamped down on my thumbnail. Ouch! Live and learn. My nail turned blue as a reminder that it is not a good idea to try to pick up a live crab by the carapace.

Anyway, we finally cooked our crabs, laid them out on a newspaper on the porch table and started fully enjoying the fruits of our labor. It was a great experience in spite of the heat, the mud, the smell of rotting meat, and the pain that I suffered through my ignorance.

PRIDE AND PLEASURE IN TEACHING

I was very involved with music during the 1975-76 year, but I was also really enjoying my new teaching position at J.J. Kelly High School. These were the days before SOLs, when good teachers were trusted to be creative and inspire their students to reach their full potential. There were some terrific students during the 70s, 80s and 90s. I carried one of the creative ideas all the way from my high school days with Quinton Franklin as my biology teacher. I loved taking the students on local walking field trips and talking to them about the many species of trees, as they collected some of the leaves for their required collection. This all changed when the state mandated the SOL plan and students were required to restrict their learning to a set of plans proposed by the State Department of Education. Teaching was less fun or rewarding after this requirement, and most teachers found themselves "teaching to the state test." We all wanted to make sure that our students were successful on the state tests. During my latter years as a teacher, the state even provided practice tests for the students, so they could memorize answers. Hmmm!?

**Lecturing to biology class in the forest
behind J.J. Kelly High School**

I always enjoyed teaching young folks. For anyone planning to teach:

1. Make sure that you know your subject matter. This comes from studying seriously while in college.
2. Make sure that you love young people and being around them.
3. Make sure that you love to share what you know with others.
4. Make sure that you see teaching as a serious profession.
5. Make sure that you take pride in what you know and how you present yourself and your subject matter.
6. Love it or leave it. Don't stick with it if you don't enjoy it!

For me, the greatest pleasure in teaching was helping students to gain enough understanding of my particular discipline to aid them in making decisions about their future. It was always very rewarding to be able to stimulate a talented student to pursue a future which was related to biology, chemistry or TV production. Luckily, it happened a lot for me, and these students are successful professionals that are still good friends.

Another joy for me was the fact that I made such good friends in the profession. Some of the teachers are still such good friends, and I will never forget them.

There were so many special students, and I would love to be able to list all of them. It is a joy for me to hear that they have done well in life. It is very special when they tell me many years later that they enjoyed my class, that they learned so much, and that they have selected a related field of study for their higher education or for their occupation.

Ronnie and Ginny had a home in Ridgefield Acres in Wise. Their two children, Ron and Allison, attended school at J.J. Kelly High School during my first few years as a teacher there. It was a pleasure to get to know them and be involved in their education.

MORE EDUCATION

I was now fully certified in biology and general science, endorsed in chemistry, and now had a post graduate degree, but I wanted a little more. I began to enjoy teaching chemistry more than any other subject I had ever taught. Most of the time my students were the cream of the crop and they had their sights set on college and a professional career. It was a challenge to keep them interested and occupied, but I was doing it, and I was proud of it. My students were going on to college and training to be high level professional people in engineering, medicine, pharmacy and higher education.

I signed up for a chemistry teaching course at Gilford College. Later I enrolled at Clinch Valley College and took extra courses in chemistry to help gain full certification. I am very appreciative of the help I received from Dr. Van W. Daniel and Roy Wells. They helped me to have a better understanding of organic and physical chemistry. My students continued to flourish.

Best Years In Music

PERFORMING ONCE MORE

What I love most about playing music is sharing it with others that want to listen. Whether I play for a small or large audience, I get a special feeling. If I am on stage in front of a large audience and the whole crowd seems to be locked in, the electricity between the people and me is indescribable. It gives me great joy.

Finally, in the early spring of 1978, things had begun to happen again musically. My friend Jack Wright had brought his friend Gary Stewart over to Gary Slemp's studio for a visit. They had invited several of us up for a jam session and to meet Gary Stewart. We had a great time that evening, and Stewart became a close and good friend to many of us. He asked Tommy Miller to go on the road with him. Stewart, just an old hillbilly born in Dunham, KY, had become a well-known country/western recording artist for RCA. Much to the dismay of "Blue Sky," Tommy accepted the offer.

We started to jam again in Richie's basement with the remnants of the "Blue Sky" band, but with a totally different sound. Thomas Countiss (from the popular old "Nite Beats" group) on vocals, Richie on keyboards, Mark on bass, Sutton Riggs on drums, and I was on guitar and backup vocals. The music was country flavored, and I had enough background to enjoy it somewhat, but Mark and Sutton didn't care for it. Jerry Miller, ("Nite Beats") who was Tommy's brother and fresh back from Vietnam, came up and jammed with us on bass.

Danny (Tuck) Robinson ("Nite Beats", "Cardigans") played drums. With Thomas' vocals, this five-piece group was sounding good. We were playing some of the most mellow and good feeling music I had ever played. I sang a few lead vocals, sang harmonies and played a lot of lead. I was really enjoying it! We were almost ready to start booking.

Then along came John Ryder. He was acting manager, roadie, and a hired bodyguard for Cova Elkins from Dickenson County. Cova was a coal baron that wanted to be an Elvis Presley type star. John met me at work at J.J. Kelly high school. He told me that he had heard about my music ability. He asked me if I would like to become a stage musician for Cova and his cousin, Virgil Fleming. Doubtful at first, I went to Clintwood a few days later and was offered the job as lead guitarist. The band mostly backed Virgil but sometimes tried to back Cova (totally unrehearsed). I was on the coal company payroll. The money was more than I had ever made per night, so naturally I stuck with it.

Other than the good money, the best part of being in Virgil's "Young Country" band was being around John. He was a loyal friend. I also enjoyed getting to play with the drummer, Raymond, the bass player, Richard (Dickie) Sumter, and the steel guitar/fiddle player, Garman Mullins. I usually played both Friday and Saturday nights. For fun, I continued to jam with Thomas, Tuck, and Jerry, and we soon became a real band!

I don't remember exactly how it happened, but Virgil heard Thomas, Tuck, Jerry and I playing together at the Endzone one Wednesday night and we worked out an agreement for us to all become the backup band for him and Cova. Thomas and I rejected the "Young Country" name and told him that we needed another name instead. It was a name that Thomas had been wanting to use. We all agreed and settled on the "Fallen Stars" for the name of our new four-piece group. Richie was not interested in playing c/w music with Virgil at that time. When we played with Virgil, we were still allowed to play several of our own covers during any performance.

THE BEST BAND

We were all grateful to Virgil and for Cova when they paid the studio bill for Thomas Countiss and I to be provided our first major recording experience. In the process, Thomas and I traveled to Nashville with Virgil in November of 1978 to help Cova and Virgil on some of their recordings. We worked at Bradley's Barn where we met and laid tracks with some of the biggest studio names in the business at the time. We were able to record tracks with the "Anita Kerr Singers," "the Nashville Edition," Buddy Harmon (Elvis' drummer), Sonny Garrish (steel guitar), Ray Edenton (rhythm guitar), Henry Stryzlenski (bass), Hargus ("Pig") Robbins (piano), Harold Bradley (producer), and others! Bradley's Barn was owned by Harold and his brother Owen, producer for Patsy Cline, Loretta Lynn, Johnny Cash, K.T. Lang, and many others. I was asked to play some of the leads on Virgil's recordings, and Thomas and I both were asked to sing with the big vocal groups on backup. We thoroughly enjoyed our stay at the barn, and we were grateful for this maximum learning experience. Thomas and I were also allowed to record our own songs because Cova didn't show up. We ended up doing two of our cover songs ("Blind Marie" and "July") with those great studio musicians that have backed many of the biggest stars in Nashville.

Thomas and I vowed to return to Nashville. We did, that same fall of 1978, when we were involved in an overdubbing session! Gary Stewart stopped by the studio to offer his support. Tim Cox was also present during some of the overdubbing time. It was a special time in all of our lives, and the memories live on. Tim took several photos, documenting our unique tracking efforts at Bradley's Barn. The one seen here was taken while I was overdubbing a lead guitar part for one of our songs, "July, You're a Woman." A new friend, Bub Province, was with us during these sessions. Thomas and I rode back to Wise County with him after the work was finished. Bub stayed with us a few days. We returned to Bradley's Barn Studio in 1979 and recorded these same two songs again with our own six-piece "Fallen Stars" band.

A 'Selfie' taken by Tim Cox at the overdubbing sessions at Bradley's Barn In Nashville in 1978. Top L-R: Ron Swindall, John Ryder, Tim Cox, Gary Stewart. Bottom L-R: Thomas Countiss, Virgil Fleming, Bobby Bradley

THOMAS COUNTISS AND JERRY MILLER

Thomas Countiss was, without a doubt in my mind, the finest professional vocalist to work in any local band here in the last half of the twentieth century. His vocals were unique, strong, and always right on key. The tone quality was unusual, identifiable and exceptional. What a joy it was to get to work with him! He was such a natural musician with a great ear for music. Thomas loved playing, and played several instruments (guitar, flute, trombone, even a pedal steel) in addition to his great vocal work. He had been in the high school band. His first venture into performing rock 'n roll was with the "Mistakes." He was involved with other bands, i.e. the "Nite Beats," "Tom Earl Tucker," and the "Fallen Stars." He often said that the "Fallen Stars" band was the best that he had worked with during his life. Thomas was the lead vocalist in this group. Luckily, he leaves behind a legacy of recordings made with this band which offer proof of his exceptional talent.

What fun it was to play music with Jerry Miller. He was a quiet gentleman in so many ways, but at the same time, he loved good humor and political satire. He was an especially complete and wonderful musician. Jerry mostly played bass and guitar and provided some backup vocals. He was efficient and precise as a bass player in the "Fallen Stars" Band. Tuck always said that the two of them worked together as one, always together on the tempo and feel of any song. Everyone loved Jerry and his involvement with music, but he also had other talents. Jerry was an artist and a draftsman, as well as a fine woodworker. He worked in the print shop in Wise with Thomas Countiss for a few years before going on to work with the Maxim Engineering Firm in Coeburn. Jerry developed the logo for the "Fallen Stars" Band. He and Thomas were involved with some of the same bands through the years.

The last time I saw Thomas, we had a chance to talk for a few minutes about Jerry and the old days. I had heard from Thomas and others that things were not going well for Jerry. Tom Davis and I visited him at home one time during his illness. Other than that, Jerry and I communicated by email, postal mail or on the phone. I knew that he was not comfortable with having visitors. If he had told me he wanted me to visit, I would certainly have been there in a heartbeat during that final time. When I had first met him in the 70s, I immediately felt a connection and felt comfortable talking with him. One of the greatest pleasures of my life was having the privilege of playing music with Jerry Miller, Thomas Countiss and Tuck Robinson in the "Fallen Stars" band. In this way, our souls all intermingled in special ways. Few people ever have the opportunity to communicate with others in this way. The world would be a much better place if folks could work and think together in a manner similar to musicians. It's like sports and other types of teamwork, whereby the common goal is reached only through such cooperation. It is a way to experience and learn something that is valuable in life. I had that with these men for a precious period of time. I thanked all of them for allowing me to be a part of that. It has been one of the high points of my life. It drew us all very close.

Jerry made a guitar for me! I have several guitars and other instruments, but my Miller #4 is the most valuable instrument in the house. To me, this instrument is priceless. I still maintain that it is the truest, and has the best tone, of any guitar I have ever had in my hands. To have a real musician and craftsman of Jerry's talent to design and build something of this caliber was very special to me. My son Nathan will inherit this guitar and he will relish the ownership as I do. He is a very fine musician and thoroughly enjoys playing.

All the times that Jerry and I talked through the years, I felt like I always gained something from the conversations, which were interesting and insightful. I believe we thought a lot alike, and saw some things that the general population seems to overlook. We were both slightly liberal conservatives. We seemed to be looking for intelligent common-sense approaches to solving problems instead of all the BS. I always wanted to hear what he had to offer. It seems like we're placed on this earth for a short time for a little bit of pleasure and happiness (if we're lucky) and quite a bit of discomfort, pain, and suffering. I can't begin to imagine what Jerry went through, and I know that he never wanted to dwell on that. I feel lucky. I was a little older than Jerry. I've always said that we all should soak up the good parts of life whenever we get the chance! We still have my 92-year old mom (Alzheimers) and have cared for her daily for 9 years now. We do get away occasionally when we can hire someone to sit with her while we're gone, and she has spent some time in Heritage Hall, the local nursing home in Big Stone Gap. I know that Jerry also experienced this aspect of life when his parents became ill. For what it's worth, I loved Jerry and cared for him. I hope that he knew that he was one of a few of the most significant people that I have encountered on this life's journey.

DANNY ("TUCK") ROBINSON

Danny Robinson began his musical career in the early 60s when he became friends with Eddie Dockery, Roy Dockery, Spanky Gilliam, Mike Gilliam and Tommy Mullins. They formed a band called the "Cardigans." They had their first public performance at the Club House in Wise. Their music was mostly instrumental, and much of their influence came from the "Ventures," a California band. They later patterned after the British Invasion, with the "Beatles," and the "Rolling Stones." Tuck was not only the drummer, he became the vocalist, covering the songs of the day as best as he could. His first attempt at singing was "What'd I Say" by Ray Charles. He added numerous lyrics to the original song. The "Cardigans" became the house band at the Copper Kettle, playing there Friday and Saturday nights.

In the mid-60s, he left the "Cardigans" and became a member of The "Nite-Beats." He was one of the vocalists in this band. It included Tom Countiss, Jerry Miller, Tom Davis, John Messer, Jack Passmore, and Greg Edwards. They opened a dance club which was named after a line in the Bob Dylan song, "Just Like Tom Thumbs Blues." The line was, "Don't put on any airs while you're down on Rue Morgue Ave." The club became known to the patrons as The Morgue. The club featured black lights and fluorescent painted walls. It became a very popular night spot for its time.

The late 60s came, and the military interrupted Tuck's musical career as he became a member of the USAF. Tuck rejoined Tom Countiss and Jerry Miller, along with Ron Swindall in the late 70s, and the "Fallen Stars" band was formed. Tommy Miller, the younger brother of Jerry Miller, and Richard Kennedy became members after a while.

At present, Tuck and I are the only two original "Fallen Stars" remaining. We were all close, as many musicians seem to be. The guys in the band always seemed like brothers to me. Tuck has joked about the fact that he and I are like Paul and Ringo since we are the only survivors of the original "Fab Four."

In addition to still being like another brother to me, Tuck has helped me in other ways to continue with my music. He was a member of our band, "Law and Disorder." He has participated in a few jams and short gigs with me, and he has been the drummer on several of my recordings. He is in demand by others because of his good steady timing. He and Jerry Miller, the bass player, always played together with precision, like clockwork. I am very comfortable when Tuck is on drums.

THE "FALLEN STARS"

We completely split from Virgil and the all country scene, and started making our own music as the "Fallen Stars" band in 1979. What a great band, and what a good time we had! It was good feeling music, both honest and appealing, and our great vocalist, Thomas, made it very real. Thomas, Jerry, Tuck and I could make a lot of music and had a "big" sound. We seemed to just think together and all of the music seemed to just fall into place. It is rare to find musicians with as much compatibility. Grace and Mike Stinson had opened the Endzone, one of the few night spots ever seen in the town of Wise VA. The "Fallen Stars" performed there often to large S.R.O. crowds and also had a good following when playing elsewhere.

When Loretta Lynn and the production crew for "Coal Miner's Daughter" came to our area to film the movie, Universal Studios contracted our band to play at the fairgrounds during the scene to be filmed at the fair. Unfortunately, we had a deluge of rain the entire day. They cancelled the scene and substituted something else, but they still paid us for being available. Thomas made copies of the cancelled check for all of us. I still have mine in my photo album.

The Four Original "Fallen Stars" at the Endzone in 1978

The "Fallen Stars" Band grew after this point. Tommy Ray Miller left the road band with Gary Stewart, so I invited him to come and jam with us. He did, and we all discussed it later and decided to ask him to join us. The next addition was Richie Kennedy, who had formerly played with "Spectrum," and had also played in the "Blue Sky" band. We had all jammed together in 1977 in Richie's A-frame basement when the band started. One evening in the winter of '78 when we were playing for a cakewalk in Norton, Richie walked in carrying his electric piano. He just set it up and started playing, and we were delighted that he had come.

Suddenly we were six in number, and the band evolved. We continued to play our old standards, but we started to add many new tunes which were suited to the instrumentation in the new group. We continued to gig as often as possible. In the summer of 1979 we all traveled to Bradley's Barn in Nashville and recorded tracks for seven of our tunes. Harold Bradley helped us produce the tracks, and his nephew, Bobby Bradley, was again our engineer. The band was well-practiced and amazingly tight. The seven songs recorded at Bradley's Barn were the only ones the "Fallen Stars" Band ever recorded in a big studio.

The Famous Bradley's   **Richie**   **Richie T. Ray Ron**
Barn

A few months later, the "Fallen Stars" Band dispersed, and we all went our separate ways to play in other groups, or alone. I never returned to Bradley's Barn in Nashville, but Thomas returned to RCA studio A. He was asked to do some backup work for Gary Stewart on a new RCA album that he recorded that year with Roy Dea as producer. Our friend Gary Stewart was a popular C/W singer in the 70's and 80's. He traveled and performed all over the U.S. but was probably better known in Texas. He is originally from Dunham, KY. He lived with his wife, Lou, in Ft. Pierce, Florida until she passed away.

When the "Fallen Stars" disbanded I found myself at a loss for a short time. I loved music, and I wanted to stay involved. Maybe it was a stroke of luck that a young friend of mine wanted to sell some recording equipment that he had purchased, but had then grown disinterested. I purchased a 3340S Teac recorder and a small four channel mixer from Kent Roberson, and started recording any musicians that would volunteer. I recorded myself and a lot of friends, and overdubbed and ping-ponged the tracks. Some tracks were of surprisingly good quality.

RICHARD DUDLEY KENNEDY

Richie Kennedy has been a good friend to me as long as I have known him. He is "Mr. Keyboard" in our area. He had joined the "Spectrum" band in 1975, the fall after he graduated from high school. Our band members were immediately taken by his talent, his humor, and his very considerate nature. We all noticed that at times his antics were silly and even a little bit risqué, but that was just part of the fun that we had playing with him. I feel fortunate to have played music with him, and he is, indeed, known widely for his capabilities.

He played in "Spectrum," the "Blue Sky" band, the "Fallen Stars," and the "Kennedy Brothers." Richie sat in with us for a couple of the "Virginians" reunion concerts many years later. He has done a lot of solo work, and also plays in a duo from time to time.

Richie worked several jobs as a young man. He left the area and went to T.C. Williams Law School in Richmond during the late 80s. As of this writing, he is a practicing lawyer in Wise, VA, and plays music with his daughter, Jessica, and others in a small group.

LUCIAN GUY PRIODE

Lucian Priode was my good buddy, plain and simple, and he was a faithful friend, not only to me, but to many others. I miss his good humor, as well as his devotion and love for good music. It was a joy just to sit and talk, and listen to the best of music with him. He maintained a nice sound system and stocked a wide variety of the best music on albums, tapes and CDs. He always seemed to enjoy my company.

We played a few gigs together when either he or I would be picked up by a band to fill in for someone. He played occasionally with the "Virginians," and I sat in a couple of times in his "Blue Velvets" band, but we were never in a band together. Lucian loved to play in dance and entertainment venues, and even started, as many of us did, in high school. One of the projects we did together was an album that I recorded of his very excellent high school concert and jazz band at J.J. Kelly high school. The taping was done at a concert featuring the jazz band with the great local artist, Glenn Smith. Lucian's major instrument was the trombone, and he had a very unique style which was syrupy and appealing. I hope Lucian Priode will be remembered as not only a musician, but also as one of the finest music educators ever to pass our way. Guy Lucian Priode was born Jan. 13, 1942 in Clintwood, Virginia. Lucian devoted a great portion of his life to Wise County Public Schools as the band director at J. J. Kelly High School. He received accolades and awards for his work at innumerable levels. He was a wonderfully talented person. However, part of his talent was cracking everyone up. He had such a "cool" sense of humor.

One time at a concert, a beaming Lucian Priode of Wise, 58 at the time, sidled up to get his picture taken with Bill Pinkneys. When Priode was growing up, the radio waves were filled with hit numbers by "The Drifters" and "The Temptations."

"Oh, it's a thrill and an honor to meet Bill Pinkneys," Priode said through a smile that would probably last all day. I enjoyed him and "The Drifters" for many, many years. And, I still do. I'll always remember this moment. This is special."

On Tuesday December 2, 2008, at Christmas Parades in Coeburn, Wise and Norton, the J.J. Kelly High School "Pride of the Tribe" Marching Indian Band honored the memory of Mr. Lucian Priode. All band members marching in the parades wore a black ribbon to honor Lucian. It was the desire of the band to honor his memory, and to rekindle memories with citizens in all towns in Wise County. The impact of Mr. Lucian Priode on music programs at J.J. Kelly High School and Wise County are cherished.

New Business Ventures

HOMESTEAD RECORDINGS, INC.

The "Fallen Stars" trip to Nashville paid off in many ways. I had been inspired by the equipment and techniques used by the Bradley's in the big studio in Nashville. In 1982, I was asked by Tim Cox, to write a jingle and record it. It would be used for producing local political radio spots for Jim Robinson. He was a candidate from our hometown who was running for House of Delegates in Virginia. Our long time delegate, Orby Cantrell, had passed away, and the district needed a new delegate for our representation. I had acquired a used 32 channel - 8 buss Tascam mixer from Washington Music Center. This, along with the aforementioned Teac four-channel recorder and some outboard equipment, was a nice small setup for my first small home studio. One of my communications students, Kevin Kilgore, dubbed the new business as "Homestead Recording Studio." The name stuck.

I still owned the Gretsch Country Gentleman guitar that I had played at the end of the "Wildcat" days, and also in the "Virginians" and "High Country" bands. Danny Green visited me at Guest River and brought along a Baldwin banjo. He offered to trade it even for my Gretsch. I agreed.

While Danny was visiting, I told him about my recent recording ventures, and that I was hoping to start a business. He suggested that I ask our mutual friend, Fred Adkins, who was now practicing law with the Cline, McAfee and Adkins firm in Norton, to set up a corporation for me. Fred set it all up. and I became the owner, president, engineer, and producer in the new company, Homestead Recordings, Inc.

Tim Cox suggested that I should advertise my availability in the local paper and on the radio. I took his suggestion and immediately got a call from the "Sunny Valley Gospel Singers." I quoted a price, and they agreed that they wanted to work in the studio. I assisted in production and got a nice clean multitrack recording on the first round. The tracks were mixed down and I studied several possibilities for making an LP record. The completed audio mixdown and a photo made by Tim, along with instructions for the printed material on the label and the jacket cover, were sent to National Tape and Record Company in Nashville. I was very pleased with the final product. The clients liked the work so well that they recorded two more albums in my studio. This was just the beginning. Over the next few years, I recorded dozens of individuals and groups as I helped with their arrangements and production. I also played guitar and/or keyboard on many of the tracks.

Other recording opportunities began to pop up. Charlie Mudder called and asked if I would be willing to become the radio voice for Virginia Supply, a lumber/hardware store in Norton. I told him I would. He had heard the jingle that I had written and recorded for Jim Robinson and asked if I could write one for his store. I created a CW sounding piece of music and wrote a few words describing the store and what was offered. Charlie liked it and bought the jingle which aired on local radio stations for many months.

Tim Morgan, a former student who had also been on one of my J.V. basketball teams at Pound High School, called me one day in the late 80s. He was co-owner of Morgan-McClure Chevrolet in Coeburn.

Tim said, "How come you've never been down to see me since the dealership started here? I know you must have bought a vehicle or two somewhere during this time."

I countered with, "Well, why haven't you called me about writing a jingle for your business, or about becoming the radio voice for Morgan-McClure?"

We chatted and talked more about the possibilities of working together. This started a business relationship which lasted for many years. I wrote and recorded radio spots for them during the remainder of the 80s, all of the 90s, and most of the 2000s. My work included the production of a few tv spots. I recorded my last spot for the dealership in 2009.

Danny Green's brother Don had heard some of my work. He called me and asked if I would be willing to do the voice overs for Black Diamond Savings Bank. I began sending out spot tapes for the bank and all of its branches. I wrote and recorded new spots for them. These aired on several radio stations in the area, all the way from Norton to Lynchburg for many years. Don had talked to Wendell Barnette and suggested to him that it would be a good idea to have me do a jingle and voice-overs for his business. Wendell owned several convenience stores in the area called Kwik Shop Markets. This also became a business relationship that lasted several years, even after they formed a business partnership with Double Kwik Markets. In addition, Wendell became a loyal long-time friend

Fred Adkins has always been one of my very best friends. One day while he was visiting, I suggested that he should record an album. He had seen and heard some of the work that I had done for local musicians, and he decided that he wanted to try it. We began to record some of the songs that we had played many years ago, plus some others that he wanted to do. The list included a song by Eddie Arnold called "Don't Rob Another Man's Castle." We decided to use it as the title cut. When all of the tracks were mixed down, I sent the mixdown tape and a photo made by Tim Cox to National Tape and Record Company in Nashville for mastering and duplication. Tim had taken the photo inside the old unoccupied Bolling Mansion in Norton on a very cold day. The building was not heated, and our breath had to be held when the photo was taken so the fog would not be seen. This work, like all of Tim's photography, was very memorable. He produced the cover and all of the layout for the back of the album. It was very artsy and attractive.

We ordered 1000 copies. We had a big party at the Copper Kettle in Norton for our release date. We marketed the LP album in music stores and record stores locally, and in the tri-cities. Fred made contacts and sent it to several promoters and radio stations around the country. About half of the records were sold, and many were given away to friends. It is still available today.

Needless to say, Homestead Recordings did very well during the 80s and 90s. While I was still healthy, I worked diligently to build my nest egg and insure a comfortable retirement. The supplemental retirement for teachers in the state of Virginia is very nice, but an additional supplement from mutual funds, savings, etc. is also helpful. The downsides of running the business were the taxes, corporation statements and quarterly reports.

In addition to working with my business, I continued to play some music as a fill-in musician whenever and wherever I was needed. I also became a temporary biologist for a couple of former students needing biological surveys to meet the new requirements for permits to mine coal. I did botanical surveys for Mullins Engineering in Norton, and also for Terry Collier at Maxim Engineering in Norton and Coeburn. One of the projects was a stream survey, as I worked for engineer and former student, David Hughes, to seine and survey the fish population in the Guest River near Norton. Tim helped me with this work. Dennis Rasnick hired me to do a survey and write a report on the possibilities of native trout in a stream near Red River Coal Co. My buddy Mark Wooten even sent me to Logan, West Virginia to survey a stream. I never turned down the opportunity to make a few extra bucks. I am a typical Jack of all trades.

A STUMBLING BLOCK

I was 40 years old before I ever experienced any serious health problems. There were some football bang ups, and the chainsaw incident while gathering firewood. I had also experienced some very aggravating ragweed and tree allergies. Then in the spring of 1983 I went to the teacher's spring picnic. Someone had set up a volleyball net and they were already playing when I arrived. I always loved to play volleyball and basketball because of my jumping ability. My advice now would be to slow down some when you reach 40. I immediately hopped out of the car and ran to join in. I did not stretch or warm up (mistake!). I played about 5 minutes when I went up for a good slam. I was delighting in my good play just before I came back to the ground. Then, pow! It sounded like a shot of some sort as my Achilles tendon popped. I had no clue what had happened except that it hurt badly. I sat down on the ground, then got up on one leg and hobbled over to sit down in a lawn chair. James Watts, the assistant principal and former coach, helped me to take off my shoe and sock. My foot flopped downwards, straight in line with my leg.

James said, "Yep. This is pretty serious. I believe you may have broken your tendon. You'd better go and have it checked out."

Vickie took me to Norton Community Hospital. Dr. Kotay looked at it and told me I would need surgery. He scheduled me for the next day.

During the surgery, he made little incisions in the back of my leg. He fished around until he found the end of the tendon, then pulled it back down and used wires to reattach it. I was on crutches for a couple of months, but it eventually all healed up and I recovered. It did not stop me from wanting to play volleyball, basketball, badminton, etc. It was ironic that I had just lost a huge chunk of tooth filling from my childhood days at the dentist at about the same time. Vickie ribbed me considerably afterwards as she made the statement that I hit 40 and then just started falling apart.

NATHAN

Nathaniel Edward Swindall, my first son, was born June 23, 1982, less than a year before my Achilles' tendon incident. I was overcome with love for him. Nathan absorbed my attention quickly. He never struggled with speech. He soon began to correctly pronounce and understand the meaning of several rather large words. I seized the opportunity. I began to use him in some very cute voice-overs for radio commercials. Before long, he began to show an interest in music, and wanted to learn to play. Santa brought him a baritone ukulele which has four strings tuned the same as the bottom four on a guitar. Whereas I had learned "Wildwood Flower" as my first song, Nathan learned "Stairway to Heaven." His interest and talent have been joyful.

My first camping trip in many years was made when Nathan was only about two years old. We had been invited to camp at the Greenbrier campground just outside of Gatlinburg. Some of those present on that trip were our good friends Kerry Edwards, Jerry and Jamie Cox, and my cousin, Sandy Austin Richards and her husband "Dog."

REUBEN

Our third child and son, Reuben Jay Swindall, made his entrance into this world on April 23, 1986. What a wonderful addition to our lives. Like all of our three children have always been, he was another equal amount of joy. We honored our friend Jay Corder by giving Reuben his middle name. I marvel at my luck when I think about the fact that I have three beautiful and wonderful children that are all intelligent, successful and loving. They are all so different, but yet the same in so many ways. We had wanted the boys' age span to be four years so they would not both be in college at the same time.

MICHELLE

Like her brothers and others in the family, my daughter Michelle was also musically talented and had always been able to sing. In seventh grade, she decided to join the J.J. Kelly band. I had known the band director, Lucian Priode, for many years. He taught Michelle the basics on sax, and she was on her way. She had the privilege of associating with some incredible young musicians, including Robbie and Richard Priode, Kenny Stallard and Chris Henson, in the J.J. Kelly marching band. She was in 7th grade, and they were seniors, at the time. She was so impressed with their musical skills. That year, the band placed in, and won, several competitions.

All through high school, Michelle had played on the tennis team. We made it a point to be there for her at most of the matches. One of the most exciting times for all of us was when she played in the final match of the year in 1986, and the team won the Virginia State Championship. Michelle and Bobbie Jo Lawson had won the final doubles match at the Regional Tournament, clinching the 5-4 win for J.J. Kelly. Just before they went to state, I had just purchased a new converted Ford van. I volunteered to transport part of the team to the finals match. Coach Brenda Ward took some of the team in her car, and I took the new van and about half of the team and headed out for Tappahannock, Virginia. The finals were played at George Mason high school.

Michelle graduated from high school in June, 1986. There was a three-way tie for valedictorian between Veena Luthra, Mark Mullins and Michelle. She had already been accepted in early decision to the University of Virginia in Charlottesville and had called me excitedly that spring to tell me. My mother had wanted her to attend Florida College, a school affiliated with the Church of Christ, so she was not pleased at first. However, she finally realized that U.V.A. was a good choice for her. Vickie, my mother and I, along with Glenda and her husband, Ron McMurray, delivered Michelle to Charlottesville on the beginning day. The day went pretty well, except for the fact that she thought we were worrying and fussing over her too much. She particularly remembers her grandmother suggesting that she should wear her student ID and room key around her neck somehow, so she wouldn't lose it. She did not like the idea of how this would look. But looking back, she sees that five family members taking her to college meant that she was very well loved.

"REACH INTO DARKNESS"

Richie's brother, Brent Kennedy, had become somewhat of a philanthropist, and he worked with organizations in the region to secure funds for education and other causes. He was talented in other ways. Brent was an author, he wrote songs, and was also a musician. One of the stories that he had written was based on actual events. "Reach Into Darkness" was about a coal mining family and their struggles with finances as they tried to mine their own coal. He eventually converted the story into a screenplay, and he had hopes that a movie producer might be interested.

In the process of completing all of the necessary requirements for the screenplay, some ideas for a music score and soundtrack were also needed. Richie approached me with the idea of writing some songs for this purpose. I was very interested, and I told him that I would be glad to help. He gave me a copy of the play. I read it and found it to be very intriguing. That spawned some ideas for songs, and I began to try out some of my ideas.

The main theme song was Richie's idea. It was a takeoff on Pachelbel's Canon in D, but in three-four time. His idea was to start with strings and blend into a bluegrass version of the basic melody. The strings would blend back in and take over, but allow the bluegrass instruments to return in the background throughout. During the first session in the studio, Richie invited his cousin Paul Hopkins to play banjo and Paul's son David to play his dobro. I played guitar chords with them while Richie played his Greek instrument, the bouzouki. It is a plucked musical instrument of the lute family, or tambouras family. The tambouras has existed in ancient Greece as pandoura, and can be found in various sizes, shapes, depths of body, lengths of neck and number of strings. Richie's bouzouki had 8 strings and sounded a lot like a mandolin.

We played the main backup theme chords for several minutes on the track. After the other musicians left, Richie tracked a piano throughout. After Richie left, I added several tracks of single note strings with the synthesizer. I then worked with the tracks so that it would meet Richie's production specifications that I described above. The overall production was beautiful and unusual in many respects. The combination of bluegrass instruments and the sophisticated sounds of strings made it unique.

Richie and I both wrote additional original songs for the soundtrack. I wrote an instrumental, "Mountain Jam," and a ballad called "Michael's Song," which was as much about my life as it was about the story. "I Don't Apologize" and "Ain't Carin' Feelings" were songs that matched at least two of the events in the main story.

Brent was excited about the possibilities for the entire package. He took the screenplay and the recorded music to Atlanta and met with someone in the main offices of Universal pictures. They were interested in Brent's work and told him they would keep it for a while to see if anything came up. We had hopes for a long time that the movie might eventually become a reality. The overall experience was worthwhile for all of us.

CHANGING NEIGHBORHOODS

I had spent a considerable amount of time and money (I thought) on improvements to the Guest River House. I had put in some new windows, a new half bath, a concrete slab at the back with a back porch sitting area, and a new Trane heat pump. We had remodeled the rooms, painted and redecorated. We both were not fully satisfied with the house and property. One of the things that bothered me the most was the almost constant noise of the huge coal trucks gearing down as they passed in front of the house after they had rounded the curve up the road. It disturbed my sleep and it interrupted recording sessions in the studio.

We began to have dreams to either build a new house somewhere or buy one in a nice quiet neighborhood. After pursuing several ideas, we both decided that Powell Valley would be a great place to live. We would still have fairly quick access to our work, and it would be quiet and convenient for my ongoing business venture. We began looking for property or houses in Powell Valley. Most of what we found was either too expensive or impractical in some other way.

During a business meeting with Don Green, I told him about our desire to find a place in Powell Valley, and he told me that he just might have access to exactly what I had described. He told me that there had been a default on a home loan and that he might be able to work it out so that we could just take over the payments with no down payment. We went to look at the house and property which was located at the top of the hill in Country Club Estates, across the road from the Lonesome Pine Country Club. We liked the property and the house. We agreed that it would require a lot of painting and fix up, but we decided to tell Don that we wanted it. With the help of M & M Movers in Clintwood we moved into our house in Powell Valley in February, 1989. We had lived in the Guest River House fourteen years.

My heavy lifting of music equipment through the years finally caught up with me. By the fall of 1988, just before we moved, I had developed a hernia. This problem was solved with surgery by Dr. Phillips in Norton. I took a couple of weeks off from school to recover and was back to work soon.

I immediately starting making plans to do some remodeling. The former owner had been a lawyer. I did not like the location of the library on the third floor. I took all the shelves and moved them down to the second floor. The former library became a bedroom for Michelle and the former dining room became our new library. We put bunkbeds in the middle bedroom for the boys, and Vickie and I took the larger bedroom at the end of the hall as the master bedroom. I also remodeled the second floor. The former living room became the dining room. We converted the den into a combination den/living room.

The basement was unfinished when we moved in. Our corporation borrowed money from the bank for facility improvements, and the entire basement became a new studio with a sound room, a control room, a drummer's booth and a new bathroom. My business continued to flourish and I upgraded the studio equipment. I went through the fickle digital audio tape phase and then eventually moved on to digital interfacing and computer recording.

TRIALS, TRIUMPHS AND TRAGEDIES

Michelle finished her third year at UVA in the spring of 1989, and she decided that she wanted to become a pharmacist. As her chemistry teacher, I wrote a letter of recommendation to Dr. White at the Medical College of Virginia. She was accepted into the pharmacy school at M. C. V. and entered school there in 1989. Sometime during this period Michelle was visiting with me, and she had been crying.

I asked her why she was distraught, and she simply said, "We are getting another divorce."

Her mom and Ron were splitting up. A year or so later, Glenda remarried again, this time to a fellow named Eddie Giles.

During the summer of 1990, we decided to purchase a timeshare unit in Williamsburg, VA. We made a trip there with Nathan and Reuben. We toured Jamestown, Williamsburg and Yorktown. The ability to trade the timeshare has made it a real asset for vacations. It provided us with the opportunity to teach our children, and expose them to many natural wonders and historical sites through the years. While on this trip we ventured down to the waterfront during Harbor Fest in Norfolk. We all experienced some great history as the ships were returning from Iraq with soldiers. We met and talked with one of the returning servicemen. The festival was resplendent with great food, exciting air shows, and concerts by "Firefall" and the "Virginia Symphony." The only downside was a wreck in the tunnel as we were trying to return to Williamsburg. We sat and waited for hours while the wreck was being cleared.

In 1988, we camped again with some of the same folks, this time at the Cave Cove campground near Fontana dam. Additions to this trip included Kerry's wife and daughter, Charlene and Keri Beth. Jim Robinson, his son Gray and his wife Diane were there. Donnie ("Jocko") and Jonelle Stephens and our good friend, Ersie Holbrook also camped with us this time. Our boys had a great time playing in the creek and exploring the grounds with Jerry and Jamie's sons. Soon, with the guidance and camping knowledge of Donnie Stephens, we were camping in larger and larger groups for up to ten days on each trip. We camped at the Breaks of the Mountain, Hungry Mother State Park, Cave Mountain State Park, Douthat State Park, and Bear Tree campground near Damascus.

In the summer of 1990, we camped at Cave Mountain Lake. Our boys were small, ages four and eight. This was Michelle's first camping trip with us. She brought a friend, Heather Wright, daughter of John Wright from Pound, Va. During the trip, we nicknamed Heather "Devil Heather," after her renowned great-grandfather, Devil

John Wright. This was the first trip when some thought was given to naming the camping group as the "Elephant Clan." The name came about as a result of sampling some extremely potent Elephant brand beer that had been shared by Al Plisko.

At Christmas time in 1990, Vickie was in a dilemma, as usual, about purchasing a gift for my mother. She decided to go to the dog pound and find a "rescue dog" for her. She brought home a mix breed and on Christmas day she presented mom with the gift. Even though she liked the dog, she said that, for several reasons, she could not keep a dog. Thus, we named him Lucky, and he became a member of our family. This dog stayed with us for 16 years before we finally had to have him put down because of numerous ailments.

In the spring of 1991, we planned a trip to Washington, DC during the cherry blossom festival. We didn't make it. There was a 48-year-old man (me) out playing basketball with the kids during a stopover at Vickie's brother Tom's home in Charlottesville. I fell and broke my left thumb. After another quick trip to the emergency room that day and a trip back home the next day, I ended up in surgery again, this time to have a couple of screws placed to hold the bone in place. I then wore a cast for about 6 weeks (the cast came off and was sacrificed into the campfire that summer).

One of the greatest tragedies in our lives took place on December 16, 1991. Michelle had completed one and one half years of pharmacy school. Glenda had borrowed her sister Ramona's van and had traveled to Richmond to bring Michelle's belongings home for the holidays. Michelle was following behind her mom in her own car as they traveled home. Glenda pulled into the turn lane at the intersection in Hansonville, to turn left onto route 58 toward St. Paul. A car came speeding through the stop sign just as Glenda was making the turn. The car hit her full force in the side, crushing the door in, and pushing the van sideways all the way across the road and into the guardrail on the far side. Michelle witnessed all of the accident. She called me to let me know what had happened. She told me that her mom had been medflighted to Bristol Regional Memorial Hospital. Glenda passed away a couple of hours later from internal injuries suffered in the crash. I was lucky to have my Uncle Gene visiting with us that night. He stayed with us and supported us throughout the night, and all the way through the funeral services. It was a nightmare whirlwind that forced us all to be more aware of the fragility of life. It was an unbelievably huge loss for Michelle and her sister, Brandi.

Michelle was extremely distraught at the loss of her mother, but she decided to return to school at MCV that winter anyway. It was probably the best thing she could have done. She graduated from MCV with a B.S. in Pharmacy in 1992. She then had plans to enter the doctor of pharmacy program at MCV.

Vickie had been taking off-campus classes in reading for several months. She earned her master's degree from the McGuffey Reading Center at the University of Virginia on May 17, 1992.

MAJOR MEDICAL ISSUES

I had thought I was in pretty good health at age forty-nine. Dr. Renfro put me on the treadmill in the spring. After careful study, he said I was in terrific physical condition for my age. The most serious health problem thus far had been the hernia. In October, 1992, darkness struck again, and this time it hit me directly, and like a ton of bricks. Fred Adkins had purchased the Carl McAfee cabin on the grounds of the Lonesome Pine Country Club. He called me one day and asked me if I owned a chainsaw. I told him I did, and when he asked me for my help in fixing a small bridge at the cabin, I loaded it up and went to help him. About a half hour into the work I became nauseous. Soon my chest was aching and all of my teeth hurt. Fred recognized the signs, because another friend of his had passed away from a heart attack while he was with him. Fred acted quickly. He loaded me into the car and rushed me to the Lonesome Pine Hospital in Big Stone Gap. I was lucky that Dr. Ford was on E.R. duty that morning. He saved my life with an injection of streptokinase which broke up the clot. Fred had called Vickie, so she and Pat, Fred's wife, were standing over me as they loaded me into an ambulance to travel to Holston Valley Hospital in Kingsport.

At the hospital, I was taken immediately to the cath lab. Dr. Claire Hixon did the heart cath and determined that the blockage was cleared, but he also found that two serious damage spots had occurred. I was placed in intensive care for a few days, then moved to a step down. Several folks came to see me during those days, including Jocko, Ray Jones, Bob Adkins, and all of my children. I'll not forget that Nick and Jan Brewer came to visit, and Nick told me that he would do anything that I asked.

He said, "I'll even carry off the garbage," and that's exactly what he did.

I took sick days for the rest of the semester and did not return to work until after the first of the year, 1993. During the late spring, we took a camping trip with our usual camping friends, the Elephant Clan. When we returned, we found our home in a total wreck. While we were on our trip, a pipe had broken in the top floor bathroom. The water ran for days before our neighbor, Beldon Fleming, with whom we shared the well, noticed that the pump was constantly running. He turned the main valve off, but the damage was devastating. The ceilings had fallen in and studio equipment was ruined. Guitars in their cases were found floating in a pool in the basement. The whole ordeal really took a toll on all of us. We had to leave the house for months while it was being restored. The house was not totaled but the total damage assessment was about $45,000 plus personal items and clothing, much of what was Michelle's, which she had temporarily stored in the studio drummer's booth. Fred allowed us to move into his country club cabin during the restoration.

We stayed in the cabin for several weeks. Toward the end of June, the whole family including Michelle, took a time share getaway trip to a resort on Greer Lake in Arkansas. While we were there, we visited our cousins Ray and Peggy Crouse and Joyce Tomisich in Jasper. On our return trip, we visited Graceland in Memphis. We drove on that evening to Dickson, Tennessee. We were all watching a movie on tv that evening, when I felt pain in my chest again. I was having another heart attack. I tried the nitroglycerin but it did not help. My lips were turning blue when they called the ambulance. I passed out but regained consciousness on a table in the emergency room, with the nurses calling my name. They were telling me to breathe, after they had already shocked me a couple of times with the paddles. They gave me morphine and something else to calm me down. The doctor told me the next morning that I had about 90% blockage in a couple of arteries. He said that if I wanted to live I would need surgery immediately to unblock the arteries. Naturally, I did not argue about this.

An ambulance transported me to Baptist Hospital in Nashville. The next morning I was prepped, and Dr. Kenneth Laws performed bypass surgery on the two errant arteries. I don't remember much about the time that I recovered from surgery, but I was told that Dr. Ray Jones and our friend Jim Collie were with Vickie and Michelle during and after the operation. The worst thing that I remember was spending the night in the recovery room while on a respirator. I fought the respirator all night. It seemed to me at the time that hell could not be much worse. Vickie's dad, my mother and her sister Rebecca had arrived after my recovery room nightmare. They left after one day and took my sons back to Pound to stay with my mother. After a day or two, they had me up and walking a few steps, which we all thought was amazing. Michelle and Vickie stayed in a hospitality house nearby. My hospital stay lasted several days, and I remember spending the fourth of July in the bed. On a hot day near mid-July Vickie loaded me back into the van and we made the trek back to Virginia. We went to my mom's trailer to stay first because it was air conditioned. While there, I called Jim Bowman and asked him to go to Sears and get an AC unit and install it in my bedroom at home. I soon left my mom's home and returned to our home to finish recovering.

We took a different type of camping trip that year. The clan was camping at Douthat State Park. Greg Hamilton invited us to stay at their cabin in Goshen and commute in and out to camp from there. I returned to work that fall.

Michelle, because of her concern for my health issues, decided to stay home and not attend M. C. V. that fall. To relieve her, I had taken over the bookwork involving bill payment and financial matters that involved her mother's passing. Fred helped with all the legal issues involving a court settlement on damages. Michelle and her sister received a life insurance payment from VSR. Glenda's condominium was sold and all issues were complete. Michelle decided to gift me with a membership in the Lonesome Pine Country Club. We enjoyed the pool and tennis. I bought a set of Lynx golf clubs and tried to play golf. The game was not relaxing to me, and I was frustrated by it. I decided later (after Michelle's wedding) to forego the country club membership and spend my energy and resources on camping and fishing. These diversions were both always more satisfying.

SERIOUS ENJOYMENT OF LIFE

Many folks stumble along through life, working hard, accumulating stuff, being successful, and perhaps ignoring their children. Some overlook the many wonders that God has placed here for us to see and enjoy. Vickie and I have had jobs that allowed us more free time to travel. This luxury also allowed for spending quality time with our children. We have always loved travel, music, concerts, fishing together, camping, and picnicking.

We have both always been blessed with numerous good friends with whom we are somewhat compatible in philosophy. We love spending time with those that especially love the outdoors and good company. These folks became the ones with whom we have chosen to spend the majority of our free time. We had already had a few camping trips before we eventually started to enjoy roughing it a little more. We ended up with a good consistently dry tent, furnished as a thoughtful gift from our friend, Jay Corder. We selected air mattresses, cooking utensils, chairs and coolers that provided us with most of the conveniences of being at home. Jocko became the coordinator and planner for our trips. He assigned duties and kept everything running smoothly. He was dubbed our Cap'n. During one trip, to his dismay, Vickie sneaked and borrowed his waterproof Kevlar cap. She cut out the logo from a box of Cap'n Crunch cereal and sewed the logo, "Cap'n," on the front of the cap above the bill. We were all shocked that she had ruined his very expensive cap, but the act became another one of those wonderful moments stamped in time that we still talk about today.

We camped a few years at Douthat State Park and really enjoyed the group campground there. After they demolished the bathhouses and totally remodeled the camp, we were no longer attracted to camp at Douthat.

We eventually settled on a favorite spot where we camped consistently for several years running. The idea developed this way: Several members of the clan decided to rent canoes and make about a five-mile float trip down the New River. They rented canoes from Mr. Lester Halsey, a long-time resident of Mouth of Wilson, VA. He owned a strip of land there which bordered the river. He had suggested that the canoers launch above the confluence of the north and south forks of the river and float down to his property for taking out. This was about a five mile float. Jay and I decided not to float. We found a comfortable spot and sat in our lawn chairs, enjoying the day and a cold beer while we waited for the rest of our crew. As we talked about this and that, we eventually got around to talking about the property, and what a nice spot it would be for group camping. When we all gathered again, we suggested it to the group, and everyone was in favor of the idea. Even though it would add a few more miles to our drive from home, it was an ideal spot for many reasons.

We began camping for over a week at the end of each summer at Shady Shack campground on the New River in Mouth of Wilson, VA. Mr. Lester Halsey loved to have our group come and camp in his campground. We tried to take a group picture during camp through the years, but we always missed someone. Our friends arrived at the beginning or near the end of the trip, while some stayed the entire time. Others came and left and then came back as need be, and the numbers fluctuated. One year we counted nearly 40 campers in our group at one time.

The shibboleths and tales grew in such numbers that we still use the sayings and tell the stories today. When we're sitting around in a group, especially by a campfire, talking about the good ole days of the Elephant Clan, we many times laugh uncontrollably, sometimes to the point of crying. There's not a good way to describe the intense pleasure and fun we had during our camping years with the Clan. I don't need to mention everyone's name here, but those that were present have no problem in relating to these descriptions.

Some of the original core group are seen in the portrait below. Vickie was one of the major cooks, but everyone helped with that task from time to time. Kurls was dubbed the "Sunshine Man." He was the first to rise on most mornings and he always built a fire and had fresh coffee brewing.

In 1999, Cap'n surprised us with new t-shirts. The shirts had been designed by Corrie, Jonelle and Jocko's daughter. They bore our elephant clan name, and the back had a beautiful drawing with our song slogan, "It Couldn't Be Better."

Some of the clan members were: Jocko and Jonelle Stephens, Kerry and Charlene Edwards, Ron and Vickie Swindall, Corrie and Casey White, Kerry Beth and Brad Hallberg, Michelle and Evan Sisson, Nathan and Amanda Swindall, Reuben Swindall, Brandi Lawson, Terry Mason, Rex and Teresa Boggs, Anne Newlun, Rickie Newlun, Jay Matthew Cantrell, Greg and Pam Hamilton, Wyatt Hamilton, Will Hamilton, Al and Val Plisko, Aerial Plisko, Heather Wright, Tyler and Linda Fleming, John Fleming, Maria Fleming, Becca Fleming, Laura Fleming, Jim and Betty Peters, Dillon Peters, Garry and Debbie Roberson, John Griffin, Jay Corder, Jason and Karen Riggs, Kent and Lynna Estep, Anna Estep, Eddie and Ruth Elkins. Other folks may have shown up for one or even two trips, but were not with us long enough to be invited into the Elephant Clan "membership." Some of the original clan members are seen in the photo below.

L to R: Charlene (Charlene Darlin') Edwards, Kerry ("Kurls") Edwards, Me, Don ("Cap'n") Stephens, Jonelle (Jo) Stephens, Vickie Swindall

It was a peaceful, wonderful place and time. There was a special closeness as we shared this experience each year. This seemed like the prime of life for us, and we were soaking up every drop of it. We floated the New River in canoes and kayaks. We fished in the waters and caught many bluegill and smallmouth bass, and a few trout. There were fish fries that fed the entire clan. The cool clean river water became a great place to spend long chunks of time in lawn chairs, just letting the world roll by. This photo illustrates so well the relaxation and enjoyment that we experienced. Cap'n Jocko is seen in the center below. On the right are Theresia, Jay, me and Rex.

We ate like kings at every meal during our camping trips. When we didn't want to cook a meal, we went "out" to eat, mostly to Shatley Springs, a short drive south on the North Carolina side of the River. We had huge campfires at night and sat around the fire, warming ourselves on the cool nights, listening to music, telling funny stories, laughing uncontrollably, sipping beer and eating peanuts.

During the evening hours, musicians like Jay, Tyler Fleming, Nathan and I, and Rex, entertained the group around the campfire. We all sang our clan camp song, "It Couldn't Be Better." Sometimes rowdy, always civilized, and loving each other's company, Vickie always said, "I just love being with you all and breathing the same air." Our great friends with whom we shared these times will always be precious to us.

LIFE ON THE LAKE

We were still loving our camping days with the clan, but we also still loved fishing at Cherokee lake in our MFG. We purchased a tiny two bedroom/one bath cabin on a hill above Cherokee Lake in the early 90s and spent as much time there as we possibly could on weekends and during the summer. Naturally we fished a lot and our whole family caught loads of fish. It was a terrific pastime. During the school year when the boys were still small, we would leave Wise County on Friday evening and return either Sunday night or Monday morning in time for work. We always kidded that we were so reluctant to leave the lake that we were holding on to the door frames until the last minute.

Then after a couple of years in the tiny cabin, I was walking on

Lakemont drive beside the lake, and I met Mr. Burch Bullock, an older fellow that told me he was interested in selling his property without being involved with a realtor. I was immediately interested, and we came to an agreement. A few weeks later we moved our few belongings into the lake house at 351 Lakemont Drive, and soon sold the small cabin to Randy and Jackie Seals. The lake house became our home away from home and we again loved spending time there.

The View from Our Lake House Window

It wasn't long before some of our friends began also taking an interest in our lake getaway. Some of them would occasionally come and spend a night or two with us at our house. Before long, they were buying their own getaway on Lakemont Drive, the same street and strip of lake. Vickie was so pleased when the house next door was purchased and occupied by one of her best friends, Theresia Mason. Jocko, Jonelle, and Kurls and Charlene decided to share a lake house about 200 yards east of ours. As of today, they still own this nice getaway and use it often. We now have several other neighborhood friends at the lake, including Garry and Debbie Robertson, and Bill and Kaye Long.

Time became a whirlwind in the 90s as Nathan reached his teenage years and began playing sports. He participated in J.V. basketball, varsity basketball, golf and cross country. Naturally it thrilled both Vickie and I that he was so involved. We tried to attend every game/

match that was played with competitors. To say that we enjoyed it would be an understatement. He was also becoming more and more interested in music, and we both found that to be very exciting as well.

Our family still traveled a lot in the 90s, making time share vacation trips to Las Vegas, Sedona, Arizona, the Grand Canyon, Mesa Verde, Arkansas, Memphis, Disney World, the Baseball Hall of Fame, Hershey, PA, the Martin Guitar Factory, baseball games, the Poconos, and many beach trips to Edisto Island.

MICHELLE AND EVAN TIE THE KNOT

Michelle continued her education, and she entered the doctor of pharmacy program at MCV. She and her future husband, Evan Sisson, both received their Pharm Ds in 1996. He was a classmate and had become her fiancé.

L-R: Me, Vickie, Michelle, Evan, Janet Sisson, Mack Sisson

She and Evan were married that summer on June 22, 1996. The wedding took place at the Wise Baptist Church and our Rev. Ray Jones officiated. The reception was a rather large affair. My mother baked a huge beautiful wedding cake, complete with a water fountain and staircase built in. Our guests included family, friends, and church congregation members, and some of them had traveled from several other states. Our friend, Jay Corder became the main photographer.

I was able to talk a few of my friends into becoming a temporary band at Michelle's wedding reception. Fred Adkins, Jay Corder,

Randy Wyatt, Tuck Robinson, Bud Stewart and Nathan helped with the music. We had fabulous finger foods, catered by the country club staff, and we had a cash bar.

Michelle's room at home became an empty nest after this, and Nathan claimed it as his room, giving Reuben more space in their former room.

Into The Twenty-First Century

REUBEN'S VENTURES

When our boys first started school, Vickie and I decided that they would benefit more by attending Norton elementary school. Afterwards, we made plans for them to start school in Wise in seventh grade.

Our son, Reuben Jay Swindall, has musical talent like his sister and brother, Michelle and Nathan. While he was in elementary school he joined the band. My old friend, Buddy Stewart had become the band director in Norton after Dave Tipton retired. He was Reuben's music teacher. Reuben played alto saxophone. Vickie and I were proud of his efforts in music, and we attended any and all events when the little band played for the public. But alas, he began to lose interest soon after he finished sixth grade at Norton. He made a move to L.F. Addington Middle School in Wise. He was still in the band there under Mr. Donnie Sorah, but this came to an end when he started intently playing football, which he loved.

When Reuben was 12, in 1998, his friend Jon Willis wanted him to join the feeder team and play football. Vickie was opposed, but I wanted him to make the decision. I was in favor of his involvement in team sports. Nathan did not play football, but he had enjoyed his time with the basketball team. Reuben chose to play.

The first day he put on the pads and went to practice, I told him that it was a rough game and that it was meant to be that way. I taught him how to get down in a stance. When he took the position, I went toward him and pushed him down roughly. He looked a little surprised. I asked him to bend forward and used my palms to charge into his shoulder pads.

He staggered back and I began my lecture. "Son, the secret to success in this game is to always charge forward, never back, and hit the man in front of you harder than he hits you. Always be the first to get a good lick and keep driving until he's down. Do your best to intimidate him and get the upper hand."

He soon learned that this and a positive attitude worked for him. Of course, his 6'2" 200-pound frame in high school was also quite helpful. I couldn't help but think about how it would be to try and push him over now like I did when he started in 7th grade. Ha!

Even though Reuben had dropped out of band for football, he often demonstrated that he had a musical ear. He had briefly picked up the bass guitar and picked a little bit with Nathan and I. He seemed to understand the noting and he was beginning to move around the neck some. Other activities then captured his attention, and he once again lost interest. As a sophomore, he became semi-serious about a young lady in the class below him and they started going steady.

Reuben listened and learned the basics of the game very quickly. He became a very good football player and started in the line as a sophomore. At different times in his high school sports career he played guard, tackle and middle linebacker. Reuben made All-District by his junior year. He graduated with honors from J.J. Kelly High School in June,  2004. He was invited to play on the team at UVA's College at Wise where he entered school and played one year at the college level before deciding that he would rather concentrate on academics. This turned out to be a very good decision.

During his senior year in high school, Reuben shocked us somewhat with another talent. The nine o'clock club, sponsored by a teacher, Jan Thompson, had been producing very high quality musical dramas each year. Reuben decided that he wanted to be a part of the club during his final year at J.J. Kelly. He had the idea that he wanted to be a stage hand and help with the props, etc. However, when Ms. Thompson first realized that he was becoming a club member, she had other ideas.

Reuben was only 17 at the time, but he was growing a substantial beard (them ye adulate, ye emulate). She immediately told him that she had wanted for years to produce "Fiddler on the Roof."

She said, "Reuben, finally! You are my Tevye!"

He actually didn't know what Ms. Thompson had meant, and when she explained that she wanted him to play the lead role and sing the songs, he just told her, "no way."

She insisted however, and they began to build the sets and work on the music. He did it! When Vickie and I went to see the production, we were shocked. We had no idea what a quality voice our son had. It was totally amazing and so much fun.

Y2K AND BEYOND

We prepared for the great Y2K prediction and the millennium changeover by staying home. We, like everyone else, had a relatively uneventful evening. Jay joined us for a couple of days. We just made some good food, had some of our best EtOH, watched tv and enjoyed the time together.

Nathaniel Edward Swindall graduated from J.J. Kelly High School in June, 2000. He graduated with honors and was the salutatorian for his class of well over 100 graduates. He played and sang for the crowd and presented his speech to his classmates, and his mom and dad were very proud of their son. As planned, he entered Virginia Tech that fall.

I have learned by now that increased age brings additional health problems to most of us. We have joked a lot about the fact that older folks have plenty of conversational topics, and that one in particular is the discussion of ailments and medications. Also, that the so-called golden ages don't really seem very golden. My doctor at the time was still Tom Renfro. He kept a fairly close watch on my health. He discovered that I had the beginnings of heart failure, had gastric reflux, and that I had hypothyroidism. Other than this, I felt pretty well, and even though my late 50s took a toll on my overall strength and stamina, I was doing well considering what I had been through.

I saw my high school best friend for the final time at our 40th class reunion in 2001. He was still telling tall tales and had everyone laughing. He had driven up from Florida along with another classmate, Ann Polinsky, just for the occasion. I enjoyed sitting and talking with him, catching up on at least some of his life during all of the years that we had skipped. Several of our classmates gathered around him that day and listened. He had many tales to tell. (lol)

Another tragical event made its ugly mark in history on September 11, 2001. Nineteen militants associated with the Islamic extremist group, al-Qaeda hijacked four airliners and carried out suicide attacks against targets in the United States. Two of the planes were flown into the towers of the World Trade Center in New York City, a third plane hit the Pentagon just outside Washington, D.C., and the fourth plane crashed in a field in Pennsylvania. Often referred to as 9/11, the attacks resulted in extensive death and destruction, triggering major U.S. initiatives to combat terrorism and defining the presidency of George W. Bush. Over 3,000 people were killed during the attacks in New York City and Washington, D.C., including more than 400 police officers and firefighters.

Most events of this magnitude are certainly memorable, and

many people remember where they were and what they were doing when the event occurred. In our case, we were preparing for a trip to Southgate, Michigan to attend the funeral services for Geneva, My Uncle Gene's wife. We drove from our home to my mom's home in Pound, and found her very sick. She was nauseous and had trouble with her balance. We immediately turned around and took her back to the ER at Community Hospital. It was determined that she had an inner ear infection (labyrinthitis). We were unable to follow through with our plans to make the trip.

I stayed in the waiting room while Vickie went in to the ER with my mom. While watching the Today Show on NBC, I witnessed the plane crashing into the twin towers.

I also remember seeing Don Powers in the waiting room, and saying to him, "Don, it looks like we are at war."

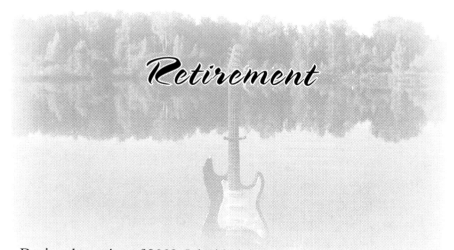

Retirement

During the spring of 2002, I decided that the teaching profession had suffered too many changes. I had also been offered a very attractive retirement option. I made plans to retire at the end of the following school year. Reuben was scheduled to graduate in 2004. After 37 total years in the profession, I said goodbye to my teaching career in June, 2003. Vickie continued to teach and her income along with my retirement check was substantial for us.

Without elaboration, I will say that my health problems continued to mount during the 2000s. I had to have another hernia operation in 2002 (uncomfortable, but no big deal).

Afterwards, my health concerns included atrial fibrillation, a defibrillator implant, addition of a third wire for a pacemaker, mitral valve prolapse, valve replacement surgery, circumflex artery bypass surgery, several shocks from ventricular tachycardia, several cardioversions, and ablations. I am currently living with a complete heart block and near 100% dependency on the pacemaker.

I am thankful to the Lord for modern technology and Cleveland Clinic! I am here today because of these things and because of the expertise of Dr. Mihhaljevic, Dr. Eileen Hsich, and Dr. Osama Wazni. My regular visits to see these wonderful doctors at the clinic are always encouraging and comforting. Most of the time I feel better when I leave than I did before arriving there. They are more personable to me than my local doctors have been. Dr. Hsich especially seems more like a family member or good friend to me.

In 2004, Reuben was gifted with a beautiful black Labrador Retriever. We tried to allow him lots of freedom to roam in our neighborhood, but this proved to be his downfall. Benji disappeared one rainy day and we never saw him again. I thought it best that we probably should not try for another dog at this juncture, but both Vickie and Reuben wanted another dog. In 2005, their desire for another pet resulted in a trip to Skeetrock in Dickenson County. A full-blooded collie named Diamond, owned by Mr. Bennett, had given birth to a litter of puppies that were a collie/Australian Shepherd mix. Reuben selected one of the males and brought him home. He gave him an old Irish name, Seamus (Vickie spells it 'Shamus'). After Reuben left home, Vickie and I adopted Seamus. He has been like a child to us, and he has absolutely been one of the sweetest dogs I have ever known about. He was our precious pet until April 27, 2017, when we had no choice but to call the vet and have him put to sleep.

We continued to travel as much as possible during the 2000s as we ventured further with our timeshare. One of our trips in 2006 took us to a timeshare resort at Seeley Lake in Montana.

We visited the U. of M. in Missoula and took a trip to Kalispell to visit my cousin, Ronnie Carl Swindall and his wife Margaret. We also met Ron's son Russell, his wife Jean, and their children. We spent one night with Ron and Margaret. They took us to Glacier National Park. The following day Russell took us fishing on Lake McDonald. I caught a 13 lb. lake trout.

Vickie caught a big lake trout on this trip also, as did another of our friends that made the trip with us. The visit, the trip, the scenery, the experience... Ah, life has been good much of the time!

CHILDREN'S EDUCATION

While we were in Missoula, we walked on the campus of the University. We decided to see if Reuben might be interested in getting his M.A. there. We sent him on a scouting trip later and he applied to the school. He was accepted and received free tuition and a teaching assistantship.

Nathan had returned to Wise and graduated in 2005 from UVA Wise with a degree in chemistry. After Nathan graduated, he decided to work on a master's degree at ETSU. He received a teaching assistantship, and began his studies there in 2005. He decided to withdraw and return to UVA Wise the following year to earn a teaching certificate. Success in this training program landed him a job at West Hampton High School in Greer, SC. He teaches chemistry, and AP chemistry.

We have been blessed to get all of our children through college with no college debt. They all received scholarships from Slemp, General, Victoria Whitaker and other sources which allowed them to pay tuition without borrowing money. Other expenses were paid from our savings for them.

Reuben graduated a year later from UVA Wise with a double major in French and history. After a year in France as an English teacher, he completed his master's degree at the University of Montana in 2008. By the end of that year, Reuben had taken up kayaking. He now loves whitewater and goes with his friend, Daniel Helbert at every chance. His favorites are the Gauley, Russel Fork, New River Gorge, the Green, and the Guest.

GRANDDAUGHTERS AND JOY

2008 was a busy year for the Swindalls. Michelle and Evan had wanted children for a while and they had not been successful. They were lucky that a friend volunteered to be a gestational carrier.

After one trial of in-vitro fertilization, it was successful, and the embryos of twins were implanted. Our beautiful granddaughters arrived into this world on February 17, 2008. They are fraternal twins. At this point in time, we feel so lucky and blessed that they have been able to grow and cope with life in a very positive way.

Isabella and Sophia are both very intelligent little beings. They are honor students in school and are both always very busy with varying interests. Our love for them is indescribable. We relish the times when they can come and spend time with us. We are very proud of our granddaughters.

Due to health problems and overall lack of inspiration, I went for several years through the 90s and 2000s without music being in the center of my life. In the studio, I was writing an occasional jingle and doing some overdubbing. I was also recording other groups. I was occasionally sitting in and playing guitar or bass with groups that needed an extra or replacement musician. As my son, Nathan, became more interested in actually performing, I was inspired to once again think about the band music scene. I had the help of my old friend Tuck Robinson from the "Fallen Stars" on drums. Randy Wyatt became our bass player. Randy and Tuck had been deputies for the county and Randy was a campus policeman at UVA – Wise. With me on lead and Nathan as lead singer and rhythm guitarist, we formed the group, "Law and Disorder." We had great fun and enjoyed playing out several times before Nathan left to attend ETSU. This all happened in 2006.

It was during this time that we met two new friends that have become an important part of our loop. One hot summer day while Vickie and I were enjoying some time on our deck at the lake, we observed a couple taking a walk through the neighborhood. When Vickie saw them, she immediately waved and we all introduced ourselves. They had recently purchased a house at the end of our neighborhood road. We spent several minutes talking with them, and soon we had made arrangements for a visit with them. Debbie and Garry Robertson have become fast friends of ours. That time together led to our introducing them to some of our other friends at the lake. They have since become very important people in all of our lives.

NUPTIAL NATHAN

 It wasn't until early 2008 that we finally realized that Nathan was very serious about the girl that he had been dating. Amanda Banning was from Greer, SC, near where he had gotten his job. Nathan had met her while he was starting his graduate studies at ETSU. They were married in a nice outdoor setting in downtown Greenville. We had family and friends there, and many of them had traveled a considerable distance. Dr. Ray Jones again led the ceremony, which was very tastefully done, and beautiful!

There were over 100 guests: Nathan's friends, Amanda's friends, Vickie's and my friends, and family from both sides. Some of our family traveled all the way from Michigan just for the wedding. The reception was held in a building on the same grounds as the wedding ceremony.

They lived in a rental house at first, and they were soon looking for a more permanent dwelling. They bought a home just out of Greer on Pleasant Oak Drive. Nathan continues to teach at West Hampton and work in two musical groups in the Greenville area. Amanda works in banking with Bank of America.

THE RON SWINDALL BAND

When Nathan left, I was in musical limbo for a while. After a period of time, I decided to try to start a band up once more, this time with a different drummer and bass player, two very fine musicians. Gary McGonagill, the drummer, was originally from the Florida panhandle. I nicknamed him "Flash." He had gigged with a lot of people through the years, some notable. Even after this band dissolved, he has always been my loyal friend. He lives close by and is always ready to help me in any way he can. We have recorded several tracks together.

**L-R: Bill Smith, Rex Boggs, Gary McGonagill,
Me, Jay Corder**

The bass player in this group was Bill Smith. Bill was also a seasoned musician. Bill's wife is a distant cousin, Nancy Countiss. Nancy is Thomas Countiss' sister, so it was nice to still have this connection to the old "Fallen Stars" band. Bill, and my friends Tuck and Richie were with me when we played tribute music during the celebration of life for Thomas.

Our sax player was my childhood and lifetime friend Jay Corder, a real asset to anybody's group. Jay and I had played together in the "Shadows" band as kids, and again occasionally in the "Wildcats" band. He was a member of a very significant blues band called "Bad Influence" when he lived in the D.C. area.

Rex Boggs replaced Nathan on vocals.

The band booked a few gigs around the area as the "Ron Swindall Band." The name was Bill Smith's idea. He thought it would help advertise the band because I was known by a lot of people (probably simply because of my age and teaching experience). Even though the sound was very professional and rather unique, the band was short lived. The members of the group had different ideas about the direction the band was taking. This led to a dissolution. It was fun while it lasted.

JUST ANOTHER FISHING STORY

What a great day I was anticipating! My youngest son, Reuben, was finally home from Montana and was planning to stay close for a while. My wife and I were thoroughly enjoying having him with us. He had also brought his very significant friend, Ann Coble, to stay with us in Virginia. This would be at least until their financial situation improved enough for them to find gainful employment. They were hoping to make wedding plans, and eventually settle into a place of their own. We really love Ann and it was a joy to have her with us. Our other son, Nathaniel, was meeting us at our Cherokee lake house in Tennessee for a special visit with his brother, and a father/sons fishing trip.

We were all up at the crack of dawn. Well, almost at the crack of dawn. The boys had already doubted that I would get up so early. But I proved to them that I could still handle the early rise by stumbling out of bed at 7:00AM (sunrise that day was only at 6:00AM, so I came close). Luckily, my wife, Vickie, is a bona fide "early to bed, early to rise" enthusiast and she had coffee ready before we left.

When I was finally fully awake, I donned my UT cap and I found myself on the boat with my boys, and I was really beginning to enjoy myself as we motored across the lake in heavy fog to one of our favorite spots. Good natured banter filled the air as we began plugging the bank with crank baits, and shortly afterward Reuben connected with the first fish of the day, which was a pumpkinseed sunfish about five inches long. We laughed that such a small fish would try to swallow a plug that was nearly as large as the fish itself.

We kidded Reuben, "It looks like the really big ones have started to hit now."

We continued to move slowly down the bank, pausing occasionally to detach a plug from an underwater log or rock.

Nathan made an errant cast into an overhanging tree and we proceeded to make him live hard. "Hey Nate, are the fish starting to bud?" or "You need more practice son, then maybe you can wrap it all the way around that limb."

Nathan took all the ribbing in good nature and shortly afterward he paid us back by hooking a nice bass.

He released the 13.5 inch largemouth and I heard him make a comment that, "We might be able to catch several fish today if I could just get a little help."

After a few minutes, we decided to move to another one of our hotspots. We placed our rods in the boat and moved down the lake about one mile.

Reuben and I took the two chairs on the front deck and Nathan started casting from inside the railing about halfway back. We began plugging the bank and in a short time I landed a foot-long bass. I released it and on the next cast I was hung up, or at least I thought so. I kept my line tight as we moved back toward the hang-up. Suddenly the hang-up pulled back.

"Guys, it's a fish, and I think it's a big one. Get the net," I exclaimed. Reuben had been running the electric motor as we were moving back to the spot. He switched the motor off and grabbed the net.

"The fish is still on and I think it's also hung up, but it still feels like a big one when it pulls back," I told them.

The boat had turned in the breeze and was moving too fast, and we were drifting back over the spot. In a floundering effort to save my plug and the fish, and try to keep my best rod intact, I decided to move inside the boat railing. The front gate on the pontoon boat was closed, so I decided to climb over the gate. That was a bad idea. I tripped over the gate and went sprawling inside between the seats, dropping my rod in the process.

The boys were both concerned that I was injured. I was, a little bit, but mostly just my pride.

Reuben yelled, "Dad! Are you alright?"

I assured them both that I was OK.

Poor Reuben, who had been holding the net over the side in preparation to retrieve the fish, so worried and distraught, dropped the net into the water (it sank). I quickly told Nathan to grab my rod before it went over the side. Nathan got the rod as I pulled myself together somewhat and stood up. In the meantime, the line had gotten wrapped around the electric trolling motor as Nathan held the rod over the side of the boat. He moved to the front as I took the rod and pushed the tip of the rod as far as I could down and around the back of the motor, freeing it. It was still hung, and I could still feel the fish pulling back. At this point, I was thankful for Stren 12-pound test line, but other than diving in, how could we catch this fish (which we hadn't even seen yet)?

We could now all see the tree that had been the source of our agony for the past few minutes. The boat had drifted against the bank and totally stopped moving. Reuben and I both moved back to the front deck. I held the rod in one hand, with the line wound tight. I laid down and reached into the water with my other hand, lifting the branch. We saw the fish! I told them, "It really is a nice one boys. Let's try our best to get it."

Reuben reached into the water and down near the fish. The plug was in its mouth and the line was wrapped around the branch several times. I told him, "Watch out for the hooks and try to get a thumb-hold on him."

He tried, but to no avail.

"I need a knife or some cutters," Reuben said.

Wouldn't you know it? We could not find a cutting tool. Finally, at last resort, Reuben, with his "Swindall strength," pulled the branch, the line, and the fish just above the surface and began chewing on the line. He succeeded in cutting the line with his teeth, and we finally "landed" the fish, a four-pound largemouth bass. I was a little "worse for the wear," and ended up with "barked shins" and a bruise on my thigh. There was, however, a positive side to the story. I was able to get 20 nice fillets that would certainly taste "better than a big snowball" this winter (a quote from my dad). Our stock of freezer fish had improved, and my wounds were healing. We replaced the net, my boys and I had a memorable morning together, and we had a "tale to tell."

If this story wasn't already so long, I would tell you about the rest of the day. Here's an abstract: Vickie loved the story, we had a wonderful breakfast with biscuits and gravy. I cranked up the big smoker on the patio and cooked three racks of ribs (dry Memphis Rendezvous style) mmmmmmm! Everything was going pretty well until we visited our friend Bill and Kay, after which I backed my 4 X 4 side by side down the driveway and wrecked in the ditch, turning the sucker over. Luckily the dog was unhurt and I was only unconscious for a few seconds. When I later thought about all of the things that had happened that day, I concluded that I'M QUITE SURE IT WAS ALL BECAUSE OF THAT DARN BILL DANCE CAP!!! Lol.

Traveling

TEXAS

I hadn't been to Texas since I was too young to remember, and it was on my bucket list. Vickie booked us into a timeshare resort near Austin at Canyon Lake. From here we were close enough to drive to both Austin and San Antonio. Good buddy Jay Corder and I decided to make the trip from home by car. Vickie only had a one week of spring break, so she decided to take a flight from Knoxville.

Jay and I left Wise County on Thursday night and drove to Nashville, where we spent the night. That evening we walked down Broadway and enjoyed the music. The next day we drove on to Memphis and spent the night there. While in Memphis, we visited Beale Street, and popped into several bars and heard a lot of great music. The Rendezvous, one of the most famous barbecue and rib restaurants in the country, was our choice for supper that evening. The following day we drove on to Tyler, where I had first gone when I was a baby. We drove on to Austin and met Vickie at the airport, then went to Canyon Lake. Jay and I were in a wonderfully different world in the midst of this famous music venue.

Our first road trip away from the condo was made to Austin. Jay, Vickie and I had a meal at one of George Bush's favorite hangouts, Iron Works BBQ. We spent the evening on 6th Street, which is famous for the music venues. We heard every style of popular music that night. To say that we all enjoyed it is an understatement.

The next day we decided to travel to San Antonio. We walked down the River Walk and had lunch at Landry's Seafood Restaurant, then we visited the Alamo. It was haunting. I have always gotten a sort of strange and special feeling when visiting historical sites.

We had a cold one in the famous bar in the Menger Hotel. It was once the site of more cattle deals than any place else in Texas. The Menger Bar has been voted one of the top 10 most historic bars in the United States. It's also where Theodore Roosevelt recruited his Rough Riders before heading off to fight the Spanish-American War.
The bartender here showed us a bullet hole in one of the support posts that was made by someone in Teddy's rowdy party.

We were so glad that we had decided to spend a small bit of time there. As you see, we had our own photographer (Jay).

We rode the elevator to the top of the 579-foot Tower of the Americas that looks down on the Spurs coliseum and the surrounding area. We sat in the lounge there for several minutes while checking out the view and taking photos.

Our other vacation days were spent exploring the Texas hill country around the Canyon Lake vicinity.

BEACH TRIPS

Vickie and I had resolved many years before, that if we were able, we would try to go to the ocean at least every other year. It was great to experience the Outer Banks of North Carolina and the beautiful national seashore there on about 4 trips. Time was spent studying the history and the museums on Roanoke Island. Kitty Hawk was on our agenda and we walked the land where the famous Wright brothers worked. We stayed in Rodanthe one time. The Cape Hatteras lighthouse was one of our destinations. We have taken the ferry over to Ocracoke 3-4 times and have had lunch on that island.

Our favorite beach, first recommended by our good friend Mark Wooten, is Edisto Island Beach in South Carolina. The pace there is slow and there's very little of the carnival like atmosphere that can be found at many other beaches. We have occasionally found our way to other ocean getaways in North Carolina, South Carolina, Virginia, Maryland, Florida, Maine, and Texas. I have walked the beach at Mission Bay in San Diego, California. Vickie has walked on the beach at San Francisco. We are always grateful for these experiences.

Michelle had formerly been diagnosed with ovarian cancer. Vickie had left me and my mother and had gone to stay with Michelle, Evan, and the granddaughters during the time that chemotherapy was scheduled.

Darkness struck again while we were on one of our beach vacations at Ocean City, MD. Our son-in-law, Evan, called us while we were there to let us know that there was a problem. We cut our trip short, left immediately and drove to their home in Richmond. Michelle was required to return to the hospital, so we stayed with them until the problem was resolved. This was a difficult and scary time for our family. We are all thankful that no symptoms have returned at the present time.

CRUISING

Our first cruise ever, and our second trip out of the continental USA, was into the Caribbean. We left from Charleston, SC on a Norwegian Cruise ship.

Georgetown, Grand Cayman

We considered the adventure to be quite a bargain. The food aboard ship was wonderful and we were treated like royalty. The nightly entertainment was of high quality and just being aboard the ship and cruising through the ocean was splendiferous. The day trips from the ship allowed us to visit Cozumel, the Grand Caymans, and Key West.

We made a second cruise with friends, but this time the countries we visited were more in the western part of the Caribbean. We flew into New Orleans on Easter Sunday and experienced their annual Easter Parade.

We were surprised at how long it took us to travel down the Mississippi River and into the Gulf of Mexico. We learned that New Orleans is actually not down on the Gulf, but instead is about 100 miles upstream.

We were able to visit Honduras, Guatemala, and the Mayan ruins in Belize before stopping by the Keys on our last leg home. The trip made us more curious about the people that had once occupied the dwellings and the city. We had first heard of this civilization while in elementary school. They were "civilized" and lived in cities, but their religions and barbaric practices were quite astounding. The temples and sacrificial alters were very thought-provoking.

MAINE

When our son, Reuben, graduated from UVA Wise, one of our gifts to him for his success, similarly to Nathan, was a getaway vacation. He chose to go to Maine for one week by using one of our timeshare weeks. His original plan was to have one of his good friends to accompany him on the trip, but the friend backed out a few days prior to leaving. I lucked out and was able to make the trip in his place.

Reuben and I drove to Charlotte and took a flight to Portland, ME. We rented a car and drove to Samoset Resort in Rockport. It was still cold in Maine at that time of year and we had to dress warmly when we were outside. Rockport, Camden, and St. George's Peninsula were some of our tour destinations. Live lobsters were purchased from an old salty guy that was selling them out of his truck on the highway. We took the lobsters back to our unit and cooked them up. There's nothing quite like a lobster feast.

Our main road trip was a trek northward to Bar Harbor. While we were there we had dinner in the famous Getty's Restaurant in the town. Many pictures were taken around the town of Bar Harbor and the surrounding areas. We visited the famous Oyster Bay lighthouse and took a picture like one of those used in the Red Lobster Restaurants.

FORT LAUDERDALE

Vickie and I took a vacation trip to Fort Lauderdale, FLA in 2011. Neither of us had ever been to that city before. We flew down from

Knoxville and landed at Miami/Ft. Lauderdale. A car was rented as usual and driven to our timeshare which was just across the road from the beach. The unit was small but it had lots of character. We had a Murphy bed and a small kitchen, but we didn't spend much time in the unit other than for sleeping and a few meals. In the Everglades, we took a ride on an airboat, where we were able to see some of the wildlife up close and personal. We ate some great food, spent quality time at the beach and heard some great music at some of the clubs. Fred and Pat were nearby at Boca Raton, so we visited with them and had a meal. We made it a point to plan another trip to Ft. Lauderdale a couple of years later.

TEXAS AGAIN

I always tell everyone that Vickie is my "travel agent." She has planned and booked some wonderful trips for us. She first booked us into a timeshare in Brownsville, TX. We had been able to visit Mexico when we went to Cozumel during our cruises. On our first trip to southwestern Texas area, we went into Mexico again, just by crossing the Rio Grande River. Brownsville is just across the river from Matamoros, Mexico. We walked around the city for a few minutes and made some purchases that we considered bargains. It was a hot day and we decided to stop into a bar and have a beer. The door was open and there was nobody in the bar when we went in. The lights were off, but they turned them on immediately when we entered. The decor was very bright and colorful with paintings and fancy fixtures. We sat down and ordered our refreshments. In a couple of minutes, a young man came around carrying a guitar. We had seen this before, even with whole bands offering to entertain. He asked if we would like to hear a song. It is a tradition in many Latin American countries. It is also customary to give them a tip for the song. I quickly asked if I could see his guitar. He hesitated, then he reluctantly handed me the guitar.

I strummed a chord. He asked me if I played the guitar. I didn't answer. The guitar was noticeably out of tune. I started twisting the tuning keys. The young man looked grief stricken. I told him it was alright, and that I would get it in good tune for him. I strummed an E minor chord and starting singing Leon Russell's "Manhattan Island Serenade."

He watched and seemed to be fascinated and impressed. When I finished, he applauded. He took the guitar and started nervously singing the old Hank Williams song, "My Bucket's Got a Hole in It." When he finished, we applauded and I reached him a tip. He thanked me, and I thanked him for allowing me to play his guitar. We finished our refreshment, and then we left to do some more shopping.

When I travel to a place that I've never been, I enjoy exploring some of the history of the region. This particular part of Texas has a wealth of such history. Much of the Mexican-American War was fought in this region. On May 8, 1846, shortly before the United States formally declared war on Mexico, General Zachary Taylor (1784-1850) outwitted and defeated a superior Mexican force in the Battle of Palo Alto. The battle took place north of the Rio Grande River near present-day Brownsville, Texas. We visited the Palo Alto Battlefield National Historical Park and studied the events that took place over 170 years ago.

We had briefly visited South Padre Island on the first trip To Brownsville, and we wanted to go there again, and spend more time. The island is just up the coast from Brownsville. It is part of a chain of barrier islands that runs up the coast past Corpus Christi and on to Galveston. South Padre Beach is very attractive and it is a tourist destination. We booked a timeshare week on the island. When we arrived, I happened to notice that there was a concert in the courtyard of one of the restaurants on the island, and that Gary P. Nunn would be performing there that evening. We bought tickets in the front row and went to the show. I have always loved the original theme song on "Austin City Limits." It is a long-running TV program on PBS that features good music from all over the country. The theme song, "London Homesick Blues" was recorded by Gary P. Nunn. The music that evening was wonderful and nostalgic. We purchased a couple of CDs. After the concert, we met Gary and talked with him. A picture was made with him which we now have in our album.

LOSS OF MY FIRST BEST FRIEND

As John Lennon said, "Life happens while you're making plans." We may wonder, but most of the time we really don't have any idea what other friends and family are doing at the same time. While we were living our lives, taking vacations, and mostly enjoying ourselves, I had given very little thought to Kennith and what he might be doing that fall. I heard from Larry and Brenda that he had passed away. He did not have a long illness, and when I asked Aaron about it, he simply said, "He died October 17th, 2011. His death was quick. His ashes are in the Gulf of Mexico."

It was unexpected. According to Kennith's request, there was no funeral, no service, no life celebration. That's the way he wanted it. I have had many close friends in my life, but Kennith was the first really close friend that I had. We were indeed very close when we were in school at Pound., and I was greatly saddened by the news of his passing.

ANOTHER UNEXPECTED TRAGEDY

A few years ago, one of my best friends and brothers met with misfortune. Fred had just gone through a colonoscopy. A couple of days later he was out mowing the yard and he passed out. When he regained consciousness, his wife Pat took him down to the Lonesome Pine Hospital ER. He laid on the table there for a few minutes without medical care, and he had another blackout. It was later determined that he had both a heart attack and a stroke. He was transported to Holston Valley Hospital where he laid for several days before he finally regained consciousness. He never fully recovered from this trauma. His speech was affected and his physical ability was permanently damaged. I tried to work with him occasionally to see if I could get him interested in music, but to no avail. He became disabled and was forced to retire from his law practice. It seems that "when it rains it pours." Pat had just gone through a serious bout of ovarian cancer and was in recovery mode. Fred had really made sure that she received the best of care. He had taken her to Johns Hopkins in Baltimore for treatment.

CAMPING AGAIN

The original camping group that we had been with lasted well over ten years, and we created many wonderful memories together. After Mr. Lester Halsey passed away, the group slowly dispersed. We no longer went out on the large group camping trips as we had in the "Elephant Clan." We were not comfortable with the idea of camping by ourselves. Vickie retired in June, 2011 and we schemed about traveling. Vickie and I talked occasionally about owning a little self-contained camper so we could take camping trips.

One day while looking through an auto sales brochure, I ran across an advertisement. A company in Manchester, Tennessee was advertising that they had a special price on a new small Shasta camper. It had been sitting on their lot for two years and nobody was willing to pay the MSRP. It was an '09 model that was made in a retro style, like the original Shasta of many years ago. I called about it and gave the guy $100 on master card to hold it until we got there, at which time we would have first option to buy. We drove to Manchester the next day and loved the camper as soon as we saw it. We bought it. They installed all of the necessary towing equipment on my truck that day and we headed for home.

The camper has a dining table that seats six people. This table and pads folds down into a queen size bed, so it sleeps two persons comfortably. It has a little kitchen with a tiny sink, a hot plate, coffee maker, toaster, and a small refrigerator. It also has a small bathroom with commode and shower. There is a small couch in the end next to the entrance door.

Our first camper trip was in the spring of 2012.The trip was made to Breaks Interstate Park just to try it out. We even took our dog, Seamus, with us. Since that time, we have enjoyed the camper on a few more trips, and it has always been a pleasure. Unfortunately, it stays parked most of the time.

That summer we took a trip that we had always wanted to make. We pulled the camper to Cherokee, NC and entered the Blue Ridge Parkway. During the next week, we ambled up the parkway, stopping many times to see the sites and take short hikes. We ate in a couple of the park lodges and saw beautiful views of the mountains. We sometimes cooked our meals in the camper, but occasionally drove into a town for a sit-down meal. After driving to the end of the parkway at Afton Mountain, we entered the Skyline Drive, a part of the national park system overlooking the beautiful Shenandoah Valley.

REUBEN COMMITS

When Reuben had enrolled at the University of Montana in Missoula, he had been able to secure a fellowship to work on his master's degree in history. Part of his duties required him to teach some classes in Freshman history courses, and to maintain office hours to assist students. His office mate was Ann Coble. She was from Livingston,

MT. Reuben made a lot of friends while going to school in Montana, but Ann quickly became the closest of all. After a few weeks of seeing each other at work every day and even helping each other with a couple of problems off-campus, they discovered that they were attracted to each other. This attraction developed further, and before long it became a serious relationship.

When Reuben finished his degree, he returned home to Virginia and again enrolled in classes at UVA-Wise. This would lead to teaching credentials. Ann had traveled back east with Reuben. Their plan was to be married as soon as their financial situation improved. This meant getting jobs, hopefully for both of them. Reuben took the necessary tests to obtain a teaching certificate. He landed a job at Franklinton High School in the little town of Wake Forest, in far eastern North Carolina.

Reuben and Ann were married near her hometown of Livingston on July 13, 1913. The wedding was an exceptionally beautiful affair. The actual wedding took place atop a ridge in the middle of Paradise Valley with a view of the mountains in the background.

There were several friends and family in attendance to observe and witness the marriage. The Methodist minister from Ann's mother's church conducted the ceremony. The ceremony also included the planting of a tree. The soils from Virginia and Montana were mixed into the  planting barrel. They both later took the tree and planted it on her family's property.

The reception was held at a center in Livingston. There was lots of food, fun, dancing, and camaraderie. A serious large canvas tent was set up for the couple just outside of the reception hall. It was stretched securely over a beautiful bed in which the couple would spend their wedding night.

We had all flown in to Bozeman. Vickie and I enjoyed some additional time while we were in Montana. Ann's mother Valerie had made a reservation for us at a large lodge in the valley, where we shared the accommodations with many family members. Michelle made the trip from Richmond, and I picked her up at the airport. Since the flight was not due until the afternoon, I took advantage of the time and had lunch at Ted Turner's Restaurant. I ordered a buffalo filet mignon. Yum!

Our crew included Vickie's brothers, Tom and Don, and their wives, Ruth and Anne. Nephews and nieces were also there with us at the lodge. Side trips were made to Yellowstone National Park in Wyoming, with Val as our guide. We also enjoyed the famous Chico Hot Spring a few miles away. The guests also included our friends Al and Valena Plisko from Vienna, VA and Ben and Terri Mason from home. Many of Ann's Montana friends and Reuben's good buddies from home came to the wedding.

MORE CAMPING

In October of 2013, Vickie and I took another camping trip. We again took our dog and made a trip to Edisto Beach in October. It was unusual for us to be there in the fall, and even more unusual to not be staying in a condo. It was a very pleasurable trip.

In 2014, we took a big camping trip to Pipestem State Park in West Virginia. The park was beautiful and we made a few side trips that are very memorable. As I described before, one of these was made to Camp Summers, my childhood summer 4H camp. Another trip was taken to view the New River Gorge and the bridge there.

We did not take a camping trip in 2015, and we only took one in 2016. We made a trip to Unicoi County in Tennessee and stayed at the Woodsmoke Campground. It was short but very sweet. From here, we ventured down the Nolichucky River over to Jonesborough on SR 81. During our trip, we passed a huge multi-acre tomato farm. We stopped at a stand to buy a few veggies and learned that the tomatoes were being picked green that day and were destined for a trip all the way to Paris, France. Neither of us had ever been to Roan Mountain, so we took a trip there on one of our days. The scenery and the leaf colors were breathtaking. We went into Elizabethton and found the famous old covered bridge that we had heard so much about. Historic Sycamore Shoals where we viewed the artifacts and the artwork, was also on our tour. On another day trip, we drove to Gray, TN and visited the fossil site and museum. It was remarkable to think about all of the activities that we had been able to cram into just three nights.

Occupying My Time

I am a believer in staying busy with something. This attitude is good for everyone, young or old. It is one of the healthiest things that I can do for myself. So many people say that they can never retire because if they did, they would not know what to do with themselves. I have never found that to be a problem in my case.

"WILDCATS" REUNION

In April, 2014, Herb Short prepared our income tax return. While we were there he asked me about music and the old "Wildcats" group. He wondered if there might be a possibility of getting them all back together for a performance. I just told him that I would ask some of the guys if they could do it. They were all interested in trying to do the concert. We made an effort to get together a couple of times for practice. This was difficult because we were so spread apart. We worked out a set list, and the folks in our original little hometown of Pound tried to spread the word that it was happening. Even though Fred was not up to par, we all still wanted him to be a part of our reunion concert. On August 2, 2014, we played for a crowd of about 400 (est.) in the Performing Arts Center at Adams Elementary School in Pound. It was a success. We got together one more time that fall for a Dewey school reunion in Flat Gap.

It seems that old musicians never really die, they just fade out at the end. I say that because if they are real musicians, then they leave a legacy. Perhaps it is just the memories that we have of them. Some leave recordings that we can listen to after they have passed on.

Fred is not healthy enough to continue playing, but all of the rest of us in the "Wildcats" still try to play as often as we are able and someone wants us. Donnie plays with a little combo in Gloucester, VA. Coy plays with different folks when he is in Morristown and still others when he is in Florida for the winter. Labo jams with us whenever he gets in, and he is open to playing in his hometown of Defiance, Ohio whenever he is asked. Jay is also still musically active and plays in a blues band in the tri-cities area. I try to pick a little bit every day. I play in church, schools, and I am willing to perform for others when asked, and feeling OK. My desire is to continue pickin' and singin' as long as I live.

L to R: (front) Donnie Mullins - drums & vocals, Fred Adkins - guitar, Jay Corder - tenor sax, (back) Me - guitar & vocals, Coy Boggs - keyboard & vocals, Larry Bolling - bass & vocals

LEGENDS CONCERT

During the summer of 2016, I was asked by my friend Wayne Mefford if I wanted to play in a concert honoring the "Music Legends of Wise County." I told him that I would certainly try to be there. I collected some musicians, including my son Nathan, Randy Wyatt, and Caynor Smith. We played in the convocation center at the college. Except for Tuck, that was on a beach vacation during the concert, the band configuration was the same as the original "Law and Disorder" band.

It was a great honor and it was so enjoyable to get to play in the "Legends" concert with all of the other great musicians that were in attendance that evening. Just to name a few: Wayne Mefford, Chris Fleming, Angel Mefford, Richie Kennedy, Mark Wooten, Ron Flanary, Lisa Roberson, Randy Wyatt, Caynor Smith, Nathan Swindall, Garland Collins and many others. I was very impressed by the quality of our sound and mix that was engineered by Ben Mays, a real sound professional. The most complimentary tribute to our group was the standing ovation that we received when we finished our set. We were honored to have a large number of our family and friends to come and offer their support.

L to R: Ron, Caynor, Nathan, Randy

At the "Legends" concert, I made an effort to recognize a few of the great legendary local musicians from the past. Some of these are still around. Others have passed on and are no longer with us. I did this by dedicating songs to their memories. I made it a point to mention Fred Adkins, Kenneth Duncan, Glenn Smith, Thomas Countiss, and Jerry Miller. I am proud to say that I was involved in documenting some of their music on tape and on CDs.

NATHAN'S CAREERS

I hope Nathan doesn't mind being told that he's following in his daddy's footsteps. It is true to a certain extent, and it is a compliment to me. I know that it's not really acceptable and that it's boring to others when we brag on our kids. I also know that we are not supposed to be prideful, but I'm going to do it anyway. First, his interest and aptitude in math and science are exceptional. It was such a pleasure to be able to have all of my kids in my classes in high school, and Nathan was an exceptional student in chemistry. He loved the material and was constantly seeking ways to improve and impress. This interest carried over into college. He succeeded in earning a BS degree in chemistry, and this became the subject that he was destined to teach. I had happily played music from the time I was 12 years old, and then became a biology and chemistry teacher. Nathan is now enjoying the same path.

It was obvious from the time he was old enough to hold the little baritone ukulele in his small hands that he had musical talent. Since that time his interest, effort, and determination have earned him a nice ride in the ranks of music professionalism. When he left home to work in South Carolina, he took with him all that he had learned from me and others. He also took along his experience with our "Law and Disorder" band.

When he was settled in SC, it wasn't long before others began to notice his musical talent. He was soon recruited by other musicians to play with them. His first gig in a new band there was with a group called "Manic Blue." Nathan always seemed to enjoy the classic rock songs most and liked playing the old covers from Eric Clapton, "Zeppelin," "Pink Floyd," Bonnie Raitt, etc. At the same time, he takes pride in learning new covers that fit into the same vein, i.e. "Train," "Maroon 5," John Meyer, Prince, etc. He has also written some very appealing original lyrics and melodies. The old and new mixture have become a trademark. The versatility and creativity have been productive and satisfying.

The first band broke up and Nathan soon became a singer/guitarist in another band, "O'Neal Township." The members in this group are mostly from Greer, SC near where Nathan's home is located. They are also known as a classic rock group. Their bookings reach from the Greer/Spartanburg area to Greenville and beyond to Simpsonville and Clemson.

Since Nathan was neither the lead singer nor the lead guitarist in "O'Neal Township," he wanted to expand his duties as well as meet other musicians that were interested in some other songs that he liked. He became involved with three very fine musicians that began to challenge him to learn more and more. The new group is named "Darwin's Radio," and they are booking in several clubs around the area. He began playing in two groups. When one of the groups books a gig, he obligates himself to play with them, and vice versa. Both groups have become notable and both play some fine dance and listening music. Vickie and I continue to enjoy trying to schedule visits with Nathan and Amanda during the dates when he is playing.

**Chris (lead guitar), John (bass), Kenny
(drums), Nathan (Vocals and guitar)**

Both bands have sites on Facebook and they keep the media updated on current information and gigs. Other than gigging, their current plans include studio time and maybe an album of original material.

My Ongoing Projects

FIRST PERSONAL COMMERCIAL RECORDING

In 2007, after the "Ron Swindall Band," I decided not to try to form another group. Since then, I have only played a few "pickup" jobs, but I have kept on playing, recording extra tracks, and overdubbing on new and old former material that I had recorded. My mother became ill, had an auto accident, and was diagnosed with Alzheimer's. She

was now living with us. The music and the recording were all good therapy for me. I released my first CD in the fall of 2007. It only contained my original songs.

A NEW SWINDALL CD

Seven years later, in the fall of 2014, I decided to produce another album of some songs that I had played often. The new CD featured all cover songs except one that I had written. The album was entitled "Some Love Songs and Other Stuff." The CD was released in the spring of 2015. It was done just for fun. At first, I ordered 200 copies. I got a lot  of nice compliments. So many of my friends purchased a copy of the CD that I ordered an additional 200 copies. The photographer for the album cover was Shannon Scott.

"FALLEN STARS" NOSTALGIA

Thomas Countiss came to visit me in the fall of 2014. We talked about the "Wildcats" reunion concert that past summer. He said, "I'm really glad that you did it. People really enjoyed it, including me."

We sat and picked on our flat tops that day and Thomas told me the story about his dad packing the little Gibson guitar up and sending it to him overseas while he was in the army. He showed me a song by "Moby Grape" that Jerry had liked and asked him to learn. Thomas told me about his Wednesday evening neighborhood pickin' sessions.

I returned the visit a few days later, this time to his home in Wise. We talked about the old "Fallen Stars" band of the 70s and the quality of the music. We both agreed that the band was far ahead of its time in many ways. He played and sang a couple of songs for me. Then we listened to some of the old practice tapes that he had saved. He had a few that I did not have, and he vowed to make copies or bring them to my place where we would make copies together. On this day, we talked about the possibility of collecting the best of the recordings with the intention of making a CD for distribution to a few people that had enjoyed the band.

The third visit by Thomas the following spring, 2015, resulted in a long visit in my studio. The time together involved listening, copying and even placing some of the recordings into my digital multitrack. We both began to see the possibility of cleaning up the homemade recordings and having them professionally mastered. Our final goal at this point was to produce a CD with 12-15 of the best songs. Our plan was to share the cost and have a few dozen copies duplicated and distributed.

Here is an email (4/8/2015 9:13 AM) from Thomas to Vickie, after one of my scary passing out incidents:

"After my last visit down there with Ron, I felt that we still have some things to take care of. I got caught up in the excitement of archiving more music history that we have between us. We still have more to do!! I just want to say what is on my heart. When Ron and I met (long after I knew who Ron Swindall was) I started playing with him, backing up Cova Elkins and Virgil Fleming at the Steak House in Clintwood. We seldom saw Cova. It was a good "gig." We got payroll checks from Elkins Brothers Coal Company. It was different than any arrangement I ever had before. As I remember, we drove to Clintwood sometimes on Thursday nights to practice, then again to play on most Friday and Saturday nights. On one of those nights Ron paid me a compliment. He said he thought I was a good rhythm guitar player and a good singer. Coming from him, that meant more to me than he'll ever know. The rest is history. By the way, I attached a recording of one of my favorite songs we did. In our prime, we were 'tight'."

Take Care,
Thomas

On the fourth visit during the summer, Thomas brought a friend, Robbie Skeens, with him. We all listened to my recordings of the "Fallen Stars." I had been doing some EQ work and volume adjustments. Robbie seemed to be very impressed with what he heard that day. We talked once more about our planned project and vowed to get together and work on it again soon. That's the last time that I saw Thomas.

Thomas had been very ill for many months with a painful stomach problem. He had gone to many doctors to try and have the problem resolved, but to no avail. That summer he went to the doctor with extreme pain in his arm. He had a blood clot. They tried to dissolve the clot but could not. In the process, he had a stroke, and they induced a coma from which he never recovered. He passed away a few days later. I was very distraught. Naturally, his family and friends were devastated by this news.

I resolved that I would continue with our project and produce the CD myself. I had known before I started that this would be a difficult project, and that it would require a lot of my time. I knew that the work would help me in accepting and having closure about Thomas' death. I'm sure that it comes as no surprise that Thomas' wife, Wanda insisted that she still wanted to pay a portion of the cost of the projects.

I began "woodshedding" the "Fallen Stars" recordings, making a bona fide effort to save as many as possible. I planned to produce a CD just as soon as I had enough songs. Some of the recordings that Thomas had given me had been recorded during practice sessions on a little Radio Shack cassette recorder. The little machine had an increased speed. Software was purchased that could be used to change the speed of the recordings while still maintaining the original key of the song.

The first CD was named "The Fallen Stars - A Taste of Nostalgia. Vol.1." It featured the voice of Thomas on seven cuts, Jerry on one, and the other four by me. This CD was a rendering of songs recorded by the  first four original members of the band. The cover picture had been taken at the Endzone by owner, Grace Helen Edwards Stinson in 1979.

The CD had a total of twelve tunes that we recorded either in practice sessions, live at the Endzone, or at another gig. Looking ahead, I decided that I would at least try to place our Nashville recordings on a separate CD later.

I finished and ordered 200 "vol. 1" CDs. Payment was made for mastering, duplication and copyright royalties. Several hundred dollars had been invested, but I was determined to continue with the work. The work was going far beyond what Thomas had perceived. I felt that if he could know what was happening that he would have been very pleased.

The first CDs arrived from California in a few days and I was very excited about the product. Immediate plans were made to produce a second CD. Arrangements were planned to distribute the CDs. Since I now had a personal investment, I couldn't really afford to just give away the recordings. Facebook was used to let all of my several hundred friends and family know about the project and the availability of the album. This led to many mail orders. A few people came by the studio to pick them up, I decided to place some in a few retail stores around the area. The Clapboard House has now sold dozens of CDs. They were also stocked at the June Toliver House gift shop, the Bookstore in Big Stone Gap, the Southwest

Virginia Museum, Brenda's Nookbooks in Pound and Donna's Nails in Wise.

The second CD, "Fallen Stars - A Taste of Nostalgia. Vol.2" was my next project. This CD contains fourteen cuts, and features the sax of Glenn Smith on three of them. The  others are vocals mostly by Thomas, and two by me.

In 1979, Glenn Smith had invited the original four of us to accompany him to a gig that he had booked for a wedding reception. We recorded our practice session on my Sony TC-377 reel to reel tape recorder. Most of it was either too noisy or contained too many errors, but the three that I chose to include on the CD were fairly clean. Even though Jerry had already passed away, I must give him credit for the beautiful lettering on the cover. It is gold on a black background.

I was having more luck with restoring the old recordings than I ever thought possible. Thomas and I had originally thought that one CD would be sufficient for the amount of material that we could accumulate. Even after the first two, I was already projecting the likelihood of two more. Work on volume three had already begun even before volume 2 was released.

The third CD in the series, "Fallen Stars - A Taste of Nostalgia. Vol.3," was quite different from the first two. The recordings had also been done in practice and during gigs, but this time it included the two new members that we added in 1979. In addition to Thomas, Tuck, Jerry and me, this one also included Tommy Ray Miller and Richie Kennedy. With fourteen cuts in all, this became the last of our own taped archives that were of sufficient quality to be presented to the public.

The cover photo had been shot by Sharon Hatfield. She was working with the *Coalfield Progress* at that time and had decided to do an interview with us for a large article to appear in the paper  later. I found the old newspaper picture and scanned it. I loaded it into Photoshop and converted it to grey scale so I could brighten it up and make it presentable. I left most of the original faded yellow colorization in the newspaper picture. Since the book pictures are black and white, that aspect does not show up here.

I had been working on the final "Fallen Stars" CD when I had yet another setback in my health. It started the day after Christmas. This time, after several ventricular shocks, I ended up in the Cleveland Clinic. The defibrillator was changed out. Unfortunately, I had ventricular tachycardia the very next day. A 6-hour ventricular ablation was performed, and the pacemaker was now set to supply 100% of my heartbeats. During a four-day loading period I was placed on two new drugs for a-fib and I spent a total of ten days in the hospital. I was very shaky and filled with anxiety when I got home. It had been one of my scariest experiences.

A few days later, I once more set about to finish my CD project. Working on the final CD was probably some of the best therapy that I could have experienced.

The CD was to be labeled, "Fallen Stars - The Nashville Sessions - A Final Taste of Nostalgia. Vol.4." This CD contains ten songs. Eight of them were recorded by the six members of the "Fallen Stars" in the  summer of 1979. The last two cuts were recorded in 1978. Thomas Countiss and myself worked with studio musicians on the first tracks. All of the recordings were made at Bradley's Barn in Nashville with Harold Bradley helping with production, and Bobby Bradley as the recording engineer.

I didn't have as much work to do on these tracks as I did on the others. The quality of the big studio sound was superb and even the rough mix that we were given was radio quality. Thomas and I were pleased with the sessions there and relished the experience to work with some very high level pros. This was the only recording ever made in a big studio setting by the "Fallen Stars." I had made the cover photo during our first trip to Bradley's in November, 1978 with Virgil Fleming. We rode down on the bus which is sitting in front of the barn in this picture. I used Photoshop to repaint the picture and give it an appearance more like a drawing.

These CDs were the last ones made in 2016. I want to do more, both for myself and others. As long as I am able to do so, I want to continue to experience as much music, both playing and listening, as possible.

Latest Ventures

TRIPPING AGAIN

Our timeshare week in Williamsburg has been an asset, and it has encouraged us to travel at times, and to places which we probably would not have experienced otherwise. All of these trips have certainly not been mentioned in my writing. In April of 2016, Vickie exchanged our time in Williamsburg for a week at the Samoset Resort in Maine, the same resort that Reuben and I had enjoyed a few years before. Having already had the experience of traveling to this area, I was able to do some planning about our excursions. We were able to enjoy the seafood, especially the lobster, and we got a feel for the general atmosphere as we drove around to the little towns and to Bar Harbor. Maine is a beautiful state, especially the coastal part.

As we flew back from Maine, I experienced a very thought provoking and exciting view. I saw the Statue of Liberty for the first time from the air as we flew into Newark, N. J.

Our senses allow for impressions to be formed each time we see a new place. I have been lucky to have traveled by air to several spots around the U.S. My idea of the airport in Newark is that it is one of the dirtiest I've ever witnessed. It is huge and sprawling, and it gave me the feeling of insignificance and almost hopelessness. I felt sorry for the people that worked there every day, and for the commuters that had to go through the terminals so often. It made me thankful once again for the place that I grew up and have lived most of my life.

Many of my friends have retired. For health and comfort, some of them have chosen to spend a portion of their yearly time somewhere south of here. I love my state of Virginia and the mountains, but one of my dreams has been to leave here during the winter months and spend three to four months in Florida. Maybe someday that will happen.

In January of 2017, my travel agent (Vickie) booked a one week time share in Destin, Florida. We spent our week enjoying the white sands of the beach and eating great seafood. We made a day trip to Pensacola and visited the Naval Museum. In addition to a large number of interesting artifacts, we were pleased to see a Kingfisher plane like the one that Vickie's dad flew over the Pacific during World War II.

One of our sayings in the mountains is, "Lord willin' and the creek don't rise," as we talk about plans that we have made. Obviously, these plans are contingent upon lots of other possibilities between now and then. Seeing and experiencing new places and things are stimulations that benefit a healthy mind and body. We feel lucky to be able to do this as much as possible.

DAILY ACTIVITIES AND PLANS

Friends and family are always curious, "what are you doing? where do you work? what are your latest plans? where are you going? do you still play music?"

Our days at the Swindall household are pretty much routine. We are both retired, but it is difficult to notice any degree of retirement in my wife. She is up at 6:00 AM each morning, and after her morning devotion, she busies herself with a large variety of tasks and interests until an early bedtime. Besides the daily house and yard work, she is nursemaid to me. She also spends at least an hour at the nursing home each day, helping my mother with her evening meal.

When we first moved to Powell Valley in 1989, I made immediate plans to remodel the basement of our home. It first became the studio for my business, Homestead Recordings. It was the practice room for the "Ron Swindall" Band and the "Law and Disorder" Band. It was the jamming/party room for my musician friends and music lovers. When I fully retired in 2009 and shed all of my business responsibilities, the basement area was renamed and designated as the Man Cave. I have kept my digital recording equipment intact, with plans for more recording, but the main studio room has become an entertainment center for my family, friends, and me. I have now installed a big screen tv and a quality quad sound system.

I like to watch a few tv programs and movies, but my wife and I especially enjoy sports. We love the college football games in the fall, the basketball games and March Madness during the winter months, and baseball during the warm months.

Because of my heart failure and surgeries, in 2009, we started making a few trips to Cleveland each year. We have found that there are many diversions in the city, and if we have time, we always try to do something interesting. We have visited Little Italy many times, where we can have a sit-down meal for some excellent authentic Italian food. We have enjoyed the huge West Side Market, where it seems that one can find every fruit, vegetable, meat, poultry, cheese and baked good that is in existence.

We have been to see the Browns play in Cleveland and we have been to several major-league baseball games. Our latest infatuation is with the Cleveland Indians baseball team, that won the American League pennant in 2016. We really enjoy going to Progressive Field to see them play.

On Euclid Avenue, that runs by the hotel where we sometimes stay in downtown Cleveland, is Playhouse Square, one of the largest theatre districts in any city other than New York. We have enjoyed major dramas, musicals and more in the big theatres there. We have listened to street concerts in the square and have visited several other attractions in this city, which always seems to have a lot to offer.

We have visited the Rock 'n Roll Hall of Fame twice, and I never seem to have time to look at everything that I want to see. If you know me at all, you must know how much it means to me to see the instruments, written lyrics and music from original compositions, clothing, and personal items that were used by my music heroes from the past.

Besides planning for long vacation trips, we want to spend as much time as possible at our lake cabin. We both still love to fish, and to stock our freezer with fresh fish from the lake. We are so lucky to have the assistance of our sweet Aunt Carol and our friend Kristin when we are away from the house. We depend on both of them to stay with our dog or with my mother when she's here.

My everyday projects vary from day to day, but since I am very restricted physically by heart failure, I mostly do my work and projects sitting down. The writing of my memoirs is one example of the type of thing that occupies my time. I enjoy writing, and I find myself often writing songs, poetry, and philosophy. I have even started writing a novel, which I have a dream of finishing someday.

It is now 2017, and I still love to play my guitar and sing. It gives me peace and a great deal of pleasure to just sit and strum some of the old songs that I have accumulated in my head over the years. I have written a number of original lyrics and melodies and I continue to do that as well. My plans include the production of a couple more CD recordings this year. All of these things depend on the approval of the Lord and a creek that don't rise.

My Final Thoughts

MORE PHILOSOPHY

Music, along with my faith, a wonderful wife, my children, grandchildren, best close friends, fishing, camping, traveling, and enjoying great food are the loves of my life. "It Couldn't Be Better." Vickie and I have always believed in making plans even though we know there is no promise of a tomorrow. When those around us that we love pass away, it is tragic and sometimes even traumatic. It has been especially difficult for me during the past five years. During this time, I have now lost beloved relatives: my Dear Uncle Gene, Uncle Roy, Aunt Virginia, Aunt Thelma, and Aunt Rebecca. Some of my closest friends which were like brothers to me have also passed on recently, including Kennith Ellison (2011), Ronnie Clark (2016), Thomas Countiss (2015), Jerry Miller (2014), Gary Slemp, and Larry Salyers (2016). Of course, there are several others, and I don't claim to be unlike others in my grief.

Ginny Clark asked me to do a eulogy at Ronnie's Celebration of Life service. It was so difficult, but it was healing for me. It drew me closer to the Clark family and allowed me some time with Ginny's brother Larry Roberts. We have even gotten together to play some music.

Vickie and I sang a song at the Celebration of Life for Gary Slemp.

When Thomas Countiss passed, Wanda had a Celebration of Life for him in Wise at the Inn. We included Jerry Miller in our thoughts. Tuck and I, along with Richie and Bill Smith played a short tribute concert to them.

Brenda asked me to come and play a couple of songs during the Celebration of Life for Larry.

These kinds of things help us all to deal with our grief. As all of us grow older, we become more and more aware of our own mortality. We lose close friends and family that have been with us most of our lives, and we begin to realize that life is really rather short. One of my common statements is "Life is short. Live it to the fullest. Sponge it all up!"

But, in the process of living, one bit of advice in the Bible for us all to live by is: Matthew 5:21-25. Be good to your friends and other people.

VICKIE LYNN STURGILL SWINDALL

What a lucky and blessed man I have been, in so many ways. My most dynamic stroke of luck was to experience the complete love of a wonderful woman. She has been the most loving, caring, helpful, sacrificing, considerate, unselfish companion that any man could ever hope for. These words are insufficient to describe my wife of over 42 years. I always relish the time I get to spend with her, and I still look forward to being with her all night and all day long the next day, and...

We love each other's constant presence and companionship, and we enjoy dozens of different activities together. We have never been apart for very long, and when that is necessary we don't like it. I have considered that it is probably a rare occurrence to see a wife that seems dedicated to the participation in the things that her man enjoys, to the extent that she is also involved fully in those activities herself. The photo on the right illustrates the point.

I told her just recently that most men probably would not believe it if I told them all the things she does for me. She insists on mowing and weed-eating the large yard in the summer, raking and blowing leaves in the fall, then shoveling and clearing the driveway of snow in winter. Grocery shopping and cooking great meals is a common occurrence for her. We sit together and enjoy them as we talk or watch a favorite tv program. I like to give her relief from this chore, so I do try to make sure that we go out to a restaurant and eat occasionally. She is the nurse for me and my aging mother with Alzheimer's, as she dispenses medicine very early in the morning, during the day, and in the evening. The house is swept and cleaned. In an effort to perk up our spirits, she places tasteful decorations around the home in all seasons. Flowers outside and inside the house are available for us both to enjoy because of her efforts. She makes donations of food and money in both of our names to individuals and organizations that need help. We attend church almost every Sunday, and she participates in church activities like the choir, in which she is an important soprano voice. The choir usually presents a wonderful Christmas cantata to the community which has required many hours of intensive practice. Yes, she does all of this, yet I can still look in my drawer tomorrow and find plenty of nice clean socks, underwear, and handkerchiefs. Clean shirts and pants are always available in my closet. Since my illness, I prefer not to drive, so she is also my prized chauffeur. I really don't know how she does it, and you must see by now that there's no way I could live without her.

Vickie respects me not only as a husband, but she loves me and is proud of the fact that I have been a successful educator. She thinks I'm intelligent, which is, of course, questionable. She shares my love of music, and is proud that I have been able to call myself a professional musician. My efforts to perform, to write songs and music, and to produce recordings for myself and others have her full support.

I have totally shared my life with this woman. We talk and have fun together, sing together, fish together, travel together, enjoy theatre together, watch sports together, watch the same tv programs together, share our thoughts with each other, plan for the future together, and we laugh and cry together. She is a very interesting and intelligent person, and I respect her knowledge, wisdom and suggestions.

My wife has always been an avid reader. Her interest in reading sparked her desire to get a degree in education and to teach children to read. Our children could read before they started school. Vickie read to them from infancy. While she was still working, she strengthened her teaching skills by securing a master's degree in reading from the University of Virginia. She was recognized as a dedicated reading specialist.

We share three wonderful children together, and within the past few years, we have been able to enjoy two twin granddaughters (we're hoping for more). Vickie is the love of my life and the joy of my life. She has made my life comfortable, fun, and well worth living. I am far from perfect, but she has made me a better man. I've never regretted a single day that I have spent with her. Need I say more??!

Bibliography

Addington, Luther F. *The Story of Wise County.* Wise, VA: Wise County School Board, 1956.

Brummett, Jack D. *John Gilliam: Pioneer, Patriot, Soldier and a Leading Citizen of Wise County, VA*: Austin, TX: Jack Brummett, 2008.

History.com Staff. *9/11 Attacks.* http://www.history.com/topics/9-11-attacks: A &E Networks, 2010.

Sutherland, Hetty Swindall Sutherland and Sutherland, Elihu Jasper Sutherland.

Swindall-Austin Families of Virginia and North Carolina 1622-1995: Clintwood, VA: Hetty Sutherland, 1995.

Sutherland, Elihu Jasper. *Pioneer Recollections of Southwest Virginia.* Clintwood, VA: Hetty Sutherland, Gregory Vanover and Joan Short Vanover, 1984.

Printed in the United States
By Bookmasters